Dedication

This book is dedicated to my wife, Grace, my sons Robert and Michael, stepdaughters Heidi and Kasey, my grandchildren, Robbie, Ryan, Mikey, Randy, Christopher, Stevie, Ashlyn, Morgan and Vivien, and my great-grandchildren, Kaelyn and Logan.

Contents

Preface

In his book, *Why Do Criminals Offend? A General Theory of Crime and Delinquency* (2005), noted criminologist Robert Agnew outlined a comprehensive theory drawing from sociology, psychology, genetics, neuroscience, and evolutionary biology. Although comprehensive, it is also parsimonious because it focuses on just two traits that are arguably the strongest individual-level traits associated with criminal behavior to be found in the literature—low self-control and negative emotionality (which Agnew calls irritability). People take these traits with them into all life domains—family, school, peer groups, marriage, and work—and these traits affect how others in those domains react to them in a process of what behavioral geneticists call evocative gene–environment correlation.

Although it is an excellent book, Agnew writes in a later work that he came "to realize that it is built on a weak foundation" (2011:vii). Agnew has no quarrel with himself about what is in the book but, rather, with what he left out. What he did not pay attention to is what he calls "foundational issues," which are the unspoken assumptions with which criminologists carry out their trade, and are what I call philosophical issues in this book. The issues Agnew explores in his new work (*Toward a Unified Criminology: Integrating Assumptions about Crime, People and Society*, 2011) are determinism versus agency, the nature of human nature, the nature of society, and the nature of reality.

Agnew was much too hard on himself; how many books on criminological theory have you read that inquire about those things? Most such books simply assume that any philosophical assumptions underlying the various theories are either settled or are unproblematic. He was quite correct in his assertion that we must pay attention to foundational issues if the discipline is to progress beyond the deep divisions it now suffers and the constant recycling of old ideas into new "theories" that lead us nowhere.

The present book examines all of Agnew's issues from a more philosophical angle and adds many others, such as justice, moral responsibility, rationality, emotions, punishment, ontology, epistemology, rationalism, empiricism, relativism, essentialism, realism, reductionism, and nominalism. Philosophers such as Aristotle, Plato, Kant, Hume, Descartes, and Schopenhauer long ago wrote about the same issues we struggle with today, and they provided answers that few modern writers, if any, have bettered. I thus introduce topics of interest to criminology and criminal justice with reference to philosophical traditions that emphasize the continuity of thought from the philosophical past to the scientific present.

This book should therefore be read as a philosophical look at criminology and not as a criminology theory text. It offers no systematic overview or analysis of criminological theories or perspectives; rather, it examines aspects of certain theories and perspectives for their philosophical assumptions, which may or may not be explicitly stated in them. Philosophy provides many nails to hang our conceptual hats on, clarifies many aspects of our thought, and helps immensely in developing critical thinking tools. Philosophy examines the grounds of our convictions and beliefs without providing definitive answers because that is not its task. Its task is rather to make us aware of them and to think more deeply and more precisely about them.

Chapter 1 points out that many physicists, the grand masters of science, have found that philosophy provides a useful foundation for their thought, and that criminologists could benefit even more because, as Agnew notes, we rarely question our underlying assumptions. Philosophy has the ability to clarify our thoughts for us, to inform us of why we think about things the way we do, to solve some contradictions in our thinking we never knew existed, and even to dissolve some dichotomies we thought were cast in stone. One of those dichotomies is free will–determinism. I make the case that criminology can live with both free will/agency, as posited by some theories, and determinism, as posited by others.

Chapter 2 examines social constructionist and postmodernist thought in criminology. The agenda of those drawn to such approaches is not so much knowledge production as knowledge destruction/deconstruction. I address suggestions by others that perhaps they are drawn to anti-science positions by a genuine fear of knowledge they find distasteful. The main concern of this chapter is whether crime and criminality are social construction or palpably real, and it suggests from a critical realist's position that the answer is both.

Relativism, rationalism, and empiricism are addressed in Chapter 3. Relativism denies there is truth or avers that there are many truths, all veridical in their own domains. Rationalism and empiricism are different epistemologies telling us that truth is attainable—the first using top-down analytic methods and the latter using bottom-up synthetic methods. Thomas Kuhn's work on the nature of science and paradigms, with emphasis on his concept of the theory ladenness of data, is the primary focus of this chapter.

Essentialism and reductionism are the topics of Chapter 4. I argue that searching for generalities, patterns, similarities, and differences is the goal of science, and that anti-essentialists fail to make the distinction between Aristotle's *per se* and *per accidens* essentialism. Reductionism is searching for causal explanations at fundamental levels. I show that chemistry, biology, and psychology went through an anti-reductionist phase in their youth, fearing for the autonomy of their disciplines, but finally accepted that the more fundamental science had much to offer and so fully integrated with it. When they did, their knowledge base increased enormously.

Chapter 5 explores ontology and epistemology—the things we accept as real and the assumptions we have about how we uncover facts about those things. Ontology clarifies the structure of the knowledge we claim to hold and provides a vocabulary for representing that knowledge. The epistemological question of the reliability of knowledge is addressed by examining the question of social class and crime in the context of labeling theory, a theory that I argue is based on ontological gerrymandering and a thoroughly flawed epistemology.

The issues of idealism versus materialism are taken up in Chapter 6, using the works of Weber and Marx as exemplars. In criminology, the idealism/materialism divide involves attributing criminal behavior to either structural (materialism) or cultural (idealism) factors. Structural theorists tend to view cultural explanations as "victim blaming" because culture is embodied in people. I explore the structural/cultural issue in terms of African American crime because it is important to structuralists not to attribute black crime rates to black cultural practices. The chapter argues Robert Sampson's point that structure and culture are cause and effect of one another, representing an ever-changing dialectic of objective material reality and subjective ideational meanings attached to that reality.

Chapter 7 examines conflict and cooperation. Conflict and cooperation are processes deeply embedded in human nature, and thus we should expect both to characterize human affairs. As many ancient and modern philosophers have opined, both processes are necessary for stability and change in society. I examine Marxist and Weberian conceptions of conflict as they apply to alienation and inequality. Marx viewed capitalism as the progenitor of both; Weber saw capitalism as a cure for alienation and was not overly concerned with inequality. Alienation is a concept central to Marxist conflict theorists, but even though Weber was concerned with it, it is hardly touched on at all by Weberian conflict theorists. The inequalities of relative deprivation appear to be a more central concern among conflict theorists than absolute poverty.

Chapter 8 examines the roles of emotion and rationality in criminological thought. Social scientists tend to pose rationality and emotions as opposites, with rationality being privileged over emotion. The role of emotion in social life has been vastly underappreciated, and if analyzed at all, it has been as a toxic producer of anger, hatred, and violence. Emotion is more evolutionarily relevant than rationality, a fact underscored by the ratio of neural fibers running from "emotional" to "rational" brain regions than *vice versa*. Cultural criminology gives a central role to emotion, but emphasizes emotion as a motivator of crime rather than as a powerful source of crime prevention. Fear, disgust, empathy, guilt, and shame are viscerally felt before they are cognitively articulated, and they are vital to social life. Criminology would do well to pay closer attention to the role of emotion as both a stimulator and an inhibitor of criminal behavior.

The fascinating process of acquiring a moral conscience is addressed in Chapter 9. The acquisition of a conscience is a complex process that involves the coming together of cognitive and emotional processes that have evolved to help our species to navigate social life. I examine the neurohormonal underpinnings of this "internal police officer" we carry with us from situation to situation and that is learned via the classical conditioning of the social emotions. Among normally functioning individuals, how well these lessons are learned depends primarily on the reactivity of the autonomic nervous system. I show that psychopaths condition poorly. Although psychopaths are perfectly capable of understanding the rules of social life, as numerous brain imaging studies have shown, they lack the emotional component of conscience.

Chapter 10 examines the fragmented nature of criminological theory. The science wars have raged for centuries based primarily on ideology. Ideology provides humans with a way of making sense of diverse matters, but it is one of the major barriers we have to obtaining knowledge. Ideology has no place in science and leads to attacks on scientists who pursue "distasteful" topics. The ideological divide in criminology consists of Aristotelian hardheaded constrained visionaries and the Platonic dreamers of the unconstrained vision. These two groups favor different criminological theories, with the former favoring individualistic theories and the latter environmental theories. If we can overcome the hurdle of ideological differences, perhaps theories that combine the individualistic with the social may hold the key to advancing criminology.

Criminologists may agree on certain "causes" of criminal behavior, but they often disagree about the "causes of the causes." This is the topic of Chapter 11, within which I argue that we must consider all of Niko Tingerben's famous four questions—functional, phylogenic, developmental, and causal levels of analyses—to get a better grasp on causation. I examine the role of Thomas Sowell's visions introduced in Chapter 10 using the ideas of Durkheim, Merton, Akers, and Hirschi and then "apply Tinbergen" to them. The chapter examines the tautology charge levied against social learning and control theories, criminology's two most popular theories, and concludes that this is not a problem because the tautology charge has been applied to some of the grandest ideas in science.

Human nature is the focus of Chapter 12. Every living thing, including humans, has a nature forged by natural selection. We may be free to forge our own natures as the existentialist philosophers insist, and we may have natures intimately and inescapably connected to our cultures as the sociologists insist, but there is a preexisting nature that puts constraints on our construction, as numerous cross-cultural studies attest. Human nature is the sum of all human evolutionary adaptations, among which is self-interest. This supports the notion of control theories that criminal behavior is the default result of the failure to properly cultivate human nature. Almost all the great moral philosophers recognized this in their concerns to discover what makes a person good.

Chapter 13 examines the philosophical assumptions of feminist criminology. Some strands of feminism reject science as a path to knowledge altogether, viewing it as a classist, racist, and "masculinist" enterprise unsuitable to feminism. Traditional feminist scholars may be particularly offended by the efforts of the neurohormonal sciences studying brain structures and hormones as causes of sex differences, believing that such a research agenda can be used by misogynists to denigrate and oppress women. I examine this body of research to determine how it stands up to the traditional socialization/sex role arguments made by feminists to explain gender differences.

Chapter 14 explores the concept of justice, a concept at the very heart of criminology. I begin by examining John Rawls's counterfactual theory of justice, which, although emotions are more important than reason in the fairness calculus, is premised solely on reason. Emotions move us to demand that we be treated fairly; reason helps us to articulate why. The sense of fairness/justice evolved via the calibration of the social emotions that function to promote cooperation in social groups. The roles of reciprocal altruism and "cheating" are examined, as are contemporary opinions about what constitutes fairness and equality. This is important because a recent survey found that an "unfair economic system" was the most popular "cause" of criminal behavior in a sample of criminologists (Cooper, Walsh, & Ellis, 2010).

The final chapter discusses justifications for punishment with emphasis in Kant's deontological nonconsequentialism. To punish criminals as a means to an end is to treat them as less than autonomous human beings for Kant, and that punishing just because they deserve it is to respect them as responsible human beings. However, most of us do things for utilitarian purposes; that is, we expect what we do will have some desired consequences and thus simple retribution does not cut it. The urge to punish has been essential to the evolution of cooperation because it gave rise to the coevolutionary arms race between cooperator and cheat that strengthened the social emotions. By helping to extinguish the negative emotions (anger and frustration) associated with victimization of self or others, and generating satisfaction upon witnessing the imposition of sanctions against the miscreant, punishment reinforces our sense of the justness of moral norms.

Books are typically written to advance a particular point of view; this one is no different. I make no claims of impartiality or of not having an agenda, although I do try to be balanced. The ideological bias I bring to this work is that which philosopher/economist Thomas Sowell calls a "constrained vision." A constrained visionary is a person who believes that there is an innate human nature that constrains human action; who believes that "solutions" to problems are really trade-offs; and who does not ask what causes negative things such as poverty and crime but, rather, what causes desirable things such as wealth and a well-ordered society.

My agenda is simple: Criminology can and should be a "natural" science with general theoretical principles and models about the nature of criminal behavior. To achieve this, we must first engage philosophical propositions about human nature and the sociocultural contexts in which that nature is expressed, lest we get trapped in all sorts of contradictory notions. Having assimilated the gifts of philosophy, criminology must engage the gifts offered by the natural sciences, such as behavioral and molecular genetics, the neurosciences, and evolutionary biology. Humans are assuredly social beings, but they also have genes, brains, hormones, and an evolutionary history that strongly informs their behavior. Criminologists have too long tried to understand the phenomena criminology takes as its domain, examining only environmental factors, but we cannot solve the criminal behavior equation by leaving out any of the terms needed to solve it. My agenda is nothing new, of course. More than 170 years ago, Karl Marx wrote of his dream that "natural science will in time subsume under itself the science of man, just as the science of man will subsume under itself natural science: There will be one science" (1978a:91). With the technology available to us today that allows us to peer into what were heretofore mysterious black boxes, this integration is no longer a dream but is rapidly becoming a reality.

Acknowledgments

I would first of all like to thank the acquisition editor Pam Chester for her faith in this project from the beginning. Thanks also for the commitment of the development editor Ellen Boyne and project manager Julia Haynes. This tireless trio kept up a most useful four-way dialogue between author, publisher, and reviewers. The copy editor spotted every errant comma, dangling participle, missing reference and misspelled word in the manuscript, for which we are truly thankful, and our production manager made sure everything went quickly and smoothly thereafter. I would also like to thank his first contact at Anderson, Mickey Brasswell. Thank you one and all.

We would also like to acknowledge the kind words and suggestions of the criminologists who reviewed this project. I have endeavored to respond to those suggestions and believe we have adequately done so. Any errors or misinformation that may lie lurking somewhere in these pages, however, are entirely my responsibility. These experts are Annalise Acorn, Andrew N. Carpenter, Walter S. DeKeseredy, and Alexander M. Holsinger for their comments on a preliminary draft of this book.

Last but not least, I would like to acknowledge the love and support of my most wonderful and drop-dead gorgeous soul-mate and wife, Grace Jean; aka "Grace the face." Grace's love and support has sustained me for so long that I cannot imagine life without her; she is to me nature's second sun, bringing forth a well of virtues wherever she shines. Facie anchors my ship and calms my storm. Szeretlek, én gyönyörű feleségem!

Online Resources

Thank you for selecting Anderson Publishing's *Criminological Theory: Assessing Philosophical Assumptions*. To complement the learning experience, we have provided online tools to accompany this edition.

Interactive resources can be accessed for free by registering at: www.routledge.com/cw/walsh

Available assets include:

- **Test Bank** Compose, customize, and deliver exams using unique questions created for *Criminological Theory: Assessing Philosophical Assumptions*.
- **PowerPoint Lecture Slides** Reinforce key topics with focused PowerPoints, which provide a visual outline with which to augment your lecture. Each individual book chapter has its own dedicated slide show.
- **Lesson Plans** Design your course around customized lesson plans. Each individual lesson plan contains synopses, key terms, and other aids designed to spur class discussion.

1

The Usefulness of Philosophy in Criminology

Why Criminology Needs Philosophy

Philosophy is the mother of all science—indeed, of all formal knowledge. Because the subject matter she claims for herself is the whole of knowledge, she fusses around at the periphery of all the sciences, as well as that of the arts and humanities. Philosophers retain a child-like wonder about all things (after all, *philosophy* means "love of wisdom"), and they were pondering much the same kinds of questions that modern sciences ask long before they were parceled out to different disciplines. They contemplated these questions relying only on their rational faculties and on an occasional observation unaided by any of the marvelous accoutrements with which modern science is blessed. Although philosophy's domain is shrinking as the sciences advance, it still has a valuable role to play in knowledge synthesis and holding before us the continuity of thought bequeathed to us by the great minds of the past. Philosophy thus continues to monitor her offspring in childhood and adolescence, making sure that in their haste to grow up they do not lose contact with the foundational principles of knowledge seeking all her children share. Whether the practitioners of the various sciences know it or not, there cannot be a philosophy-free science.

Presumably, most criminologists have no great wish to go beyond the data they produce to struggle to understand and define fundamental principles of the "whole" within which their work is organized and situated. It is easy to agree with Williams and Arrigo's (2006:15) complaint that "criminology proper has mostly failed to contemplate let alone critically examine its conceptual underpinnings, that is, the philosophical cornerstones that support its purpose and potential." We do, however, have unlabeled suppositions of which we are only dimly aware that serve as our "silent partners" as we go about our business. It is these silent partners I wish to bring out of the closet and give voice.

Criminologists' works are judged by the explanatory power of their findings and the clarity of their presentations applied to specific problems. The philosopher's work is judged by his or her persuasive use of logic and language in articulating the whole within which these specific problems reside. Criminologists may rest content, for example, by showing that such and such an approach to punishing offenders "works" better than some alternative approach in terms of the goals they have in mind, or with arguing whether this or that practice is consistent with justice as they view it. The philosopher's motives are much more grandiose and abstract, and they direct our attention to the "first principles" of knowledge. The philosopher asks why we punish, what is the basis for it, how we justify it, what would society be without it, what is its relationship to justice, where justice comes from, and what it means to act justly, as well as numerous other fascinating and perplexing questions of interest to criminologists and criminal justicians.

Philosophy and Physics

Thinking of ourselves as empirical scientists concerned with collecting and analyzing data rather than armchair speculators, we might be tempted to think philosophy a waste of time with nothing to offer us. If we do, we are terribly mistaken. Our discipline is still in the toddler stage relative to our more mature siblings in the natural sciences (all of which have journals devoted to the philosophy of their subjects), and we can still learn a lot hanging on to our mother's apron strings. Many of the finest minds in physics, the grand epitome of science, such as Ernst Mach, Niels Bohr, and Erwin Schrodinger, were steeped in philosophy. As for Albert Einstein, arguably the greatest scientist of them all, Howard (2005:34) writes: "Einstein's philosophical habit of mind, cultivated by undergraduate training and lifelong dialogue, had a profound effect on the way he did physics." Einstein's philosophical interests went beyond the philosophy of physics; one often detects references to the works of Kant, Hume, Spinoza, and Schopenhauer in his writings (Howard, 2005). Einstein believed that all scientists should cultivate a philosophical frame of mind or rest content to be dustbowl outhouse counters unable to see the forest for the trees: "So many people today—and even professional scientists—seem to me like somebody who has seen thousands of trees but has never seen a forest." He further added that philosophical insight is "the mark of distinction between a mere artisan or specialist and a real seeker after truth," and that philosophy is most needed when the intellectual foundations of a discipline have become problematic (in Howard, 2005:34).

Not far behind Einstein in the hierarchy of great minds is Niels Bohr, of whom Galison (2008:122) writes: "Historians of physics have made much of the way Niels Bohr used the ideas, directly and indirectly, of Søren Kierkegaard as he formulated his principle of complementarity." Werner Heisenberg, a pioneer in quantum physics, lectured extensively on Immanuel Kant's ontology and epistemology, especially in terms of interpreting quantum phenomena (Camilleri, 2005), and Kurt Godel, arguably the greatest mathematical logician of the twentieth century, was deeply devoted to philosophy, especially the works of Leibniz, Kant, and Husserl (Parsons, 2010). If philosophy was valued as an adjunctive study for the likes of Einstein, Bohr, Heisenberg, and Godel, and is recommended when the foundations of a discipline are shaky, surely it is not wise for criminologists to ignore their mother.

British philosopher of mathematics and Nobel Laureate Bertrand Russell (1988:18) wrote of the value of philosophy thus: "The knowledge it aims at is the kind of knowledge which gives unity and system to the body of the sciences, and the kind which results from a critical examination of our convictions, prejudices, and beliefs." Philosophy concerns itself with examining the assumptions, methods, and ethics that apply to particular sciences and to the "grand problems" central to all sciences, such as the nature of truth and reality. It is an analytic enterprise based on deductive logic rather than a synthetic enterprise based on inductive empiricism as is science. As is the case with any other domain of inquiry, the philosophy of criminology seeks to lay bare the practices and assumptions underlying the inquiries the discipline makes, and it offers critiques with the ultimate aim of enhancing the discipline's ability to improve its understanding of the phenomena it claims as its domain. Philosophy asks criminologists to contemplate on the abstractions and concepts they work with, which are usually, consciously or otherwise, taken for granted.

Philosophers have not found the problems of crime and criminality to be worth spending very much of their intellectual energy on. However, they have expended much on pondering issues connected with the concerns of criminologists, particularly on the ontological and epistemological assumptions on which our discipline rests. These issues include human nature, justice, free will, moral responsibility, rationality, emotion, punishment, the nature of reality and knowledge, determinism, essentialism, realism, reductionism, and nominalism. It is for this reason that "criminology is fundamentally wedded to philosophy in countless ways, and the crossroads for criminology and philosophy are ripe for exposition and assimilation by scholars in both camps" (Williams & Arrigo, 2006:2). The same point about exposition and assimilation was made to physicists by both Einstein and Heisenberg in earlier times (Camilleri, 2005), so Williams and Arrigo are in excellent scientific company.

Although it is often said that there is nothing new under the sun, it is obviously not true in many areas of science where knowledge is increasing exponentially about what we did not even know we did not know. It is probably true, however, that there is very little that is new in the fundamental understanding of human nature that cannot be found in the works of long-dead philosophers. Humans have contemplated what it is to be human and how they are to behave toward one another from time immemorial. Even those things revealed to us by the remarkable advances in the genomic and neurological sciences have tended to corroborate what one line or another of philosophical thinking has long asserted. I will thus introduce topics of interest to criminology (and criminal justice) in this book with reference to some philosophical tradition to emphasize the continuity of thought from the philosophical past to the scientific present.

Many topics in criminology engage seemingly dichotomous either/or positions. One of the aims of this book is to try to bridge some of these dichotomies. Aristotle's principle of the golden mean, by which he meant that virtue lies at the midpoint between the polar vices of excess and deficiency, is something always to be kept in mind when assessing seemingly irreconcilable philosophical positions. There is no universal mean applicable to all positions, of course, only to reasonable positions for which there are often compelling arguments on either side. The most extreme positions defy any sort of compromise, so it is wise to leave them alone. With this in mind, we begin with a metaphysical question for which science offers no real support for strong versions on either side but for which there are compelling argument on both sides: the perennial issue of free will versus determinism.

Free Will and Determinism

Both the free will and determinism positions are embraced or disdained by different groups of scholars across the social sciences. This philosophical issue does not necessarily disturb natural scientists *qua* scientists, but because the theories and practices of social science disciplines tend to be predicated (wittingly or not) on one side of the debate or the other, it is an important issue for us to explore. Social scientists as a group seem to think in terms of extreme positions on free will and determinism, as exemplified by behaviorists such as B. F. Skinner, who insisted that we do not have free will but keep pretending that we do, and existentialists such as J. P. Sartre, who insisted that we do have free will but keep pretending that we do not. The positions on the issue supported by these two men were extreme versions that brook no compromise. Thus, we often feel that we are confronted with a Manichean choice on this issue: Either our behavior is completely determined or (in Sartre's words) we are "condemned to be free." Here we search for Aristotle's golden mean.

The classical eighteenth-century founding fathers of criminology and criminal justice, such as Cesare Beccaria and Jeremy Bentham, were certainly a lot closer to Sartre than to Skinner. For classical thinkers, a God-given free will enabled humans to purposely and deliberately calculate a course of action that they were free to follow absent external restraints. Given the classical assumption that we are free to choose how we will behave and that we know the difference between right and wrong, if we choose to engage in illegal activities, society has a perfectly legitimate right to punish us. The act of holding criminals responsible for their actions both deters an unknown number of potential wrongdoers and affirms the humanity of offenders by treating them as free agents rather than mindless automatons blown hither and thither by capricious circumstances and events external to them. The assumption of a rational free-willed individual that emerged during the Enlightenment is the assumption that underlies all modern legal systems.

The nineteenth-century founding fathers of our disciplines, such as Cesare Lombroso and Raffaele Garofalo, were children of positivism, a philosophy pioneered by Auguste Comte that maintains that authentic knowledge comes only from sense experience that is subject to "positive" verification. This was the great age of science, and science was (and is) deterministic. Even though there was a great enthusiasm for science in general during the nineteenth century, there were enemies of determinism as it is commonly understood by scientists. The modern counterparts of these folks may call themselves by names such as postmodernists, humanists, existentialists, radical feminists, and social constructionists. This coterie of intellectuals values creativity and spontaneity, and tends to view science with all its rules and methods as a numbing rationality lacking in emotional quality. Saint-Amand (1997:96) describes the anti-science writings of these scholars as "a refutation, as well the negation, of the heritage of the Enlightenment." Modern anti-science individuals are heirs to the fears of science that such champions of Romanticism as Wordsworth and Shelly railed against in the early nineteenth century. The Romantics believed that the idea of determinism detracts from human freedom and dignity, and they tended to equate the determinism of Newton's age with universal determinism, a view usually associated with eighteenth-century French mathematician and astronomer Pierre Laplace, who wrote:

> *An intelligence knowing all the forces acting in nature at a given instant, as well as the momentary positions of all things in the universe, would be able to comprehend in one single formula the motions of the largest bodies as well as the lightest atoms in the world, provided that its intellect were sufficiently powerful to subject all data to analysis; to it nothing would be uncertain, the future as well as the past would be present to its eyes. The perfection that the human mind has been able to give to astronomy affords but a feeble outline of such an intelligence.*
>
> *(in Bishop, 2006:2)*

These two sentences look a lot like fatalism, or perhaps Calvinistic predestination, because only an almighty God could possess such an intellect. But Laplace was well aware of this and posed this hypothetical as true in *principle* but impossible in practice. He posed this impossible scenario precisely to propose how science should proceed in the absence of perfect knowledge about all possible influences on a phenomenon of interest. He wanted to contrast the concepts of certainty and probability to introduce his statistical physics (Bishop, 2006). Yet some enemies of determinism claim that Laplace's purposely constructed absolutely deterministic straw man is the kind of determinism that scientists actually embrace (Saint-Amand, 1997).

When scientists speak of determinism, they usually mean causal determinism, which simply means that every event stands in some causal relationship to other antecedent events. Determinism is a position relating to how the world is said to operate and is a position held by all scientists; what would it be for a scientist *not* to be a determinist? Scientific determinism does not state that X will lead to Y absolutely and unerringly; rather, it says that given the presence of X, there is a certain probability that Y will occur, which was exactly Laplace's conception of statistical determinism. Surely we are all determinists in this sense. There are certainly unique events and random happenings, thus we cannot always speak of statistical regularities, although even unique events and random happenings have causes. The world is not all chaos and randomness; it has a great degree of predictability about it, and the more science discovers about it, the more predictable it becomes.

On the other hand, when it comes to investigating any kind of human behavior, our most inclusive models do not come near to explaining even one-half of the variance. This is true even in many of the recent models that include genetic as well as a slew of personality and demographic predictor variables. We can continue to blame this on misspecified models and/or inadequate measuring instruments, but I am more inclined to opt for locating the "missing" variance in human agency and pure chance. Although I am more allied with Sartre than Skinner on this question, Sartre's radical freedom does not cut it. Rather, Karl Marx got it right when he asserted that humans make their own history, but they make it from a cloth they did not weave themselves. Left realist Steven Box (1987:29) puts this in more modern context in asserting that people *choose* to act criminally, and "their choice makes them responsible, but the conditions make the choice comprehensible."

Atoms and the Origin of the Controversy

According to Pamela Huby (1967), the Greek philosopher Epicurus was the originator of the free will/determinism controversy. Epicurus took the free will position based on Democritus' atomic theory within which the "swerve" of an atom can occur without cause. Roman philosopher Lucretius developed his theory of free will based on the same idea, and he wrote, "The atoms do not move in straight or uniform lines; there is in their motion an incalculable declination or deviation, an elemental spontaneity that runs through all things and culminates in man's free will" (in Durant, 1944:150–151). The modern version of this argument is based on Heisenberg's principle of uncertainty (unpredictability), which is said to destroy determinism and affirm the unfettered freedom of the will (Schuster, 2009). But would you want the kind of freedom in which no one can probabilistically predict your behavior? The random, unstructured firing of neurons is one of the defining features of schizophrenia, and being in that unfortunate condition is not my idea of freedom. Max Weber wrote of the kind of freedom championed by Lucretius as the "privilege of the insane" (in Eliaeson, 2002:35). If free will means action without a cause, all actions would be unpredictable and chaos would reign.

Writing of the uncertainty principle and the way it has been misused to affirm a sort of "new age" free will, Nobel Prize-winning physicist Richard Feynman says that the prediction of an emission of a photon from an atom is probabilistic but still deterministic, and that "this has given rise to all kinds of nonsense and questions of freedom of will, and the idea that the world is uncertain" (in Corredoira, 2009:450). The indeterminacy of quantum phenomena is not in the system itself but exists "only when the measurement is carried out" (Corredoira, 2009:450). There are no "uncaused causes" miraculously free of nature, and we do not live in an "Alice in Wonderland" world.

Determinism is the operating assumption of criminological theories usually defined as positivist, such as social learning theory or strain theory. Free will—or human agency—is the operating assumption of such theories as rational choice theory and age-graded life course theory. These latter theories are not radically free-willed in the sense that they disavow behavioral causation. Their free will is more akin to the compatibilist free will of philosophy, a position that insists that free will and determinism can peacefully coexist. What is meant by agency or free will is that people are free to do what they want unless constrained by external circumstances. In affirming this position, compatibilists are in complete agreement with Schopenhauer's position that "you are free to do what you want, but you are not free to want what you want" (in Clark, 2007:96). In other words, we are free to wish for that which is compatible with our nature, a nature that is the product of a configuration of our genes and developmental history. We are not free, however, to choose wishes or wants that run contrary to our nature—that is, wants that would disgust, harm, or terrorize us. A weak, introverted, and fearful man, for instance, may wish for a nice, quiet, and safe career in accounting or computer science but never for a career in the police or the marines. Even if the choice is between two options congenial to our natures, we will follow the strongest inclination. We are thus free only to follow our strongest inclination, and for some that is not freedom of the will.

I see no problem with this kind of freedom. After all, my strongest inclination is *my* strongest inclination, and no one else's. My nature is me and my will is mine; so if I follow the direction my nature nudges me in, am I not following my will? To ask for freedom beyond that is meaningless; how can one be free of one's nature? As Weber says, it would constitute insanity, and that is not freedom. A determinist might reply that nonhuman animals also engage in goal-directed behavior dictated by their natures, and no one invests them with free will because they are instinctively compelled to do so. A compatibilist would reply to this that humans, however, have the unique ability to take ownership of their natural desires and to control them. They have the ability to reflect actively on their desires to form judgments concerning their desirability in light of many other moral and pragmatic considerations. A simple example will suffice. Suppose the "animal" appetitive desire to eat a donut overcomes me (call this a "first-order" desire). The rational part of me then leads me to forgo the pleasure for the sake of future considerations of health (a "second-order" desire). In taking control of my first-order desires—which are more "natural" in that we share them with all other animals—I believe that I am as free as it is possible to be in this world of cause and effect.

It might well be that determinism is necessary for human agency. If I did not think that the things I do produce (determine) meaningful consequences, why would I do anything? All rational action and education is deterministic in the sense that it is designed to produce effects (not eating the donut makes me healthier). I know that I am a free agent and that living according to that position is necessary, but I also know that my agency is constrained and/or enabled by my temperament, upbringing, knowledge, conscience, physical and cognitive abilities and disabilities, and the size of my bank account, as well as the formal and informal constraints imposed on me by others. Without a belief in free will or agency—our ability to shape our own worlds—our minds would be imprisoned by the kind of deadly *que sera, sera* fatalism that Walter Miller (1958) found infecting lower class neighborhoods in his focal concerns theory.

As noted previously, there are some folks who believe that any kind of causal talk about our behavior detracts from our freedom and dignity, which I find to be counterintuitive. Let us say that I know you have found a wallet in the library containing a considerable amount of cash and predict that you will turn it in at the counter. Have I, by predicting your behavior, thereby impugned your free will and thus insulted you? I have certainly made a prediction about you based on my knowledge of your moral character, but rather than insulting you, I have praised your character, and praiseworthiness and blameworthiness are the pillars that support the free will concept. If, on the other hand, I said that although I have known you for several years, you are a free autonomous agent and therefore I do not know whether you will turn it in, I have insulted your moral character by implying that you might decide to keep the wallet.

This is not to say that we do not also have instances of excessive determinism. One often gets the impression that some criminologists, in their eagerness to blame everything for crime except those who commit it, view criminals about as free as leaves blown hither and thither by the vagaries of the November winds. To illustrate this point, Walsh and Stohr (2010:232) quote a Calvin and Hobbes cartoon to illustrate what correctional psychologists call "stinkin' thinkin'." Calvin says to his father:

> *I have concluded that nothing bad I do is my fault.... Being young and irresponsible I'm a helpless victim of countless bad influences. An unwholesome culture panders to my undeveloped values and it pushes me into misbehavior. I take no responsibility for my behavior. I'm an innocent pawn of society.*

People like Calvin are part of today's cult of victimhood, a cult for which social science must accept some responsibility by giving folks like Calvin authoritative excuses for their behavior. Criminals and defense attorneys are glad to take advantage of what Richard Felson (1991) calls "blame analysis," which can become the ingrained patterns of thought ("stinkin' thinkin'") that frustrates treatment efforts (Sharp, 2006). If we think of ourselves (or of others) as victims rather than as autonomous agents, as well as absolving ourselves and others of responsibility, we rob ourselves and others of humanity and exercise what existentialists call "bad faith" (the practice of disowning our freedom to act as authentic human beings).

Compatibilists can also steal from physics to buttress their position in the form of Niels Bohr's principle of complementarity—that is, the wave-particle dual nature of light. There was much initial resistance to this counterintuitive wave-particle duality, but as it became increasingly more empirically endorsed, it led to modern quantum theory (Polkinghorne, 2002). Albert Einstein and Leopold Infeld (1938:262–263) had the following to say about this supposed conundrum:

> *But what is light really? Is it a wave or a shower of photons? There seems no likelihood for forming a consistent description of the phenomena of light by a choice of only one of the two languages. It seems as though we must use sometimes the one theory and sometimes the other, while at times we may use either. We are faced with a new kind of difficulty. We have two contradictory pictures of reality; separately neither of them fully explains the phenomena of light, but together they do.*

Substitute human action for light, and free will and determinism for waves and particles, and we can likewise conclude that neither free will (agency) nor determinism alone is sufficient to understand human action; we need both concepts to do so. Just as there is no longer any paradox in the wave-particle duality of light in physics, there should be no paradox among criminologists about humans being both agenic and determined. Determinism gives us the only kind of free will worth having. It is a free will that follows the reasoned dictates of our natures (albeit, natures "caused" by the interaction of genetic inheritance and developmental experiences) and lays on our shoulders the responsibility of owning our actions.

According to neuroscientist Bjorn Brembs (2011:933), free will is a quantitative trait with some having more of it than others: "The question is not any more 'do we have free will'?" but rather "how much free will do we have'?" I find this position congenial. Conceptualizing free will/agency as a quantitative thing, it is logical to think that most of us will tend to become freer as we become more self-assured by the sum of our life experiences and our bank accounts. Becoming increasingly freer of external constraints as we move from childhood to old age means that we are able to live progressively more in accordance with the natural proclivities of our natures leavened by the wisdom of age. Behavioral genetic studies consistently and robustly find that as we age the influences of shared environments (environments in which individuals are under the considerable control of others) on our personalities and cognitive abilities fade to almost nothing, while the influence of genes (which belong to us) and nonshared environments (which we partly create) become stronger (Beaver, 2009; Bouchard & McGue, 2003; Moffitt, 2005; Walsh, 2009a). I am reminded of the wise old saying here: "The older I get, the more I become myself."

Genetics, Determinism, and Free Will

It would seem that most social scientists *qua* scientists are determinists if we judge by the content of their textbooks and journals and by the curriculum they provide for their students. It is thus safe to assume that they are not against the concept of determinism in general. However, when most social scientist use the term *determinism* they are heaping scorn on what they call "biological" or "genetic determinism"; environmental determinism appears to be perfectly acceptable, however. Genetic determinism is seen as implying that social behavior is a *direct* outcome of genetic programming absent any influence from the environment. Colin Trudge (1999:96) opines that such reasoning represents either mere rhetoric or simple ignorance: "No evolutionary psychologist [or geneticist or neuroscientist] doubts that a gene is in constant dialogue with its surroundings, which include the other genes in the genome, the rest of the organism, and the world at large." Criminologists who incorporate genetic, neurological, or evolutionary factors into their work include environmental factors, using such concepts as gene × environment interaction and neural Darwinism (the process of "softwiring" the brain by selective elimination and retention of synaptic networks according to environmental experiences). These criminologists are well aware that without an environment, genes and brains have no place to go because they depend on the environment for their expression. If only those who rail against biological and genetic determinism would learn something about human biology, they would not embarrass themselves by reflexively bandying that naive accusation about.

Ironically, there are philosophers and scientists who see genetics as the foundation of free will. This position is couched most often in terms of free will being the evolving freedom to follow the inclinations of our own natures. Matt Ridley, the heavyweight champion of nature *via* nurture, had something quite astute to say about the fears of "genetic determinism" and why social scientist should rid themselves of such fears:

> *Genes are not puppet masters, nor blueprints. They may direct the construction of the body and brain in the womb, but they set about dismantling and rebuilding what they have made almost at once in response to experience. They are both the cause and consequence of our actions. Somehow the adherents of the "nurture" side of the argument have scared themselves silly at the power and inevitability of genes, and missed the greatest lesson of all:* The genes are on our side.
>
> (2003:6; emphasis added)

Ridley is telling us a truism of genetics, a truism that is directly the opposite of what those who fear "genetic determinism" believe: *Genes are at our beck and call, not we at theirs.* Genes are constantly responding to our needs by making the hormones, neuro-transmitter, and cell-structure proteins we need as we meet the many challenges of our environments. Badcock (2000:71) goes so far as to assert that our genes "positively guarantee" human freedom and agency. If they incline us in one direction rather than another, we are being nudged internally, not by something wholly outside of our beings. After all, our genes are *our* genes. Neurobiologist and avocational social scientist Steven Rose (2001:6) likewise writes, "Individually and collectively we have the ability to construct our own futures, albeit in circumstances not of our own choosing. Thus it is that our biology makes us free." The more we come to appreciate how natural scientists view issues of human agency in relation to biology, the more we will appreciate how erroneous the charges of biological determinism and the more we will appreciate the necessity to study criminal behavior and the human nature that it issues from at multiple levels of analysis from neurons to neighborhoods.

Conclusion

Just as physicists, mathematicians, and other physical and natural scientists have found that philosophy provides them a useful foundation for their thought, so can criminologists. We should be able to benefit even more than other scientists because we are an extremely young discipline, and we within it rarely question the underlying assumptions upon which we rest our work. Philosophy has the ability to clarify our thoughts for us, perhaps inform us of why we think about things the way we do, perhaps solve some contradictions in our thinking we never knew existed, and perhaps even dissolve some dichotomies we thought were cast in stone. Let me be quite clear: "The alternative to philosophy is not no philosophy, but bad philosophy. The 'unphilosophical' person has an unconscious philosophy, which they apply in their practice—whether of science or politics or daily life" (Collier, 1994:17). We will see how these "unconscious philosophies" seep into the works of social scientists in terms of ideologies and "visions," and how modern geneticists and neuroscientists are pinpointing how these things lie in our temperaments.

One of those dichotomies that have bedeviled social science is the free will–determinism argument. This fight has been going on for centuries and may never be resolved to everyone's satisfaction. Criminology can live with both free will/agency, as posited by some theories, and determinism, as posited by others. After all, we all do so in our own lives as we look for cause and effect in our work, while at the same time living our lives as we want to within normal constraints. Free will and determinism are very much in the same category of the wave-particle duality of light, and Schopenhauer's view of free will is a wonderful compromise between false dichotomies. It is certainly much preferable to Lucretius's view that implies unpredictability, which, as Max Weber said, would put us in a rubber room. If I am free to follow the dictates of my nature, then I am as free as it is logically possible to be because the dictates moving me are mine and mine alone. It is in this sense that I join a host of eminent scientists in claiming that our biology, far from imprisoning us, makes us free.

2

Social Constructionism Versus Science in Criminology

What Is Social Constructionism?

Social constructionism has a long history, with its many instantiations dating back many centuries. The postmodernist tradition grew out of social constructionism and shares its blend of skepticism, nihilism, relativism, and its penchant for almost incomprehensible prose (Einstadter & Henry, 2006). Postmodernism and social constructionism have infiltrated criminology and strongly challenged its claim to be objective in any sense of the term. For anti-science scholars, science is as irrational as any other system of human thought. Like all terms ending with *ism*, there are many varieties of postmodernism and social constructionism that range from the reasonable, most of which empirical scientists can happily live with, to the outrageous. We are only concerned here with claims of social construction as they apply to features of criminology, such as the nature of crime and criminality.

Broadly speaking, social constructionism is a philosophy of knowledge maintaining that concepts, practices, beliefs, and sometimes facts are artifacts of a particular time and place and are defined into existence rather than discovered. These artifacts (constructions) are said to be contingent on human representations for their existence rather than on some inherent property those things possess. It emphasizes the socially created nature of truth and knowledge, and it serves as an ontological–epistemological critique opposed to realism, reductionism, determinism, and essentialism. It is popular with the most radical of dreamers because it challenges almost everything that *is* and champions that which *should* be. It is also optimistic in its assumption that because humans have constructed things the way they are, they can deconstruct them and then construct something they consider to be better.

There are six degrees of commitment to social constructionism, according to the eminent philosopher of science Ian Hacking (1999:6–7). The weakest constructionists (he calls them *historic*) do not judge a concept or a practice (call it X); they merely claim that X is the result of certain historical events and could have been otherwise. The *ironic* constructionist points out that X could have been otherwise, and anyone who believes that X is inevitable is naive, but we are stuck with it. Next is the *unmasking* constructionist who exposes the ideology and power relations that underlie X and is content to simply expose X, but not to refute it. The *reformist* constructionist takes a negative view of X and seeks to modify it by pointing out the contingency of the disliked aspects of X.

The *rebellious* constructionist wants to get rid of X altogether, and the *revolutionary* constructionist is an activist in the cause of eliminating X.

The major difference between the weak (the first three degrees) and strong (the remaining three) versions of constructionism is that whereas the weak version maintains that people's *representations* of things and concepts are socially constructed, "strong social constructionism claims not only that representations are socially constructed, but the *entities themselves* to which these representations refer are socially constructed" (Goldman, 2006:11). This is known as fact constructionism. Paul Boghossian (2006:25) maintains that fact constructionism is the most influential form of constructionism, which he finds "surprising given that it is the most radical and most counterintuitive. Indeed, properly understood, fact constructivism is such a bizarre view that it is hard to believe that anyone actually endorses it. And yet, it seems that many do." It may be that it is precisely its radical and counterintuitive nature that attracts those whom Bruce Charlton (2009) calls "clever sillies." I cannot believe that any postmodernism–social constructionist criminologist is a fact constructionist, although some come dangerously close.

Although the idea that humans construct their reality by common agreement has been around at least since Plato, Peter Berger and Thomas Luckmann's *The Social Construction of Reality* (1966) arguably marked the beginning of a major interest in constructionist thought in sociology. So many of the social things and practices Berger and Luckmann addressed were so obviously social constructions (money and newspapers) that a modern reader may find it superfluous to have mentioned them at all. Yet at the time their unmasking of so many things was revelatory and enlightening in their assertions about the tenuousness of social reality. Berger and Luckmann were not radical constructionists in the sense that they believed everything is arbitrarily socially created. Although they often stressed the biological substrates of many social constructions about humans, they urged us not to confuse the socially constructed referents of these things for the things themselves. Their main point was that people interact with the subconscious understanding that their perceptions of reality are shared with others, and when they act on this understanding, their faith in their reality is further reinforced. As far as I could see, their only agenda was to stop us taking our realities for granted and reifying them. Unlike so many modern social constructionist critiques, nothing in their book was about substantive claims about the existence of things but, rather, about how those things are (mis)represented as natural.

The Power of Language

Hacking (1999) lists at least 50 tangible and intangible things, ranging from mental illness to quarks, that someone or another has claimed to be social constructions. We could add many items to Hacking's laundry list of things created from social stuff. Following Daniel Dennett's (1995) famous metaphor for natural selection as a "universal acid" eating through all worldviews that preceded Darwin, I have (Walsh, 2013) metaphorically described social constructionism as a "universal sponge" soaking up all sorts of concepts from A to Z and squeezing them back out in mutated form. Constructionists grant themselves this right of concept cleaning because, with Immanuel Kant, they are skeptical about the extent to which language is referential to an external reality. Language is flawed in its ability to take us unerringly from Kant's noumenal world (the "really real" world of things-in-themselves) to the phenomenal world (our perceptions and interpretations of these things). Something can have a quite different meaning to different people based on the language used to describe and understand it. This is why language is so important to postmodernists and other associated positions. Berger and Luckmann (1966:37–38) make the unassailable assertion that language is essential for understanding the reality of social life:

> *The common objectivations of everyday life are maintained primarily by linguistic significations. Everyday life is, above all, life with and by means of the language I share with my fellowmen.... I encounter language as a facticity external to myself and it is coercive in its effects on me. Language forces me into its patterns.*

It is undeniably true that language enables us to represent our taken-for-granted worlds, but our representations and categories of it have developed from our experiences of the actual world. Our world shapes our categories, even if our understanding of it is limited by our perceptual abilities and influenced the categories provided by others, as Kant claimed. Kant's noumenal/phenomenal distinction can be misleading, however, because many of the things of science that were once "noumenal" (bacteria, atoms, genes, and hundreds of other things) are now phenomenal as our raw perceptual abilities have been augmented by technology. Nevertheless, the sometimes arbitrary nature of our classifications is exemplified by the familiar Thomas theorem: "If men define situations as real they are real in their consequences" (in Merton, 1995:380). In some senses, the "reality" is as much constituted by talk as it is mirrored by it. We cannot deny that the reality we perceive and act on is constructed from common experience and communally validated, so we are all social constructionists in this weak sense.

Steven Pinker (2002:202) provides many examples of things that "exist only because people tacitly agree to act as if they exist. Examples include money, tenure, citizenship, decorations for bravery, and the presidency of the United States." Constructionists do not deny the reality of these things and practices, but their point is that they are not products of nature, and thus are not inevitable. They may be ontologically objective in that they produce real consequences, but they are also ontologically subjective because they require human input in order to exist.

We could, of course, get by without tenure and bravery decorations, although they are rather nice to have. On the other hand, it seems inevitable that social groups competing and trading with other groups had to develop formal systems of leadership and efficient systems of barter lest we remain in Hobbes's chaotic state of nature. Yet they are still human products rather than products of nature. But before we go too far with this, let us acknowledge that at one level *all things*, including the gifts of nature, are socially constructed. Nature does not reveal herself to us ready sorted and labeled, so humans must do it for her. Social construction in this weak sense means that humans have perceived a phenomenon, named it, and categorized it according to some taxonomical rule (also socially constructed) that takes note of similarities and differences among the things being sorted and classified. Because things are *necessarily* socially constructed in this vacuous sense, it does not mean that the process of categorization is arbitrary and without empirical referents and rational meaning.

However, as we have seen, there are strands of social constructionism that go far beyond examining how people interpret and refer to the world to embrace radical refutations of almost everything, including science itself. Hacking (1999:67) characterizes folks drawn to radical constructionism in quite negative terms:

> *What is true is that many science-haters and know-nothings latch on to constructionism as vindicating their impotent hostility to the sciences. Constructionism provides a voice for that rage against reason. And many constructionists do appear to dislike the practice and content of the sciences.*

Extreme constructionists make preposterous statements, such as "the validity of theoretical propositions in the sciences is in no way affected by factual evidence" (Gergen 1988:37). Social constructionism is so seductive to people like this because it puts no constraints on them, and it is thus more generous than science in what it allows them to claim. If nothing is real and objective, if there are no universal standards with which to judge truth and falsity, they need not produce evidence to support their position when a paragraph or two of impenetrable prose will sweep it under the rug. If everything is relative, they are relieved of coming to terms with the theories and methods of science with its claims of objectivity, and they are blessed with the freedom to deconstruct concepts not to their liking. As Wright and Boisvert (2009:1232) characterize this intellectual freewheeling: "without scientific reasoning as the core value, 'theoretical imagination' is allowed to run amok."

Postmodernism/Social Constructionism and Criminology

Wright and Boisvert's (2009) complaint highlights a major problem with postmodernist approaches in criminology. So many of the pronouncements made by criminologists in this tradition sound so naive and are written in such convoluted prose that I often feel that they have followed Alice down the rabbit hole and jumped on the mushroom to share the caterpillar's hookah. This is a pity, because in some ways social constructionist thought can be useful if not stretched to the breaking point. The value of social constructionism is that it gives us pause when we start to believe that our social practices are natural and inevitable rather than contingent, but it is not a useful epistemology to guide us in our search for new knowledge. Social constructionism is a brake preventing us from going too far in our claims rather than an accelerator moving us forward. It is too often off-putting in its belittling of the importance of science, in its universal condemnation of almost everything about the status quo (from which most of them benefit handsomely), and its imperial quest to deconstruct everything in its path. As Hacking (who calls himself a weak social constructionist) remarks about this imperial overstretch: "so many types of analyses invoke social construction that quite distinct objectives get run together. An all-encompassing constructionist approach has become rather dull—in both senses of the word, boring and blunted" (1999:35).

Postmodernist/Peacemaking Criminology

Postmodernist criminologists reject the "modernist" view aimed at understanding, explaining, predicting, and controlling crime and appeal for a diversity of views in which none are disparaged and all are legitimized. They reject the notion that the scientific view is any better than any other view, and they disparage the claim that any method of understanding can be objective because there is no mind-independent reality:

> *Postmodernism questions whether we can ever "know" something objectively; so called neutral science is considered a sham and criminology's search for causes is bankrupt because even the question is framed by androcentric, sexist, classist, and racist definitions of crime, criminality, and cause.*
>
> *(Pollock, 1999:146)*

The bedrock principle of postmodernism is that all worldviews are mediated by language, and the language of the modernist worldview is science. Rather than liberating people, they claim that the products of science, such as industrialism and modern weaponry, have oppressed people because they have "extended and amplified the scope of violence in the world" (Schwartz & Friedrichs, 1994:224). Postmodernists claim that the dominant language discourse of society is the language of the rich and powerful, and by virtue of "owning" the dominant language, their point of view is privileged. The views of reality shared by criminals and the mentally ill, for example, are rejected and replaced by the views of the criminal justice and psychiatric systems, because the latter have the power to enforce their view of reality, and "this replacement of languages eclipses reality as lived and spoken by others" (Arrigo & Bernard, 2002:251). Lutz (2000:230–233) augments this by saying "language is a tool or weapon that can be used by those in power to achieve their ends at the expense of others.... It delivers us into the hands of those who do not have our interests at heart." The exposure of the dominant language system as a source of oppression and then to "deconstruct" and supplant it with "replacement discourses" is high on the postmodernist criminological agenda. These replacement discourses are supposed to authenticate all of society's pluralistic viewpoints and to grant primacy to none.

Peacemaking criminology is in the postmodernist tradition and has a compassionate and spiritual spin that attracts a hodgepodge of dreamers and disenchanted types both spiritual and secular. It relies heavily on the concept of "appreciative relativism," which means that all points of view, including those of criminals, are relative, and all should be appreciated. Peacemaking criminology's basic philosophy is similar to the Hippie adage, "Make love, not war," without the sexual overtones. It shudders at the current "war on crime" metaphor and wants to substitute "peace on crime." This idea is captured by Kay Harris's statement that we:

> need to reject the idea that those who cause injury or harm to others should suffer severance of the common bonds of respect and concern that bind members of a community. We should relinquish the notion that it is acceptable to try to "get rid of" another person whether through execution, banishment, or caging away people about whom we do not care.
>
> *(1991:93)*

For peacemaking criminologists, an emphasis on punishing criminals escalates violence. Richard Quinney has called the American criminal justice system the moral equivalent of war, and notes that war naturally invites resistance by those it is waged against. He further adds that when society resists criminal victimization, it "must be in compassion and love, not in terms of the violence that is being resisted" (in Vold, Bernard, & Snipes, 1998:274).

Critical Realism: A Middle Ground

I do not propose a complete dismissal of the postmodernist perspective. Our thinking should be sufficiently tinged with postmodernism to recognize that there is a certain precariousness involved in the relationships between our theories, our perceptions, and our data (see the discussion of Thomas Kuhn's concept of the theory ladenness of data in Chapter 3). It is naive to suggest that by following the "scientific method," what we discover directly corresponds to a big-T Truth about the world, especially the social world. While the natural material world is intransitive (or nearly so), the social world is transitive. Our theories always depend on our preconceptions about the phenomena to which they are applied and the ways we measure them. While the successes of science, particularly of the hard sciences, strongly suggest that they tell us a lot about the complexities of reality, it is naive to claim that what we find is uninterpreted objective reality—the way things "really" are. This is what philosophers call naive realism. By the same token, we should also rule out more extreme forms of idealism that promote the notion that mental concepts are more real than the physical.

A philosophical position at the interstices of modernism and postmodernism and strong realism and strong relativism is critical realism. Critical realism is associated with British philosopher Roy Bhaskar (1978), and is a philosophy of knowledge that claims the possibility of gaining mind-independent knowledge of the world as it is, not merely as it is subjectively perceived. It does, however, hold that science is fallible and that our perceptions of reality are functions of the mind, and consequently, that we must always critically reflect on our perceptions. This position is somewhat akin to Kant's phenomenal/noumenal distinction without the skepticism that the noumenal world is forever lost to us. Critical realism maintains that science has the ability to progressively close the gap between our views of the world and reality itself; that is, the chasm between the phenomenal and the noumenal can be bridged incrementally as scientists go about interpreting and reinterpreting their data. This is the "realism" in critical realism. The "critical" element in critical realism lies in the belief that nothing should go unchallenged; if it is not challenged, no reinterpretation is possible and no progress is made.

Critical realism wants us to remember that our theories and data are maps of reality, not reality itself. We all realize that when we look at a map, we are looking at a representation of the terrain, not the terrain itself. Likewise, when we conduct experiments and surveys, we are artificially constructing a closed world to isolate regularities between and among variables that we rarely can directly observe in the more chaotic open world. But maps, experiments, and surveys are tremendously helpful in getting us where we want to go, and they give us some idea of what it will be like when we get there. In other words, critical realism is ontologically realist (it affirms that there is a mind-independent world out there) and epistemologically fallibilistic (no theory or model of the world can ever be rationally justified in an absolutely conclusive way). I imagine all scientists agree with critical realism, even if it has to hit them in the eye occasionally to remind them when they become too dogmatic about their theories.

The Reality of Crime and Criminality

According to Ron Akers (1997:176–177), postmodern-influenced approaches:

> *take the extreme position that denies crime as such really exists. Crime exists only because it is a "discursive production," that is, a product not only of the interaction of offenders, control agents, criminologists, or other people, or simply by talking about it.... This implies that there is no such thing as crime as an objective behavioral reality to be explained.*

He goes on to ask, "Does this mean that criminal behavior would not exist if we did not talk about it?" This is a tad overstated because Akers makes it sound like fact constructionism, but it is easy to see how he could read it this way. Postmodernism/ peacemaking criminologists do not deny the harm done by what we call crime, or that it will disappear if we stop talking about it. Rather, they argue that "harm will cease to be the outcome of a world that does not invest in the realities of difference in ways that value some human subjects over others and that exploit difference as a means of domination" (Einstadter & Henry, 2006:304). Because this was written in a criminological context, I can only assume that Einstadter and Henry had in mind things like appreciative relativism, "making peace" on crime, and that we should love criminals as we love ourselves, or at least not "value some human subjects [noncriminals?] over others [criminals?]." Unless

I mistake their meaning, this seems almost as naive as saying that crime will cease if we stop talking about it.

The ontological status of crime in this tradition (shared by a variety of modernist conflict-critical theories) is that it is a social construct with no palpable independent referents, although as I have said, they do not deny that crime is real for its victims, or that it hurts. The arbitrariness said to characterize the labeling of a particular act as criminal may be traced to Emile Durkheim's (1933:81) statement that:

> *we must not say that an action shocks the common conscience because it is criminal, but rather that it is criminal because it shocks the common conscience. We do not reprove it because it is a crime, but it is a crime because we reprove it.*

Thus, Darnell Hawkins (1995:41) can write that "we cannot know what *real* crime is, or who *real* criminals are." Then we have William Chambliss's classic bait-and-switch tactic involving the nature of crime. Chambliss explained how the vagrancy laws of thirteenth-century England were implemented to favor the elite by providing them with workers and concluded: "What is true of the vagrancy laws is true of the criminal law in general" (in Nettler, 1984:197).

What Durkheim forgot to add to his statement is that there are acts that shock the collective conscience everywhere and are universally condemned (Walsh & Ellis, 2007). Saying that we cannot know what real crime is or equating vagrancy (a *malum prohibitum*) with other crimes "in general" minimizes the suffering of victims of intrinsically evil (*mala in se*) crimes. *Mala in se* crimes produce *real* palpable physiological responses in people victimized by them in all places and in all times because, except in the most bizarre of circumstances, nobody wants to be victimized by murderers, rapists, robbers, and thieves. These built-in physiological responses (anger, helplessness, sadness, and desire for revenge) are not added to and subtracted from our natural emotional response repertoires every time some political body decides to add or delete an item from its criminal code. The statute forbidding the act is socially invented, but the act forbidden is as ontologically real as the knife in the chest or the house denuded of its contents. *Mala in se* acts engage our emotions because they hammer at our deepest primordial instincts. They are evolved responses to acts that militated against our ancestors' survival and reproductive needs, and function to help us both to avoid victimization and to motivate us to punish (*pace* Quinney) offenders (Krebs, 2008; O'Manique, 2003; Walsh, 2006). This is not to deny that some *mala prohibita* crimes may engage the same emotions in some people in some places at some times. These emotions may be engaged less strongly and in fewer people if a formerly illegal act (abortion, sodomy, or flag burning) becomes legal, but *mala in se* acts engage them ubiquitously and will do so regardless of their legal status.

Then there is the issue of criminality, the name of a trait we give to individuals who commit predatory harmful acts. Criminality is a scientific rather than a legal term that is defined independent of legal definitions of crime. Crime is an intentional act of commission or omission contrary to the law; criminality is a property of individuals that signals the willingness to commit those acts (Gottfredson & Hirschi, 1990). Criminality is a continuously distributed trait that is a combination of other continuously distributed traits such as negative emotionality, impulsiveness, egoism, low empathy, and many other traits that make a person less than desirable as a friend, mate, or employee. It is the propensity to use and abuse others for personal gain that defines criminality independent of the labeling of an act as a crime or of the person being legally defined as a criminal.

Defining criminality as a continuous trait acknowledges that there is no sharp line separating individuals with respect to this trait. We are all situated somewhere on the criminality continuum, from saint to sociopath, but a small number of individuals have committed so many crimes and other harmful acts over such a long period of time that few would question the appropriateness of calling them criminals. Criminality is a very complex phenotype consisting of a number of building blocks or component parts that geneticists call *endophenotypes* (endo = "within" the phenotype). Endophenotypes are parts of the complex chain leading from genotype to phenotype, with each perhaps having only minor effects on the phenotype, and then only if combined with other relevant endophenotypes and environments. The point is that when we get down to the nitty-gritty of molecular genetics, reducing the criminality phenotype to the constituent and less complex endophenotypic parts, such as impulsiveness and negative emotionality, makes it easier to identify and study their genetic basis than if we tried to map the more elusive phenotype itself (Glahn, Thompson, & Blangero, 2002). This is so simply because constitutive traits (the endophenotypes) "sit closer to the genotype in the development scheme" (Gottesman & Hanson, 2005:268).

Talk of genes, heritability, and genomes may horrify postmodernists, but the question for criminologists on the science side of the science wars is no longer *whether* genes influence criminal behavior but, rather, *how* they do so. Meta-analyses of behavior genetic studies show a broad heritability of at least 50% for antisocial behavior (Ferguson, 2010; Guo, Roettger, & Shih, 2007; Moffitt, 2005; Rhee & Waldman, 2002). The question thus devolves to molecular genetics and becomes "which genes predispose individuals to criminal behavior in which environments?" As our brief discussion of endophenotypes reveals, there is no direct genetic route from any gene or set of genes to any quantitative trait. Heritability coefficients computed for criminality or for any other quantitative trait are actually capturing a wide variety of correlated endophenotypes. The specific genes mapping to these endophenotypes have to be identified using molecular genetics techniques. Some of these genes are discussed in Chapter 9 on conscience.

The Moralistic Fallacy

A number of commentators, such as philosophers Paul Boghossian (2006) and Mark Kalderon (2009), have written that many academics who gravitate to postmodernism and social constructionism do so out of a genuine "fear of knowledge." They do not mean fear of all knowledge, only of knowledge they believe can do harm to certain groups by using science to imply that differences between or among them are natural. This is especially true when it comes to race and gender issues (Walsh, 2013). According to Kalderon (2009:239), constructionists' fear of knowledge: "is animated by the thought that the authority of reason, and its attendant rhetoric of objectivity, is a mask for the interests of power." He further claims that any effective case against these scholars must deal with their real fear or else risk their further embrace of antiscientific positions.

Arguments from fear easily slip into the moralistic fallacy, the lesser known sibling of the naturalistic fallacy. The naturalistic fallacy, a phrase coined by the philosopher David Hume in the eighteenth century, is the fallacy of leaping from *is* to *ought*. This is the tendency to believe that whatever is natural is healthy, good, and moral; that is, no distinction is made between an empirical fact and a moral evaluation of it. An example of the naturalistic would be to say that because violence is part of human nature (i.e., part of our evolved behavioral repertoire), it is natural and therefore it is morally acceptable or at least justifiable. It is obvious that many natural things—disease, death, earthquakes, and so forth—are highly unwelcome and ample reason to reject the idea that *ought* can be determined by *is* (Buss & Malamuth, 1996). Nature simply *is*; what *ought* to be is a moral judgment. Yet, there are many in the social sciences who accuse others who use biologically based (and therefore natural) arguments of justifying, or even applauding, things such as rape and other forms of violence (see Dupre, 1992). Evolution is morally blind in that it "allows" for the selection of behavioral traits that enhance fitness, regardless of how morally repugnant they may be. It is incumbent upon us to control immoral behaviors regardless of whether scientists show them to be products of natural selection, because just as *natural* does not mean *desirable*, it does not mean *inevitable*.

The moralistic fallacy reverses the process to jump from *ought* to *is*; that is, it deduces facts from moral judgments. It is easy to see how one can slip into committing the naturalistic fallacy, but the moralistic fallacy is something one can commit with a clear conscience only if one is a strong social constructionist. Those who commit this fallacy argue that if they find something to be morally offensive, then it is "in fact" false. At least they encourage their negative value judgment of the thing or idea they disparage to be treated as factually true. An example of the moralistic fallacy would be to say that violence is a bad thing and therefore cannot be part of human nature. Violence is bad in the vast majority of instances, but this moral claim simply cannot be used to deduce from it that violence is not a part of our evolutionary baggage. The ethical principle that we should not hurt others does not and cannot rest on false assumptions that deny biology (Lahn & Ebenstein, 2009). In her concerns about the naturalistic and moralistic fallacies and their implications, Helena Cronin (2003:59) writes that:

> it all stems from muddling science and politics. It's as if people believe that if you don't like what you think are the ideological implications of the science then you're free to reject the science—and to cobble together your own version of it instead. Now, I know that sounds ridiculous when it's spelled out explicitly. Science doesn't have ideological implications; it simply tells you how the world is—not how it ought to be.

Biologist Bernard Davis supposedly coined the moralistic fallacy phrase in 1978 to counter censorial propositions being bandied about regarding what research topics should be banned as "socially dangerous." The feared knowledge of the time (and still feared to some extent today) was the genetics of intelligence. Because those who sought to prevent this research took it for granted that they have the monopoly on virtue, they believed that it granted them the right, indeed the duty, to conceal or destroy any knowledge contrary to their vision of social justice ("The idea that genes underlie variation in intelligence is repugnant to us; therefore genes *do not* underlie variation in intelligence"). Davis says that the notion of "forbidden knowledge" has a long history because it has disturbed cherished beliefs, but also that "it is a difficult notion for scientists to accept, since all knowledge can be used in various ways, and it would seem better to restrain the bad uses rather than to deprive ourselves of the good ones" (2000:5). I think this is a position that almost all true scientists would hold. As Norman Levitt (1999:315) has concluded: "All of us, scientists and nonscientists alike, must ultimately create and sustain a society and a culture that is mature enough and brave enough to handle the gifts—and the uncomfortable truths—that science affords." Let me just add to this a hearty Amen!

The intrusion of geneticists and neuroscientists into the realm of human behavior has been exponential during the past decade or so, and many social scientists do not wish to accommodate themselves to Levitt's "gifts of science." Biosocial criminologists gratefully accept the gifts of science. As John Wright and Francis Cullen (2012:237) claim: "Biosocial criminology can lead to a criminology that is rooted more in science and empirical observations than in ideology and … can link criminology to a diverse array of other disciplines and research methodologies." Constructionists may well find that the majority of social scientists will eventually come to see the invaders from the biological sciences as liberators rather than conquerors, and as robust allies in the task of coming to understand the quicksilver of human behavior.

Conclusion

It is admittedly strange to hear that there are folks in academia who are anti-science. It is strange when we realize that questions posed about the tangible world—the world we seek to understand and make better—can only be addressed reliably by the tried and true methods of science. Science has always had its enemies, be they from religion, romanticism, new age mysticism, and now postmodernism and its offshoots. Any system opposed to science and rationality draws to it people who are disenchanted with modernism and with just about everything else about the worlds they inhabit. The agenda of folks drawn to such approaches is not so much knowledge production as knowledge destruction. As some have suggested, perhaps they are drawn to obfuscation out of a genuine fear of knowledge—not all knowledge, of course, but knowledge they find distasteful. They seize on certain problematic areas in science, or at least areas problematic for them, in order to damn the whole scientific enterprise.

Although it is true that science is not the only meadow where knowledge and understanding grow, and that there is plenty of room for philosophy and the arts and humanities, it is the most fertile meadow. Science does not always get it right, and sometimes it gets it quite wrong, but scientists know that their work is always tentative and self-correcting. Any system of thought that actively seeks to prevent the march of science (as opposed to monitoring it and demanding practical and ethical justification) because it finds things in it that it fears is a system that represents the betrayal of the Enlightenment tradition of human progress. For my part, I am inclined to the opinion that fear of knowledge can be quieted by actually learning about what is feared. Fear is fed by ignorance, which is easily rectified if one is willing to spend the time and effort to learn something about what is feared. I am aware that many people are temperamentally unable to let themselves into alien worlds, but those who do so may find that there is nothing to fear from the truths that science reveals.

3

Relativism, Rationalism, Empiricism, and Paradigm Shifts

Relativism and Contingency

We have seen that strong constructionists maintain that either there is no truth as such or there is no superior truth, only different truths each veridical in its own domain. The validity of their claims jumps around according to the issue at hand, but when it comes to matters of science these claims must be challenged. Science maintains that there is knowledge and there are truths that are arrived at through procedures of rational assessment. There are domains that the methods of science touch only gently, such as history, morality, ethics, and aesthetics, where "truth" depends to varying extents on non-evidentiary criteria such as taste, politics, social consensus, individual temperament, and experience. The contested areas are those claimed by social sciences that are not sure where to fly their colors because they straddle the humanities and the sciences. Because most social sciences claim the human domain as exclusively theirs, they raise strong objections when natural scientists bring their big guns to bear on topics constructionists believe are not amenable to them. Other social scientists welcome natural scientists and their theories, concepts, and methods as robust allies who can move our enterprise forward.

One of the main sticking points in the war between science and constructionism is contingency (Hacking, 1999). Contingency is the denial of inevitability, or the notion that nothing in science is predetermined and that it could have developed in many different ways. Constructionists support contingency and physical scientists support inevitability, believing that science (at least the physical and natural sciences) would have inevitably evolved much the way it did in any cultural context. Inevitability is not Laplace's purposely constructed determinist straw man or the denial that events are contingent upon other events in order to occur the way they do. Rather, it is the position that the same discoveries, laws, and theories would obtain anywhere because there are constraints presented by the hard facts of nature to prevent contingent modifications based on historical or cultural practices. Nature largely dictates the questions of science, and most certainly it dictates its answers. Maxwell's equations, the second law of thermodynamics, and the velocity of light are examples given by Hacking of scientific knowledge that any adequate physics would find in any cultural context. Had these discoveries been made in Africa, America, or Asia rather than Europe, they would have had exactly the same mathematical values and have led to the same practical applications.

Criminology has no inviolable equations or laws, so its domain is far more open to contingency. Yet norms of conduct, later codified into formal law, do seem to be inevitable as societies evolve, and surely (and ironically) the constructionists' Thomas theorem is true everywhere. What is not inevitable is the nature of these laws and how and to whom they are applied, and "men" can define many situations that are not so. Thus, the social sciences are far more open to contingency because many things in the social world "could be otherwise." The agenda of social constructionists is precisely to strive for "otherwiseness." There will never be an $E = mc^2$ of human behavior, but the extent to which criminological concepts contain elements of the natural (genes, brains, hormones, and evolutionary history) will be the extent to which the contingency argument will be weakened but never destroyed.

The ideas of contingency and relativism are closely related, but there are differences. Contingency rather than relativism is arguably the correct antonym to absolutism. Contingency is compatible with objectivism because it only avers that events rely (are contingent) on other events to occur; thus, the truth of a proposition is not guaranteed under any and all conditions. The difference is that relativists make the claim that something can never be really objective under any conditions or, alternatively, that something can be true for some people but not for others.

Many of us might agree with either or both of these positions as they apply to the vast majority of moral, aesthetic, religious, historical, cultural, and political issues. It is this latter form of relativism that is trivially true: Is prostitution legal? Was Reagan a great president? Is Chicago east or west? Is Starbuck's coffee better than McDonalds'? Is the Bible literally true? The truth or falsity of these and thousands of other similar questions depends on where you are, who you are, and what you believe. This is a noncontroversial position, but radical social constructionists have gone beyond to make the same claims about science. It is when relativism is applied to science that it falls apart. As a critical realist, I believe it a good thing to be skeptical about claims of truth, even scientific claims. Strong claims that all claims are relative are relative and therefore self-refuting, as both Aristotle and Plato pointed out centuries ago. Relativists are absolutely (*pace*) right that we cannot have a God's eye view of the world as it "really" is, but extreme relativism provides no common ground for rational discussion and precludes any kind of knowledge acquisition. The credo of science is to question everything and believe nothing until proven beyond a *reasonable* doubt, but some social constructionists have appropriated relativism to cast *unreasonable* doubts on scientific claims for which there is an abundance of hard evidence, in order to advance an ideological agenda.

Relativism and Moral and Cultural Standards

I think it more than defensible to apply strict standards of belief to moral and cultural standards, as well as to strictly scientific beliefs. If there are no absolute standards for deciding among conflicting beliefs of right and wrong, all cultural value systems are equally valid and anything goes. This limits discussion of issues of morality and truth to descriptive and non-normative discourse. It amounts to intellectual laziness hiding behind the mask of tolerance of diversity because it leads to the conclusion that we can rest content with "truth" being whatever happens to be true for us or for the culture in question. For instance, Boghossian (2006) is appalled with the relativism of anthropologists who defend creation myths of indigenous cultures (he was specifically referring to the Lakota tribe of South Dakota) as equally valid ways of knowing about the origins of humanity as Darwinian evolution. These myths may be psychologically and culturally functional, but once they are taken beyond this to claim epistemic truth, we have a right to demand evidence. If none is forthcoming, they cannot be equally valid accounts of the origins of human beings. Extreme relativism renders it impossible to believe that anyone, including ourselves, can ever be in error, and it demolishes the distinction between what we choose to believe and what is actually true.

Paul Boghossian (2006) claims that relativism is used as a shield to protect those who wish to appear before the world as open-minded nonjudgmental liberals from their fear of inconvenient knowledge. He also wants to convince those folks to examine their motives for hanging on to positions he believes to be incoherent. If we take relativism in its postmodernist and strong social constructionist form seriously, we can never have faith in anything as real and will know nothing about anything. The "nice" thing about being a relativist, of course, is that one is relieved of the burden of being in error because there is no objective way of determining truth and error. Either there is no truth or there is a plurality of truths, all correct. This is incoherent because it provides relativists with no defensible grounds for criticizing obnoxious practices (the holocaust, the execution of homosexuals and female genital mutilation in some Islamic countries, torture, cannibalism, etc.). If relativists are to be consistent, they must judge these things "good" or "bad" only relative to the culture in question, because they believe it is arrogant ethnocentrism to judge another culture by the standards of our own.

Rationalism and Empiricism

Rationalism and empiricism are rival epistemologies, both of which stand against radical relativism to claim that we can obtain objective truths. Although they are rival epistemologies, only extreme versions claim exclusivity for their position. The primary tool for rationalism is reason, and for empiricism it is sense experience. Reason is a uniquely privileged means of acquiring knowledge for rationalists such as Rene Descartes and Immanuel Kant, because they believed that the world comes to us through the buzzing confusion of sense perceptions and must be filtered and organized by the intellect. For most early rationalists, the world could only be understood as *it is* through the intellect; the senses allow us only to see it as *it appears* (Descartes' meditation of the piece of wax is the definitive précis on rationalism). Rationalists idealize mathematics as the only true paradigm of truth because mathematical thinking is analytic; that is, it rests on *a priori* knowledge that is true by definition. Deductive "top-down" reasoning from truths considered self-evident had been taken as the ideal path to knowledge by rationalists ever since Plato. Deductive reasoning guarantees the truth of the conclusion given that it is already present in the premise ("All crimes are against the law"), and any denial of it is self-contradictory.

Mathematics is deeply connected to empirical science, but for all its usefulness, most empiricists would probably agree that it is overly optimistic to expect the tangible world to mirror the perfection of the instrument used to gain insight into it. As Albert Einstein, a rationalist who never performed an empirical study in his life, stated: "As far as the laws of mathematics refer to reality, they are not certain; and as far as they are certain, they do not refer to reality" (1923:28). On the other hand, physicist Steven Weinberg has remarked that it is "positively spooky how the physicist finds the mathematician has been there before him or her" (in Sarukkai, 2005:420). What I think Weinberg meant is that many discoveries are "rationalized" by the intellect before they are observed by the senses. For example, the heliocentric model of the solar system was a mathematical model; Copernicus could not directly experience the earth moving around the sun. Einstein's general relativity theory predicting that the light from distant stars would be bent by the sun's gravitational field was mathematical, and the predicted effect could only be observed during a solar eclipse. Arthur Eddington empirically verified the predicted effect in 1919, three years after Einstein published his theory (Okasha, 2002), and the search for the grand "theory of everything" by string theorists has been pursued mathematically since the early 1980s without any experimental guidance (Polsek, 2009).

Bacon's Four Idols

Francis Bacon was the first to radically depart from the deductive methods of rationalism and to stoutly defend the empirical alternative. In his *Novum Organum*, published in 1620, he championed knowledge acquisition that proceeds from induction, which pre-supposes nothing, rather than deduction, which assumes axiomatic truths. In his book, he describes four "idols" that represent deep-rooted biases and prejudices that contaminate reason, the first of which is the *Idols of the Tribe*. The idols of the tribe have their foundation in human nature and are the contaminants of reason and perceptions that all humans share. The human mind has a great tendency to see more order and regularity in the world than actually exists, to give substance to abstracts, and to accept things that we wish to be true and reject those that we wish not to be true.

The *Idols of the Cave* are the errors of individual beings that exist in addition to the errors all humans share. These idols are attributed to the errors to faulty learning and selective perception—the ideological goggles that let us only see certain things. The *Idols of the Market Place* are due to the ambiguities of language—words and concepts meaning different things in different contexts—and thus confuse our understanding of nature, leading people with different worldviews to talk past one another. The fourth idol is the *Idols of the Theatre*, which are derived from the grand schemes of philosophy to which individuals pledge their allegiance. Bacon maintained that humans have a strong inclination to construct elaborate theories based on nothing but our faulty reason and for which there is scant evidence from experience. As we shall see, I believe much of criminology is in the grip of Bacon's idols.

Empiricism is the path of modern science because that which issues from it can be tested by minds other than our own. Empiricists do not deny that concepts can be independent of experience, but they maintain that if those concepts refer to the tangible world, the truth about them can only be established by observation and experiment. Although it is true that hypotheses are deduced from a form of *a priori* knowledge we call theory, theories are not true by definition; they have been synthesized from numerous empirical facts and are "truths" that may not survive the tests to which they must be subjected. Aristotle's ideal method of gaining knowledge was deductive reasoning, which is rationalism, but unlike Plato, he realized that his syllogisms must predispose broad inductions to validate their major premises. A "conclusion" for a rationalist is a "hypothesis" for an empiricist. All real knowledge of the world is *a posteriori* for the empiricist; we can only achieve it with some degree of confidence after we test our concepts in the world outside our own minds. Empirical statements are thus synthetic, such as "All crimes are universally condemned." This is a statement that is not true by necessity because the predicate is not contained in the subject, and to deny it would not be self-contradictory. It is a statement that can be true or false, and one that we must refer to the stern judge of experience. Empirical science cannot produce the absolute knowledge demanded by those who identify all true knowledge with the magnificent certainty of mathematics.

Kuhn and Paradigm Shifts

Rationalism and empiricism are thus both necessary for the advancement of knowledge. Deep intuitive thought can lead to eureka moments for the intellectually prepared, and then these cognitive moments get translated into experiments for verification. The sum of empirical findings welded together as theory then supplies the deductive *a priori* arguments we call hypotheses, which by their nature are synthetic statements to be tested against data. Theory is the deductive scaffolding from which we derive hypotheses. This all sounds nicely and linearly progressive, but then along came Thomas Kuhn, who supposedly changed all that for us.

Thomas Kuhn's book, *The Structure of Scientific Revolutions* (1970), is perhaps the most influential philosophy of science book of the twentieth century. Kuhn's work was enthusiastically embraced by many social scientists because it showed that even physics was beset by the same sort of uncertainty, contingency, context dependence, and ideological biases that so bedevil their disciplinary endeavors. A number of social scientists used the book (without Kuhn's blessing) to support radical positions about the instability, relativity, and subjectivity of science. However, Kuhn was a strong supporter of science who thought a lot more like a critical realist than a relativist. Kuhn's main argument was that science does not progress in a neat linear accumulation of knowledge but, rather, that it is a messy business that periodically undergoes revolutions that fundamentally alter the way the content of a particular science is viewed.

Science seems to advance much like Gould and Eldredge's (1977) punctuated equilibrium model of evolutionary change. Based on paleontological observation, this theory asserts that evolution involves the slow accretion of adaptations and long periods of stasis that are punctuated periodically by very rapid changes. Likewise, Kuhn sees science characterized by the slow growth of knowledge during long periods of stasis, and then rapid advancement. The pace of biological and scientific evolution is dictated by environmental events. For biological evolutions, it could be something like climate change, an asteroid collision, or the introduction of a new predator. For science, it may be the introduction of a new instrument (telescope, microscope, or brain imaging technology), or the introduction of concepts from adjacent sciences, such as the introduction of atomism into chemistry or genetics into social and behavioral science. As Fromm (2006:583) notes, scientific disciplines are in "constant flux from right, to more right, to even more right. If they reach stasis they're dead." We reach scientific truths tentatively and asymptotically; we will never touch the axis of ultimate *Truth*.

Kuhn wrote that "normal science" is conducted within a paradigm, which is a set of fundamental theories, assumptions, concepts, values, and practices shared by a scientific discipline that guide its view of reality, such as Newtonian physics or Darwinian biology. Normal science tests hypotheses derived from theories shaped by the contents of the paradigm in which they exist, and it aims to extend the knowledge that the existing paradigm permits, not to look for novelties within it. Work that goes beyond what the paradigm permits is rarely tolerated by orthodox scientists within the paradigm, and it is "often not seen at all" (Kuhn, 1970:24). Unexpected results found by those embedded in the paradigm (most often by adventurous young scientists on its periphery enamored by new possibilities) that do not fit into the paradigm's assumptive framework are considered anomalies that are either ignored or explained away by guardians of the paradigm. Kuhn makes much of the role of anomalies in paradigm shifts. As anomalies that the paradigm cannot accommodate accumulate, a crisis ensues and a new paradigm vies with the old for supremacy. The new paradigm, typically championed by the young and the bold, is engaging in what Kuhn calls revolutionary (as opposed to "normal") science; when anomalies become the expected, a paradigm shift has occurred.

Before one paradigm is replaced by another, however, there is a fight for the soul of the discipline between the rival paradigms. Kuhn claimed that because the terminology and conceptual framework of rival paradigms do not mesh, they are incommensurable, and thus they cannot talk to each other. This was the case for many years in the social/behavioral sciences as "genetic determinists" and "environmental determinists" vehemently argued the now moribund nature-versus-nurture issue. Because rival theories are incommensurable, it was supposed that one cannot make a rational choice as to which is superior, a position that seems to entail that theory choice in science is irrational—that is, determined by factors external to science and thus relativistic.

This is the claim that radical constructionists have jumped on to discredit science. But they did not look closely before they leaped. Kuhn was not asserting that science is subjective and irrational, with its theory choices being made only by "mob consensus."

Nor did Kuhn mean "noncomparable" with his use of the term "incommensurable," which simple means that two things have no common measure or common standards. Kuhn's position was only that we cannot rationally choose between theories if we are in the middle of the paradigmatic crisis and are stubbornly ignorant of the claims put forth by the proponents of the revolutionary paradigm. Kuhn points out that a hypothetical observer ignorant of the chronology of events who was asked to choose the superior theory would do so every time, and that it would be the most recent theory because it would be the one best able to accommodate the known facts of a particular domain. Kuhn concluded that the preceding point is "not a relativist's position, and it displays the sense in which I am a convinced believer in scientific progress" (1970:206).

Criminological Paradigms?

A perusal of criminological textbooks, journals, and course syllabi makes it clear that criminology has no paradigm in the sense of an agreed-upon set of fundamental assumptions that could be challenged by a rival paradigm (Sullivan & Maxfield, 2003). We are at best in what Kuhn called the "re-paradigmatic" or "pre-scientific" stage—a stage that is characterized by the collection of masses of facts we have yet to fully digest. This fact-finding is guided by theory, but we have such an embarrassment of riches in that regard (see Chapter 10) that it is "no wonder different men confronting the same range of phenomenon describe and interpret them in different ways" (Kuhn, 1970:17). This is one of the major problems Kuhn identifies in his work that is particularly apropos to criminology: the *theory ladenness* of data.

An empirical theory is a formal conceptual scheme based on our interpretations of our observations obtained by testing hypotheses derived *from the theory itself.* This renders the analytic–synthetic distinction problematic because they are born of each other—that is, there is no distinction between theoretical framework and its empirical content. In other words, data are always contaminated with the assumptions of our theories, so even if our findings correspond with our theory, it is of little comfort if the data are infected with flawed theories. It is in this sense that science is relative because what we see is relative to what the theory leads us to see. But the problem lies in the Baconian idols within us, not in the world out there.

Examples of Theory Ladenness

An example of theory ladenness and of anomalies resulting from it is the profound shock to socialization/developmental research administered by the discovery of the relative unimportance of the shared environment in producing similarities among siblings (Ferguson, 2011; Plomin & Daniels, 1987; Rowe, 1994). Standard socialization theory assumes that shared experiences within the family make siblings alike in their psychological development and that the most important of these experiences is parental treatment. Traditional socialization researchers found that children who are treated affectionately are less antisocial than those who are abused and neglected, and that parents who are confident, well-liked, and sociable have children who manage their lives well and get along with others. Researchers thus got what they expected to get—the paradigm works! Then along came researchers schooled in genetics who pointed out that 99% of socialization studies observed only one child per family (Plomin, Asbury, & Dunn, 2001). These researchers noted that previous findings such as those just discussed may have had more to do with genetic similarity between parent and child than with parental treatment (Lilly, Cullen, & Ball, 2007). It simply did not occur to those doing normal science within the strict environmentalist quasi-paradigm to even consider that their data were contaminated by their theory and that they were addressing only half of a coherent whole.

Those working in the revolutionary paradigm asserted that looking at only one child per family does not allow for the assessment of child effects, and thus genetic effects, on parental behavior. Eventually it became clear that to examine the role of these effects, researchers needed twin and adoption studies to tease apart genetic and environmental sources of variation (Grusec & Hastings, 2007). When this was done, the shock was that genes accounted for more of the variance in most traits, followed by non-shared environment (the unique environment of siblings), and that shared environments (everything siblings shared, such as parents, social class, religion, and neighborhood) account for almost zero variance in almost all cognitive and personality traits in adulthood (Bouchard & McGue, 2003; Carey, 2003; Moffitt, 2005; Walsh & Bolen, 2012). Social scientists also came to know what every parent who has more than one child knows: There are different parenting styles for different children. The same parent who is permissive with a warm and compliant child may be authoritarian with a bad-tempered and resistant child, while all the time trying to be the authoritative parent that child psychologists tell us that all parents should be to all offspring. Thus, any results that issue from studying only one child per family depended on which child was the focus, which utterly confounded any meaningful generalizations.

Another example involves the conundrum formed from the widespread belief that violence begets violence, on the one hand, and the fact that the majority of abused and neglected children do not become violent or criminal, on the other hand (Widom & Brzustowicz, 2006; Wright, Moore, & Newsome, 2011). Being abused or neglected as a child certainly increases the risk factor for future criminal and violent behavior, but we would like to know what factor(s) accounts for maltreated children who succumb to the risk versus those who do not. Again, the problem has been model misspecification. Researchers have traditionally treated children as empty vessels into which were poured environmental experiences, forgetting that what is "out there" combines with what is "in" the child once the two come together. Biosocial scientists call this coming together to produce effects greater than the sum of their individual effects gene–environment correlation (rGE) and gene × environment interaction (GxE).

Alleles of the gene for the enzyme monoamine oxidase A (MAOA) have been the genetic components of a number of GxE studies in which maltreatment was the environmental component. MAOA degrades a variety of neurotransmitters (primarily serotonin) after they have excited postsynaptic neurons. There are two major varieties of this gene: low (MAOA-L) and high (MAOA-H). The MAOA-H variety evinces high serotonin transcriptional activity, which ultimately promotes higher levels of serotonergic activity at the synapse, compared to the MAOA-L allele (Chiao & Ambady, 2007). A number of studies show that individuals with the low-activity variety are more likely to react to challenges with aggression (McDermott, Tingley, Cowden, Frazzetto, & Johnson, 2009), and low serotonergic functioning is robustly related to impulsivity, one of the strongest correlates of criminal behavior known (Agnew, 2005; Fishbein, 2001). Brain imaging studies have shown that MAOA-L men show greater activity in the amygdala (the part of the limbic system specializing in emotional processing, particularly fear) and lower activity in the regulatory prefrontal areas of the brain during emotional arousal, thereby suggesting the emotional and cognitive channels that link MAOA-L to impulsive aggression (McDermott et al., 2009).

The landmark GxE study of antisocial behavior and MAOA–maltreatment interaction is the longitudinal cohort study of Caspi et al. (2002). This study found that although males with the low transcriptional activity allele (MAOA-L) who were maltreated constituted only 12% of the cohort, they were responsible for 44% of its verified violent convictions. The odds of maltreated MAOA-L males having a violent crime conviction by the age of 26 years were 9.8 times greater than the odds of the MAOA-H-non-maltreated males. The maltreatment/non-maltreatment groups did not differ significantly on possession of the risk MAOA allele, thus ruling out the possibility that the effects of low MAOA activity on children, such as impulsiveness, contributed to maltreatment via children's evocative behavior (evocative rGE).

A meta-analysis of the MAOA-maltreatment literature concluded that the interaction between MAOA and maltreatment is a significant predictor of antisocial behavior across studies (Kim-Cohen et al., 2006). Interestingly, it is estimated that one-third of males carry the low-activity version of the MAOA gene, which is located on the X sex chromosome. Because males have only one X chromosome, they only get one version of the gene (either high or low activity), making its effects easier to detect (Williams et al., 2009). Females, on the other hand, have two X chromosomes, so they are much more likely than males to get at least one protective high-activity allele of the MAOA gene. This potential advantage may partially explain why females are far less prone to criminal behavior than males.

Is Criminology Having a Paradigm Shift?

The proliferation of such studies provides a distinct indication of a major shift from strict environmentalism (which we may consider to be the quasi-paradigm under which most criminologists conduct their research) to biosocial criminology. In 2003, Frank Cullen moved from strict environmentalism to acknowledging the role of individual differences. He subsequently went further in stating the opinion that the criminological paradigm (sociological) that he loves and in which he has spent his career "has exhausted itself," and that biosocial criminology, "a broader more powerful paradigm," will be dominant in the twenty-first century (2009:xvii). Whether Cullen's prediction comes to pass or not, it should not rest on ideological decisions to accept or reject the proffered help of the more advanced sciences.

Criminologists whose allegiances are more ideological than Cullen's will resist the shift, but resistance by guardians of the discipline status quo is a good thing. Mark Warr (2002:139) writes that the biosocial sciences are breathing down the neck of sociological criminology, and that this is "disorienting and even threatening" to the majority of current criminologists. He does not try to dismiss the challenge to criminological orthodoxy but, rather, views it as scientifically healthy, which it assuredly is. The more robust the challenge mounted against biosocial criminology, the more muscular it will become. Kuhn (1970:65) is adamant that resistance to a new paradigm is positive up to a point: "By ensuring that the paradigm is not too easily surrendered, resistance guarantees that scientists will not be lightly distracted and that the anomalies that lead to paradigm change will penetrate existing knowledge to the core."

Kuhn argues that many individuals with a lifetime commitment to a paradigm find themselves psychologically unable to follow the data into alien territory. It is often just too painful to relinquish that which we have held so dear for so long and around which we have developed productive and rewarding careers, despite any and all evidence that one should: "The transfer of allegiance from paradigm to paradigm is a conversion experience that cannot be forced" (Kuhn, 1970:151). But as Kuhn intimates, those who fail to do so will find themselves irrelevant: "Retooling is an extravagance reserved for the occasion that demands it," and the wise scientist knows when "the occasion for retooling has arrived" (1970:76). What will the wise scientist find if he or she retools? According to Kuhn (1970:111), many unexpected wonders:

> *Led by a new paradigm, scientists adopt new instruments and look in new places. Even more important, during revolutions scientists see new and different things when looking with familiar instruments in places they have looked before. It is rather as if the professional community has been suddenly transported to another planet where familiar objects are seen in a different light and are joined by unfamiliar ones as well.*

Conclusion

"It's all relative" is a buzz phrase sophomores bandy about thinking that it marks them off as educated and tolerant. Everything is relative in some sense, but like so many other things, it is taken to extremes by some to claim that there can be no truths. This kind of attitude is detrimental to both science and morality. Rationalism and empiricism are different epistemologies telling us that truth is attainable—the first using top-down analytic methods and the latter using bottom-up synthetic methods. Both deduction and induction have their valued place in science. Rationalism and empiricism are forms of knowledge-seeking that lay claim to objective truth via different methods. Although these methods have traditionally been viewed as rival methodologies, we see them today as two sides of the same enterprise, particularly in the hard sciences where *a priori* mathematical reasoning almost always accurately predicts phenomena later verified empirically. In all sciences today, the predictions deduced from theory presuppose broad inductions from previous empirical work; thus, rationalism and empiricism are joined at the hip as the left and right legs of the scientific journey.

Thomas Kuhn seemed to have been an accidental radical, and certainly a false prophet to those who wish to denigrate science. Of course, science is an unstable, messy, theory-laden social enterprise, but so what? If a scientific theory is transient, it is because the scientific process has found a theory that better comports with reality. The most valuable lesson we can take from Kuhn is related to the theory ladenness of data. This was illustrated by examining how socialization research and maltreatment research had for so many years ignored the role of genes. These researchers looked at only one-half of the picture because their studies were conducted deep inside Plato's allegorical cave, well out of the sunlight. Like the denizens of the cave, as long as we were unaware of the wider scientific world outside, we could be excused. Now that the evidence is everywhere, it is shameful that some of us still treat the returning prisoner who had been led into the sunlight as an evil destroyer of criminology's status quo. If we refuse to come out into the sunlight and cast our eyes on the whole that is human behavior, we will remain imprisoned in the cave where we can see only the flickering shadows we take for reality.

4

Essentialism and Reductionism
Enemies or Friends?

Essentialism

If determinism is a slur word in social science branches unfriendly to science proper, essentialism and reductionism are terms of abuse used even by most members of its science-friendly branches (Sayer, 1997). There are varieties of essentialism and reductionism, but their enemies tend to attack only extreme versions that proponents barely recognize, such as Platonic essences tied to his perfect, unalterable, and eternal Forms. Essentialism is attacked most strongly by some feminist criminologists who believe that many social science theories "homogenize" women based on "basic, stable sex differences that arise from causes that are inherent in the human species such as biologically based evolved psychological dispositions" (Wood & Eagly, 2002:700). Believers in the reality of race are also charged with essentialism. Naomi Zack alleges that "to this day [believers in the reality of race] assume the following: (1) Races are made up of individuals sharing the same essence; (2) each race is sharply discontinuous from all others" (2002:63). I have never heard any scientist claim that racial groups share a common "essence" or that racial boundaries are "sharply discontinuous"; if they were, we would call them species (but even species are not *sharply* discontinuous). I will wager that Zack has never heard any biologist make these claims either.

Aristotle's Essentialism

Classical essentialism is best exemplified by the Aristotelian notion that things have attributes that are necessary, unalterable, and indispensible to them such that any object or subject lacking that property cannot be what it is alleged to be. Such properties are universal in every entity that belongs to a particular classification, and they are not idiosyncratic or context dependent. This does not mean that essentialism homogenizes all subjects classified into a group; those who insist that it does ignore Aristotle's distinction between *per se* and *per accidens* properties of an entity. A *per se* property is an essential property that a subject or object possesses and cannot lose without changing its nature; a *per accidens* property is a nonessential property that a subject or object may not have, or lose if it previously had it, without changing its nature (Oderberg, 2007). My neighbor could lose a leg and still be who he was before. Being one-legged *per accidens* does not deprive my neighbor of his humanity; he can still be nothing other than human, which is his *per se* property defining him at his most fundamental level.

Likewise, it is essential (i.e., necessary) that a molecule of water has two hydrogen atoms and one oxygen atom; without either, there is no molecule of water. The atomic structure is the *per se* property of water; its manifestations as a liquid, solid, or gas are *per accidens* alterations resulting from its *per se* property interacting with the ambient temperature. It is also essential to being a male or a female to have a certain karyotype (XY or XX) and a certain kind of gonads. These things define (partly) maleness and femaleness in a way that my neighbor's leg does not define his humanness. We cannot say that these properties are always and unequivocally associated with a particular sex, of course, because some individuals have their gonads removed for medical reasons, and there are a variety of intersex anomalies that play havoc with our binary classificatory schemes (Fausto-Sterling, 2002). Losing one's gonads does not change one's being any more than losing one's leg does, nor do H_2O's transitions from liquid to gas to solid change its essence. What counts as an essential property need not be necessary and sufficient for defining a kind—only necessary. It is surely not scientifically wrong to define sex according to chromosomal and gonadal status, or even to say it is essential to do so, because it is true, if we exclude loss of gonads for medical reasons, in all but the rarest of circumstances. As Odeberger (2011:89) says about definitions of natural kinds, "That definitions range from partly accurate [e.g., man is a rational animal] to completely accurate [e.g., gold is a metal with element number 79] does not militate against the fact that achieving any degree of accuracy in definitions requires attending to characteristics of the object to be defined."

Anti-essentialists often confuse generalities with essentialism, as in Janis Bohan's (1993:7) complaint that "if 'friendly' were gendered, an essentialist position might argue that women are more friendly than men ... and the quality is now a trait of women." She adds that this kind of generalizing is grounded on "problematic universalizing assumptions" portraying women "as a homogeneous class [that fails] to acknowledge diversity among us" (1993:8). This statement is a mystery. We are told in our first statistics class that when we say that group X is higher than group Y on trait W, it does not mean that all X's are higher than all Y's on W. There are differences between groups (comparison of means) and differences within them (variance) that acknowledge Bohan's "diversity among us." I wonder if the following statement by Eileen Leonard would be considered essentialist: "Women have had lower rates of crime in *all nations*, in *all communities* within nations, for *all age groups*, for *all periods in recorded history*, and for practically *all crimes*" (1995:55; emphasis original). Referring to Leonard's statement, Bohan might say "if 'prosocial' were gendered, an essentialist position might argue that women are more prosocial than men." She might also go on to call it a "problematic universalizing assumption" because, after all, Leonard did emphatically write that her statement is true across *all* age groups, cultures, and historical periods. Leonard is indisputably correct, and if anyone should criticize her on the grounds that her statement ignores variation, it would be uninformed.

To dismiss generalities is to claim the existence of nothing but context-specific differences in a sort of extreme nominalism (the rejection of abstract universals). Recognizing general features of things does not commit us to essentialism as defined by its enemies, for we all understand (don't we?) that when we make general statements, it is a given that there are exceptions to the rule without having to make it explicit. If we define essentialism as the process of generalizing, we are rejecting objective nomothetic science in favor of idiographic accounts of contingent and subjective phenomena. It is true that each individual is in many ways unique, but an atomistic "$n = 1$" is rarely useful for advancing knowledge of human behavior in general.

Neither can we avoid categorization if we are to make sense of the world. Categorization is the search for common properties, which *presupposes* diversity rather than the homogeneity of the things being sorted. The features that the category hold to be essential to being placed into it are a matter to be determined scientifically by examining various relevant properties. Andrew Sayer (1997:462) maintains that "moderate essentialism" is necessary for explanation and that it is critical for social science. He notes that critics assert that essentialism involves essences that are Platonic "unchanging eternal ones." He goes on to say that this straw man construction "helps to load the dice against essentialism." As the *per se–per accidens* distinction clearly highlights, essentialism does not claim that all members of a class of people are identical, only that they share the same essential properties that mark them as one thing rather than another. Members of a class of beings can be radically different in multiple ways in their *per accidens* properties while sharing what makes them what they are and distinct from the things that they are not.

Modern Essentialism

There has been a resurgence of this kind of essentialism about natural kinds in philosophy (Williams, 2011) and biology (Rieppel, 2010) in recent decades. This neo-essentialism is not the straightjacket of Plato's transcendental essentialism, or even Aristotle's more naturalistic essentialism. Darwin killed off the idea that natural entities have unchanging essences that make them *eternally* what they are, but that does not prevent biologists from talking about natural kinds that any geneticist can discern given sufficient DNA material. This kind of essentialism is called "origin essentialism." According to Williams (2011:154), a biological kind is "a matter of standing in a specific historical relation, perhaps to an ancestor. An animal that does not stand in this historical relation is not a member of the kind…. The essence of a natural kind is a set of (relational or intrinsic) properties." Essences are thus relational properties that biological entities of a kind take with them into all possible worlds. Although natural selection ensures continuous change and speciation over the vastness of evolutionary time, this does not gainsay accurate categorizations of biological kinds that are not contingent on idiosyncratic interpretations because they are as they are now, and shall be so, for a very long time.

Charges of essentialism in social science rarely engage the arguments made by philosophers and biologists. I once had a sociological colleague whose favorite epithet was "essentialist" when confronted with statements of generality he found offensive. When I asked him if he was railing against Platonic, Aristotelian, or origin essentialism, he just gave me a puzzled look. I believe that for the most part the charge of essentialism is so much puzzled waffle used to attack generalities that for one reason or another are not welcome. Aristotelian essentialism meant invariant only in those things that are truly necessary to something being one thing and not another, not about attributes and characteristics that regularly cross gender, class, racial, cultural, and even species lines (e.g., Bohan's "friendliness"). Surely not even the most radical social constructionist truly believes that there is anyone who thinks that anything in the social world is invariant. However, the essentialist epithet is convenient for those who use it to reinforce other hissing suffixes so beloved by those who believe that *ad hominem* bluster is a useful argumentation device.

Reductionism

Whereas determinism and essentialism are boo words used mostly by radical social constructionist and postmodern types, reductionism tends to be used pejoratively by most social scientists. By reductionism, I mean the process of taking causal explanations from higher, fuzzier levels to deeper, more precise levels. Reductionism is nothing more sinister than this, but many social scientists recoil when they hear it, as if it would foreclose on their whole enterprise if we were to reduce Durkheim's "social facts" to something more elementary. Reductionists do not suggest that the social factist paradigm lacks ontological credibility. It is readily acknowledged that although social facts do not occupy space, like gravity, their effects are real and are revealed in the enabling and constraining effects they have on human activities.

Eminent philosopher of science Thomas Nagel has pointed out that "non-reductionist accounts simply *describe* phenomena while reductionist accounts *explain* them" (in Rose, 1999:915). Steven Pinker's (2002:72) account is more irreverent, describing the differences between reductionist and non-reductionist explanation as "the difference between stamp collecting and detective work, between slinging around jargon and offering insight, between saying something just is and explaining why it had to be that way as opposed to some other way." This is not to say, however, that reductionist accounts are always preferable to more holistic accounts. According to a well-known quip that curses both their houses, a reductionist knows increasingly more about increasingly less, until he knows everything about nothing, whereas a holist knows increasingly less about increasingly more, until he knows nothing about everything.

To explain something rather than simply describing it, we have to discover its causes, and to do this we have to look at its constituent parts. Reductionism and determinism are thus joined at the hip because the reductionist goal of explanation is intimately tied to the determinist goal of prediction. The correctness and utility of any explanation (whether or not we judge it reductionist) can only be gauged by its predictive power. Emile Durkheim, often lauded as the consummate holistic social factist, believed that to unlock the mysteries of the social, we have to unlock the mysteries of human nature:

> *Although sociology is defined as the science of society, in reality it cannot deal with human groups, which are the immediate concern of his research, without in the end tackling the individual, the ultimate element of which these groups are composed.... It is impossible to explain the whole without explaining the parts.*

This appeared in his *The Dualism of Human Nature and Social Conditions* (2005:35) originally published in 1914, two decades after his famous "social facts" dictum in *The Rules of Sociological Method.* Lower-level explanations often absorb the explanatory efficiency of broad demographic categories used in sociology, such as race, gender, and class, and add incremental validity to them (Lubinski & Humphreys, 1997; Walsh, 1997), but they do not do so without remainder.

Anti-Disciplines and Reductionist Fears from Chemistry to Psychology

Fear of reductionism has infected other sciences in the past because it has been seen as a threat to discipline autonomy. Edward Wilson (1990) coined the term *anti-discipline* to describe the relationship between a young and insecure science and its adjacent older science. There is tension between the two disciplines initially as the young science tries to define discipline boundaries by identifying its appropriate level of analysis. This tension is felt most acutely by the younger science because the older science sees no threat to its status from the younger science. As practitioners of the younger science gain confidence, they feel less threatened and begin to experiment with the ideas and theories of the adjacent mature science. After a period of creative interplay, the younger science becomes fully complementary with its erstwhile anti-discipline. With integration accomplished, the young science makes huge gains in theoretical and methodological sophistication. It is able to prosper from the rocket thrust provided by the more mature science in ways it could never have done had it not shaken itself free of its adolescent anxieties and insecurities about status and territory. When this happens, we have a paradigm shift.

The process first took place in chemistry as it debated the intrusion of physics and its atomic theory in the nineteenth century. Benjamin Brodie, one of the top chemists of his time, argued for an "ideal [pure] chemistry" based on explanations involving qualitative (the transformation of substances such as a solid to a gas) and quantitative (weight changes due to transformation) changes. Brodie believed that any reference to atoms (if indeed they existed) was reductionist and unnecessary because chemical compounds possessed emergent properties not predictable *a priori* from their constituent parts (Coffey, 2008). His position that chemical compounds are *sui generis* entities that transcend their constituent parts was supported by the majority of chemists of the time (Knight, 1992). However, many changed their minds soon thereafter when "the deductive power of the atomic theory [became] evident…. The atomic theory now enabled definite predictions and detailed explanations to be made. The experimental and deductive aspects of chemistry were cohering at last" (Knight, 1992:124). An early success of this uniting of physics and chemistry was the awarding of the Nobel Prize to Svante Arrhenius in 1903 for elucidating the nature of ionic bonding. He had previously had his doctoral thesis explaining this process turned down, ostensibly because it relied on atomism (Knight, 1992).

When chemistry became consistent with physics, the pair of them ganged up on biology, bringing a molecular approach with them, much to the chagrin of Joseph H. Woodger. Woodger (1948) argued that biology has a characteristic way of thinking not reducible to the thinking of chemistry or physics—biological facts should be explained only by other biological facts. Woodger seemed to have stood on firmer ground than Brodie in claiming autonomy for his discipline because the step from the inorganic to the organic is surely the most momentous discontinuity in all nature. Yet it was only five years after the publication of Woodger's *Biological Principles* that James Watson and Francis Crick (along with the almost forgotten Maurice Wilkins) decoded the "language of life" by an examination of the chemistry and atomic structure of the DNA molecule and garnered their own Nobel Prizes.

The Watson–Crick–Wilkins and Arrehenius Nobels were won by venturing outside the constraints of discipline orthodoxy and applying insights from more fundamental sciences (Arrhenius, Crick, and Wilkins all had formal training in physics [Coffey, 2008]). It is both ironic and instructive that central concepts of modern chemistry and biology (atomic bonding and the chemistry of DNA, respectively) were once considered reductionist and outside the domains of those disciplines. Today, chemists learn physics, and biologists learn chemistry; any suggestion that they should not would be met by puzzled stares by modern chemists and biologists. Perhaps in the future it will be just as surprising to criminologists to suggest that they should not learn human biology.

Psychology has never been as anti-biology as other disciplines dealing with human behavior, but there have been many efforts to distance their discipline from biology. John Watson's radical statement that he could take any healthy infant at random and make him into any type of specialist regardless of "his talents, penchants, tendencies, abilities, vocations, and race of his ancestors" and Zing Yang Kuo's assertion that psychology "needs the concept of heredity as much or as little as the concept of god" are examples of noted psychologists discounting biology (in Degler, 1991:155–159). Psychology has not embraced biology as intimately as biology has embraced chemistry, or as closely as chemistry has embraced physics, but it is on much friendlier terms than it was in Watson and Kuo's time. Many of today's top behavioral geneticists, such as Thomas Bouchard, Absolom Caspi, Terrie Moffitt, and Robert Plomin, earned their PhDs in psychology. As behavioral genetics flows naturally into molecular genetics, these scholars have ventured into its domain also (these folks are certainly not afraid to retool). A perusal of contemporary psychology textbooks indicates that many (perhaps most) psychologists have surrendered their opposition to lower levels of analysis to agree that to fail to consider genetic, evolutionary, or neurohormonal evidence is to neglect the guidance of compasses that have demonstrated their predictive power time and again. As psychologist Christopher Peterson states: "Most contemporary psychologists prefer to regard people as biopsychosocial beings, believing that people and their behavior are best explained in terms of relevant biological mechanisms, psychological processes, and social influences" (1997:20).

Sitting on the top rung of Comte's hierarchical ladder of disciplines are acrophobic sociologists stubbornly refusing to look downward for guidance from the sciences below, convinced that monsters are at rest on the lower rungs awaiting those who would dare carry *social* facts down there for analysis. One particularly strange example of anti-reductionism that has stuck with me since my undergraduate days is Irwin Deutscher's (1968) assertion that it would be just as absurd to reduce the understanding of criminal behavior to psychology as it would to reduce it to quantum physics. In effect, Deutscher was claiming that individuals are non-agenic slaves to the vagaries of environmental forces about whom psychology has absolutely nothing to say. Yet all criminological theories that have evolved under sociology's wing are reductionist from a sociological point of view, and certainly from Deutscher's. They are reductionist because they appeal to individuals, their natures, and their motivations, which of course they must, even as we acknowledge that motivations and individual natures are partly formed and greatly developed by social experiences. A meander through our most popular theories reveals how reliant they are on appeals to individuals:

Differential association: Individuals are socialized to accept or reject "definitions favorable" (values, attitudes) to law violation.
Social learning: Individuals learn their behavior via reinforcement and punishment.
Rational choice: Individuals make choices based on utilitarian calculations.
Social bonding: Individuals are emotionally attached or not to significant others and to institutions.
Self-control: Individuals' level of self-control largely determines their behavior.
Marxism: Lower-class individuals must jettison false consciousness and develop class consciousness.
Conflict: Individuals are in constant conflict over personal and group interests.
Anomie: Individuals assess their life chances and adopt a particular mode of adaptation.
Social ecology: Individual's natural inclinations are released in disorganized neighborhoods where informal social controls have broken down.

Although all these individual actions take place in a social context, the point is that all theories must necessarily talk about what happens in individuals' minds—their evaluations of the social context or situation, as the mature Durkheim (2005) asserted. This is not to say that all issues in social/behavioral science are best addressed at individual levels. We can explain crime rates, revolutions, wars, economic systems, and so forth at the individual level only in the narrowest of senses. Phenomena such as these are far better analyzed at the macro level. But when it comes to *criminality* rather than crime, *individual* violence rather than state violence, and *micro* versus macro economic decisions, it is necessary to go from group processes to psychological processes. If we can agree on this, why can it not be acceptable to go still further and explore why different individuals interpret and react differently to identical social contexts? This is simply the next step in the causal ladder, one that engages the biological sciences.

Is the Fear of Reductionism Diminishing in Social Science?

The first decade of the twenty-first century saw some events that many who attended graduate school in the 1970s would have considered heretical. A blizzard of books and articles in sociology and criminology are delving into such "exotic" things as gene × environment interactions, cultural neuroscience, evolutionary biology, molecular genetics, epigenetics, neurophysiology, and a variety of other physiological processes in their attempt to understand all sorts of behavior. Major social science journals, such as the *American Sociological Review*, *Social Forces*, *Social Science Quarterly*, *Law and Psychiatry*, the *British Journal of Criminology*, and the *Journal of Contemporary Criminal Justice*, have published special issues on the role of biology in social science, indicating that fewer social scientists than was heretofore the case tremble in the face of reductionism. Indeed, in his presidential address to the American Society of Criminology, Richard Rosenfeld (2011:1) remarked that "the current period, with its breakthrough studies of gene–environment interactions and individual development, epitomizes the dominance of microcriminology."

There is still reluctance among those inclined to agree with James Coleman's assertion that when two or more individuals interact: "the essential requirement is that the explanatory focus be on the system as a unit, not on the individuals or other components which make it up" (in Wilson, 1998:187). It is difficult to talk about groups without talking about individuals, although it is true that a separate reality emerges when parts belong to a dynamic system of similar parts. However, although it is true that the interaction of elements—whether they be atoms, chemicals, neurons, genes, people, or whatever—produces effects that can be explained on their own terms, the claim that it is *essential* to focus explanatory efforts only on the whole unit to the exclusion of the parts is unnecessarily constraining. In response to Coleman, E. O. Wilson (1998:187) noted that biology "would have remained stuck around 1850 with such a flat perspective if it had taken seriously the claim that 'the essential requirement is that the explanatory focus be on the organism as a unit, not on the cell or molecules which make it up.'"

Wilson is correct: Cell biologists know that at bottom they are dealing with atomic particles and seek to understand their properties in order to understand the cell. But Coleman is also correct: Cell biologists also know that there are properties of the cell that cannot be deduced from those particles *a priori*, and that they require functional explanations of the whole cell and how that cell fits into a network of other cells to form the organism. We need both holistic and reductionist accounts that complement, not exclude, one another. Science poses questions and offers explanation at several levels of understanding. Natural scientists have long recognized that reductionist and holistic explanations complement one another. Useful observations, hypotheses, and theories now go in both reductionist and emergent directions in sciences; from quarks to the cosmos in physics and from nucleotides to ecological systems in biology.

It is doubtless true that there are many times when holistic accounts are more coherent and satisfying than reductionist ones. Phenomena may be *explained* by lower-level mechanisms, but they find their *significance* in more holistic regions, and thus we must be careful not to lose *meaning* as an essential component to understanding behavior by an overemphasis on explanatory mechanisms. We do not have to be poets to agree that propositions about entities such as genes, hormones, and neurons do not contain terms that define the most meaningful aspects of the human condition, such as love, justice, and morality. Neuroscientists have scanned the brains of people in love and discovered that the biological basis for romantic love is a chemical soup sparking up the brain's pleasure center (nucleus accumbens) (Esch & Stefano, 2005; Fisher, Aron, & Brown, 2005), but this in no way reduces the wonder of love as it is experienced. Only romantics who believe, with the poet Wordsworth, that science "destroys the beauteous form of things" by dissecting them would see this as reducing the awesome whole of love to the "mere" soup and sparks of brain activity.

Let us acknowledge that brain scans do not even come close to explaining why Romeo fell for Juliet. In this case, the lower-level account is more of a descriptor than an explanation because these brain processes did not *cause* Romeo to become love-struck; they only describe what happened in his brain when he did. Why he fell in love is better explained at higher levels. However, I still see more, not less, wonder in these brain scan studies of love because as Bartels and Zeki (2004:1164) opine, they bring us closer "to understanding the neural basis of one of the most formidable instruments of evolution, which makes procreation of the species and its maintenance a deeply rewarding and pleasurable experience, and therefore ensures its survival and perpetuation."

Reductionism Does Not Mean Eliminating Holism

At the back of all this concern social scientists have about reductionism is that accepting lower-level explanation automatically entails the elimination of higher-level explanations. This is eliminative reductionism, which essentially means that higher-level phenomena can be fully explained by lower-level properties, and that the higher-level properties have no causal impact independent of their parts. It might be claimed, for instance, that poverty has no impact on criminal behavior once we consider the personal traits of individuals assumed to explain both their financial status and their criminality. On the basis of such a claim, we may be tempted to eliminate poverty from consideration as an independent causal factor. Although lower-level variables may explain away the direct effects of a higher-level variable, the higher-level variable's indirect effects are not undermined. In terms of poverty, we cannot know all of the causes of each person's poverty, and surely the effects of poverty amount to more than the sum of their parts. I have elsewhere surveyed the effects of extreme poverty on neural development, epigenetic processes, and its allostatic effects on the brain and endocrine system (Walsh, 2009b; Walsh & Bolen, 2012; Walsh & Yun, 2011), and I would never discount it as a major player in its own right. Yet I would still aver that most holistic explanations in the social–behavioral sciences are ripe candidates for causal reductionism, but none is a candidate for eliminative reductionism. We cannot dissolve social and psychological reality into biological processes, but we cannot deny that these processes help to elucidate them. Neither must we confuse a part, however well we understand it, for the whole.

Daniel Dennett (1995:82) calls eliminative reductionism "bad" or "greedy" reductionism, by which he means the practice of skipping over several layers of higher complexity in a rush to fasten everything securely to a supposed solid foundation. For Dennett, eliminative reductionism is as nonsupportable as anti-reductionism. Anti-reductionists, he opines, seek a *deus ex machina* (which he calls "skyhooks" without foundations) to miraculously lift them out of scientific difficulty. There is no excuse for looking upward into the clouds for such skyhooks when perfectly grounded cranes built by the more robust sciences are available for loan, rent, or purchase. When we use these devices, we engage in Dennett's "good reductionism," which is simply "the commitment to non-question-begging science" (1995:82).

What counts as reductionism, of course, depends on where a science sits on Auguste Comte's ladder. The cognitive processes involved in making a decision to engage in a criminal act might be holistic from the biologist's point of view and reductionist "psychologism" from the sociologist's point of view, while all the time being "just right" from the psychologist's point of view. But surely each one of these levels adds something to the puzzle of human behavior, so why not welcome them all? Ladders are for climbing up and down, depending on what part of the house needs painting.

Let us re-engage Aristotle's golden mean here to attempt to dissolve (or at least weaken) the reductionist/emergence dichotomy. We can think of emergence as a series of self-organizing processes that produce qualitative "novelties" that cannot be *fully* expressed as the sums of the quantitative properties of the constituent parts. Corning (2002:26) tells us that reductionism used to mean an understanding of the parts—period—that comprised the whole, but modern reductionists "speak of parts and their 'interactions.'" Biosocial scientists favor rGE and GxE and other biologically informed models that explicitly recognize that biological variables have particular effects only when certain environmental conditions are satisfied. Corning (2002:26) maintains that by analyzing interactions among parts and the environments in which these parts operate, we are thereby analyzing emergent wholes or systems: "The 'whole' is not something that floats on top of it all." In other words, by looking at parts interacting, we are looking at wholes and therefore dissolving another false dichotomy.

As much as I appreciate Corning's argument, we cannot let it dissuade us of the necessity to understand the parts because the higher-level properties of wholes are supervenient on their lower-level properties. Think of the nightmare of twentieth-century communism and its attempts to build political systems (wholes) in ignorance of the nature of the individual human parts that comprised them. Communism seriously contravenes human nature, but millions had to be slaughtered in its name, and millions had to risk life and limb to flee from its grip, before most Western intellectuals were able to grasp this. Thus, although we will always need the social sciences and their concern with emergent meaning, only when mechanisms are discovered and understood can we more fully understand the emergent phenomena they underlie. Science has made its greatest strides when it has picked apart wholes to examine the parts and in doing so has gained a better understanding of the wholes they constitute. As Matt Ridley (2003:163) opines: "Reductionism takes nothing from the whole; it adds new layers of wonder to the experience." We shall know that the social sciences have matured when accusations of reductionism are consistently met with Dennett's mocking answer: "That's such a quaint, old-fashioned complaint! What on earth did you have in mind?" (1995:81).

Conclusion

The philosophical concepts most often used pejoratively by social scientists are probably essentialism and reductionism. These concepts are attacked in their most extreme forms, which are rarely, if ever, found today. Those who love to charge others with essentialism tend to see it as the homogenization of whatever class of subjects is being discussed. Anti-essentialists often go so far as to attack generalities as essentialist, forgetting that searching for generalities, patterns, similarities, and differences is the goal of science. They fail to make the distinction (many not even being aware that there is one, which is another good reason to value the ancient wisdom of philosophy) between Aristotle's *per se* and *per accidens* essentialism, and they prefer to attack Plato's eternal and changeless essences contained in his Forms. Essentialist thinking in its modern form is, if I may use the word, essential to scientific classification, which can only be done by sorting things according to what distinguishes them from all things they are not.

Reductionism is searching for causal explanations at fundamental levels. We saw how even chemistry went through an anti-reductionist phase when it saw the physicists' atomism as unnecessary reductionism and as threatening to its autonomy. Other disciplines have had similar tantrums when they have perceived intrusions into "their" territory by more advanced sciences. However, they all finally accepted that the more fundamental science had a bounty of gifts to offer and fully integrated with it. When they did, they found that the knowledge bases of their disciplines grew enormously. I see no reason whatsoever why criminology cannot likewise benefit enormously from integrative theories, concepts, and methods from the biological sciences. Reductionist science is simply science looking at phenomena at a deeper level; it is not about eliminating higher-level explanations. It is at higher levels that meaning is most often found, but higher-level analyses must be consistent with what is known at lower levels.

5

What Is Real and How Do We Know?

Ontology and Epistemology

Perhaps the most basic areas of philosophy are those that try to understand the fundamental nature of being and reality: Why is there something rather than nothing? What is existence and reality? How do we know? How can we understand? The nature of existence or being is a question of ontology, and the nature and mode of acquisition of knowledge is a question of epistemology. Within these broad categories lie arguments about issues such as holism and reductionism, materialism and idealism, any of which may be considered debates about ontology or epistemology depending on their context. For philosophers concerned with formal ontology as a primary area of study, ontology is the study of the fundamental categories of existence and reality. Those concerned with formal epistemology want to explore how we can know and reason about that reality and the reliability of knowledge claims.

Every discipline has its ontology and epistemology in which its practitioners make assertions about the reality of the things they study and how they explore those things, rather than asserting general statements about reality and knowing as philosophers do. A discipline's ontology informs its scholars of the fundamental categories of reality within its domain, and its epistemology defines how they should discover more about them—its investigatory techniques. For instance, if a biologist tells a philosopher that the animal specimen they are looking at is female, he or she is asserting the reality of an abstraction called femaleness and that this particular specimen is an instantiation of that universal category. If the philosopher asks how the biologist knows that it is female, the biologist has been asked an epistemological question. The biologist will then explain the methods by which sex is categorized in biology and describe the various things that differentiate one sex from the other. He or she will pay particular attention to distinctions that are necessary to place a specimen into one category versus the other, such as chromosomal, gonadal, and hormonal status, and perhaps describe the various methods by which this is done.

Nominalism Versus Realism

Nominalism and realism are separate ontologies with deep meaning for the fate of abstract categories of social science such as society, social class, race, gender, and criminality and for arguments about reductionism and essentialism. If scholars are in the process of using scientific methodology to explore some phenomenon, then it would seem to follow that its ontological status is a given, but there are folks who call themselves nominalists who might disagree. With Kant, nominalism asserts that the conceptual categories by which we organize the universe do not correspond to any inherent structure of the universe but, rather, they are products of the human mind. They obviously do not deny that the specimen the biologist and philosopher were examining was real because it has size and shape, and it occupies space. Neither would they deny the usefulness of the category in which it was placed. It is the universality of the descriptor "female" they would contest because for them there is no universal femaleness; there are only particular females. The individual specimen is a particular *subject* with material substance; the *predicate* "female" has no substance and is simply a descriptor used to place it into some conveniently named category.

Nominalists draw a very sharp line between the concrete and the abstract and aver that only particulars we can see, feel, hear, and touch are real, whereas universals (unseen properties supposedly common to various instances) are not. Humanness, for instance, is instantiated only in particular humans living in the phenomenal world; it does not exist independently in some noumenal world. Extreme nominalists reject even the notion that there is anything common to subjects or objects selected by a name (e.g., human, female, red, and cup). For extreme nominalists, all subjects or objects named are unique representations of the world, and terms indicative of a general nature (humanness, femaleness, redness, and cupness) have no meaning. Strong anti-essentialists tend to adopt a nominalist position without necessarily being aware that they are doing so, because they disdain nomothetic (quantitative generalizing) accounts and embrace ideographic (qualitative specificity) ones. In social science, of course, we arrive at the "norms" or generalities of a category of people (the term nomothetic derives from the Greek for norm—*nomos*) to thrash out general principles by summing the responses of a number of "private" (the term idiographic derives from the Greek for "own" or "private"—*idios*) responses to stimuli. Thus, the distinction between nomothetic and idiographic in social science is not as clear-cut as it is in the natural sciences.

The opposite of nominalism on this, but not on all issues, is realism. Realist philosophers claim the reality of abstract universals and the usefulness of generalities. Realists maintain that to make use of universals such as humanness, we ignore individual differences such as gender, color, size, and age and *abstract* from all instances we come across what they have in common—that is, their humanity. Both Plato and Aristotle were realists about universals, although their ideas about them were radically different (Armstrong, 1989). Plato's universals are his independently existing archetypal Forms—his perfect "humanness," "cupness," "redness," "treeness," "squareness," and so on. These Forms were ultimate reality for him and existed in the noumenal world prior to any material manifestation of them in the phenomenal world. It is easy to be anti-realist if by realism we mean this sort of realism, although it was held in various ways by other famous philosophers such as Descartes and Kant. This form of realism tends to be paired with an idealist rather than a materialist epistemology. Materialists can be, and most often are, realists about universals, but in the Aristotelian rather than Platonic sense.

In Aristotle's view, universals exist, but they only do so (become real) when instantiated. In other words, Plato's universals existed prior to any human being; Aristotle's universal abstractions, such as humanness, femaleness, strength, and intelligence, are qualities we ascribe to humans, and thus human beings must exist before we can realistically talk about things that describe them. Aristotle's view is eminently sensible and necessary if we are to talk about the world rationality. Certainly, no one has ever seen abstractions such as "strength," "intelligence," "empathy," or "happiness," but we see them demonstrated every day. We can even measure these things in a variety of ways and establish how variation in them has meaningful effects on people's lives.

An example of nominalism in social science is Georg Simmel's (in Coser, 1971:128) opinion that "society is only a name for a number of individuals who are in constant interaction with one another." In other words, for this early sociologist, the subject matter of his discipline—society—does not "really" exist, or at least it exists only as the sum of its interacting parts. Of course, it cannot exist apart from individuals, but as Durkheim stressed, society precedes any one individual, will be there long after that one individual has passed on, and its reality is indexed by the power it has over him or her. Certainly no one has ever seen the abstraction we call "society" or gazed upon something called "social class," but if we deny the reality of "social facts" we risk becoming extreme eliminative reductionists. Many theories in the social/behavioral sciences have within them ontological commitments to abstractions, the existence of which nominalists deny. If things marked by a common kind have nothing that is universally true about them save the name they are given, nomothetic social science with its talk of universal abstractions such as human nature, social class, status groups, and culture is dead, and we are left with only a series of atomized individual biographies.

Some Ontological and Epistemological Issues in Criminology: Labeling Theory

In any practical sense, epistemology boils down to how we go about generating knowledge—that is, the methodologies we use. Without an adequate methodology, we cannot have much faith in the knowledge we might accumulate. Chris Eskridge has charged that many criminological theories contain "a pinch of science (and often bad science at that) and a pound of ideology." He goes on to opine that "the primary weakness in the would-be science of criminology is the lack of basic epistemological understanding" (2005:304). A useful epistemology produces knowledge for which there is broad agreement that it constitutes evidence that can influence the policy-making process with an eye to doing something positive about the problems to which it is applied. If the fundamental disagreements and theoretical fragmentation of our discipline are any guide, Eskridge is right.

Labeling theory is a prime example of how we can be led down the garden path to nowhere when we rely on faulty ontology and epistemology. It was a popular theory in the 1960s and 1970s, and it still has a few adherents today (Cooper, Walsh, & Ellis, 2010).

The theory emphasizes the power of bad labels to stigmatize and by doing so to evoke the very behavior the label signifies. The ontological position of labeling theorists is weak nominalism. Crime and deviance are social constructs defined into existence rather than discovered, and they have no objective reality, although it is not denied that they are real in their consequences.

There is a great deal of selective skepticism in labeling theory in that it either affirms or denies the existence of phenomena according to how well it coheres with its underlying ideology. Woolgar and Pawluch (1985) call this "ontological gerrymandering" in which some things are "really real" (the labeling process and its aftermath) and other things (crimes) are not. The labeling process is constitutive of crime; there is no crime independent of cultural values and norms embodied in the judgments and reactions of others. We addressed this point in Chapter 2 on social constructionism and will not do so again. Suffice to say that labeling theory maintains that no act is by its nature criminal, because acts do not have natures until they are witnessed, judged good or bad, and reacted to as such. Rather than asking why people commit crimes, labeling theory asks why some behaviors are labeled criminal and not others, and thus shifts the focus from the actor (the criminal) to the reactor (the law and its agents).

Labeling theory distinguishes between primary and secondary deviance (Lemert, 1974). Primary deviance is the initial nonconforming act that comes to the attention of the authorities. Primary deviance can arise for a wide variety of reasons, but it has only marginal effects on an offender's self-concept, a variable crucial to labeling theory. Primary deviance is of interest to labeling theorists only insofar as it is detected and reacted to by individuals with power to pin a stigmatizing label on the rule breaker. Being caught in an act of primary deviance is either the result of police bias or sheer bad luck; the real criminogenic experience comes *after* a person is caught and labeled. The central concern of the theory is to explain the consequences of being labeled.

Secondary deviance results from society's reaction to primary deviance. The stigma of a criminal label may result in people becoming more criminal than they would have been had they not been caught. This may occur in two ways. First, labeled persons may alter their conceptions of themselves in conformity with the label ("Yes, I am a criminal, and I will act more like one in the future"). Second, the label may exclude them from conventional employment and lead to the loss of conventional friends. This may lead them to seek illegitimate opportunities to fulfill their financial needs and to seek other criminals to fulfill their friendship needs, which further strengthens their growing conception of themselves as "really" criminal. The criminal label becomes a self-fulfilling prophesy because it is a more powerful label than other social labels that offenders may claim.

I am not criticizing any of the concepts employed by labeling theorists: Self-fulfilling prophecies are real with real consequences, and labels can definitely stigmatize. My problem is with the logic of the theory, deduced as it was from faulty ontology and tested with a deeply flawed epistemology, as well as its selective skepticism. Labeling theory offers us a sterling example of how data can be so infected with Kuhn's theory ladenness that it can hinder the progress of a discipline.

The idea that so-called primary deviance is of no consequence is a position arrived at by examining self-report studies of crime and delinquency. Official statistics contained in the Uniform Crime Reports (UCR) consistently show much higher arrest rates for African Americans and the lower classes of all races than for the middle class, but self-report data from the 1960s and 1970s tended to show small or even no significant differences in race or class in offending. Taking these self-report data at face value, labeling theorists suggested that it is race and class prejudice of criminal justice agents that is responsible for the arrest figures, not any real race or class differences in actual offending (Paternoster & Iovanni, 1989). In other words, self-report data tell us that no specific group of individuals (including even males vis-à-vis females for some criminologists in this tradition) is more prone to commit more crimes than any other group; thus, the overrepresentation of some groups in official statistics "obviously" reflects police bias. This constitutes another example of the moralistic fallacy; that is, there *ought* not be any difference in rates of offending between different gender, racial, or class groups (this would rank groups in a moral hierarchy, and that is unacceptable) and therefore there *is* not. We will explore this central issue of labeling theory by examining the question of the relationship between social class and criminal behavior.

Social Class and Crime

Social class is a convenient label conceptualized and measured in different ways to categorize people so they can be compared across various domains of interest. It is shorthand for a composite of variables used to place individuals, families, and neighborhoods into categories based on such things as income, wealth, education, occupation, and property values. No one has seen, smelled, or touched social class, but it is real in its consequences. Some criminologists have denied that one of these consequences is an increased propensity for antisocial behavior in the lower classes. A major basis of the denial of a negative relationship between social class and criminal behavior was an article by Tittle, Villemez, and Smith titled "The Myth of the Social Class and Criminality" (1978). These researchers examined 35 self-report studies assessing the relationship and found an overall gamma of –0.09, and on the basis of the weak (but still there and still negative) correlation they declared that the relationship between social class and criminality was a myth. This paper drew comments ranging from being praised as a definitive work (Stark, 1979) to calling its conclusion "extraordinarily senseless" (Harris & Shaw, 2001:137).

The Tittle et al. paper sparked a great deal of interest in examining the strengths and weaknesses of self-report studies. The majority of the studies examined in the Tittle et al. article relied on students in colleges and high schools for their subjects, but some surveyed known delinquents as well. Several studies addressed the issue of the accuracy and honesty of self-reported offending with generally encouraging results, at least for uncovering the prevalence of minor antisocial behaviors. Studies have shown that officially identified delinquents and criminals self-report substantially more antisocial conduct on anonymous questionnaires than do non-delinquents and non-criminals

(Cernkovich, Giordano, & Pugh, 1985). The evidence appears to indicate that self-report measures provide fairly accurate information about minor forms of antisocial behavior and that almost everyone has committed some sort of illegal act sometime in their lives.

However, there are a number of reasons why many older self-report crime surveys provide a highly distorted picture of criminal activity. First, they tended to survey largely "captive" students who are fairly class homogeneous. High school and college students are not populations in which we expect to find many seriously criminally involved individuals and thus do not cover the very people we are most interested in gathering information about. Second, self-report studies typically ask only about trivial acts such as fighting, stealing items worth less than $5, disobeying parents, smoking, and truancy, most of which are officially classified as status offenses (if classified as offenses at all) rather than delinquency. Almost everyone has committed one or more of these acts, which are hardly acts that help us to understand real crime. Third, some researchers compounded this problem by lumping respondents who report one delinquent act together with adjudicated delinquents who break the law in many different ways many different times. Braithwaite (1981) pointed out that one such study only required students to admit to underage drinking and to having sex to be placed in the "most delinquent" category. Such sloppy conceptualization is exactly why criminologists should engage themselves with philosophy.

Although most people are fairly forthright in revealing their peccadilloes, most do not have a criminal history, and those who do have a distinct tendency to underreport their crimes (Hindelang, Hirschi, & Weis, 1981). As the number of crimes people commit increases, so does the proportion of offenses they withhold reporting (Cernkovich et al., 1985). For instance, researchers have asked respondents with known arrest histories whether they have ever been arrested and found that 20–40% replied negatively, with those arrested for the most serious offenses being most likely to deny having been (Hindelang et al., 1981).

If everyone has committed trivial offenses of the kind included in almost all self-report studies, there is no point in searching for group or individual differences with respect to those offenses. If one insists on doing so, one should not be surprised to find null or very weak relationships. Subjects from relatively class-homogeneous schools being asked about trivial offenses results in severely truncated variance in both measures that will by definition reduce the value of a correlation that may be extremely strong when assessed across the entire population range of both criminal offenses and socioeconomic status (SES).

The tendency to equate parental SES with offspring SES is another issue at the heart of the confusion about the class–crime relationship. Student subjects are assigned a class based on their parents' class, but as various researchers note (e.g., Ellis & McDonald, 2001), adolescents are already on their way to establishing their own SES, which is often different from that of their parents. In a sample with a modicum of SES heterogeneity, there will be individuals from the lower classes moving up and individuals from the middle classes moving down, with the upwardly mobile lower-class youths having lower "delinquency" scores than downwardly mobile middle-class youths (Chen & Kaplan, 2003). "Delinquency" is thus better predicted from the class the individual *will* enter as an adult than from the individual's parental class. Of course, to assess this requires longitudinal studies; there is no real way of knowing a subject's eventual SES with cross-sectional studies.

Further indicative of a negative class–crime relationship is the fact that we invariably find far more crime in lower-class areas than in middle-class areas. Each iteration of the National Crime Victimization Survey (NCVS) reports that victimization decreases monotonically with increases in neighborhood median income. A particular telling example is the study by Wilson and Daly (1997) of all Chicago neighborhoods that found homicide rates ranged from 1.3 per 100,000 in the richest neighborhood to 156 per 100,000 in the poorest—a huge 120-fold difference. Unless we believe that these differences are the result of middle-class folks trolling for victims in lower-class areas, we have to conclude that the crimes recorded in these areas are committed by those who live there.

Self-Report Data: Strengths and Weaknesses

Self-report studies have their place, but like the drunk who knew he had not lost his keys under the lamppost but looked for them there anyway "because that's where the light is," criminologists who use convenience samples and mistake peccadilloes for crimes are fooling themselves without the excuse of inebriation. Surely we should be looking for the things being sought where they are most likely to be found. Lest I be accused of being overly critical, recall that the title of Tittle et al.'s (1978) article is the myth of social class and *criminality*, not the myth of *parental* social class and *minor misbehaviors* (Walsh, 2011b). Most of us recognize that criminality and minor misbehavior are two very different things.

Let me be clear that I am not dismissing self-reports as a useful methodology. I am only criticizing those who take weak data from weak cross-sectional samples and then deduce strong (and very often strange) conclusions from them. There are excellent studies that have used self-report data but that also have copious augmenting data with which the credibility of self-reports can be assessed. For instance, Fergusson, Swain-Campbell, and Horwood's (2004) large ($N = 1265$) longitudinal study of a birth cohort verified the majority of the information obtained from subjects, parents, and teachers via multiple sources such as police records and other state agencies. The study classified children into one of six categories ranging from professional (class 1) to the lowest income category, consisting primarily of children from father-absent homes (class 6). Class-based outcomes were assessed when the cohort age was 10, 16, 18, and 21 years. The percentage of children from the lowest class who had a parent with a history of offending was 10 times greater than the percentage of children from the highest class. In terms of self-reporting, class 6 subjects reported a rate of offending 3.21 times greater than that reported by subjects from class 1, but class 6 subjects had 25.82 times more officially recorded offenses (at age 21 years) than class 1 subjects. The comparison of these two figures (3.21 vs. 25.82) supports the contention that those most seriously involved in offending do tend to report more offenses than others, but also that they are likely to greatly underreport them.

When all predictor variables associated with SES were entered into negative binomial models, the incident rate ratio of 3.21 for self-reported offending was reduced to 1.23, and the 25.82 ratio for officially recorded convictions decreased to 1.93 with all family, individual, school, and peer group factors included in the equation. The most salient point is that SES *per se* contributes little independent variance in regression models of criminal behavior once the effects of variables associated with SES are entered into them. Including additional individual-level variables in the model (e.g., genetic and personality variables) would doubtless further reduce the independent role of SES.

This does not vindicate Tittle's (1983) claim that there is no class–crime relationship, nor should it comfort the nominalist for whom class is simply a convenient abstract category with no independent existence. It might please reductionists, however, because by reducing social class to its component parts, we have elucidated mechanisms by which class exerts its influence. Locating intermediary mechanisms that account for the effects of A on B is, of course, the major goal of any science.

Controlling for variables that reduce the direct effects of class to zero undermines *direct* causation but not *indirect* causation. After all, class differences in student grade distributions would statistically disappear if we control for intelligence, motivation, and time spent studying, as would the difference between cooked and uncooked eggs if we controlled for heat. Although these factors explain the different outcomes to the satisfaction of most, students still get the grades they get, eggs remain cooked or uncooked, and lower-class individuals still commit more crimes regardless of the variables that explain why they do so. Social class can be considered a "cause" of criminal behavior if we consider SES to be the principal component derived from a factor analysis of all component variables that contribute to it, even though analysis of the component parts is a more satisfactory and comprehensive strategy (Walsh, 2011b).

I want to emphasize again that I am in no way criticizing self-report studies. Currently, a number of longitudinal studies are being performed that utilize self-reports as part of their methodology, such as the Dunedin Multidisciplinary Health and Development Study (Caspi et al., 2002), the National Longitudinal Study of Adolescent Health (Udry, 2003), and the National Youth Survey (Menard & Mihalic, 2001). These studies may use a variety of methods to verify self-report data, and many of them are collecting DNA for genetic analysis from subjects. As a result of increasingly cheaper technology, a number of ambitious longitudinal studies are being conducted that are brain imaging 400–2000 subjects at a time (Paus, 2010). Many of these studies are collecting large amounts of environmental, behavioral, and cognitive data (SES, maternal substance abuse, breastfeeding, stressful life events, IQ, personality profiles, and many other variables), and some are also collecting DNA data. As Lilly, Cullen, and Ball (2007) have pointed out, the most dramatic advances in science have not typically come from new advances in theory but, rather, from new technology (think of the major advances made possible by the invention of the telescope and microscope). The increasing use of new technology such as DNA analysis and brain imaging in the social and behavioral sciences predicts an exciting and fruitful future for them. The type of studies mentioned previously will push criminology into more evidenced-based paradigms if we can jettison our fear of letting the biological sciences into our domain. It is obvious from the wealth of data that the previously mentioned studies are collecting that they are not looking at parts isolated from the whole.

An interesting study conducted by Matt DeLisi and colleagues (2011) highlights the valuable information we lose when relying on community samples (as all the previously mentioned cohorts do), however comprehensive the data, however meticulous the study design, and however sophisticated the technology. DeLisi et al. compared a random sample of 500 adult arrestees with a purposive sample of 500 career offenders (defined as someone with a minimum of 30 arrests) divided into seven age categories ranging from 8–17 to 53–59 years. The results showed that the "normal" offenders had a pattern of arrests for relatively minor crimes that declined steadily with age, whereas the career criminals were relentlessly criminal in all age categories, with men in the oldest category (53–59 years) having approximately four times as many arrests as those in the "normal" category had during their most antisocial years (18–24 years). This pattern conforms to Moffitt's (1993) adolescent-limited/life-course-persistent offender patterns in which there is a group of minor offenders who will ultimately mature and desist from offending and another group of offenders who evidence stable pathologies across the lifespan and who will only desist with death, infirmity, or imprisonment. Community samples capture almost exclusively the adolescent-limited type of offender because the life-course-persistent types are relatively few, not likely to be available to community researchers anyway, and not motivated to participate if they are available. This is something we must always remember when making generalities about "criminals" from largely non-criminal samples.

The Police Bias Assumption: Improved Methods Yield Improved Conclusions

As we have seen, because of the discrepancy between self-report data and official data, a number of supporters of the superior validity of self-report measures have claimed that the "cause" of the class–crime/delinquency relationship is police bias (Uggen, 2000). The UCR does not break down arrest statistics by SES, but we may examine the police bias argument using black/white arrest differences as a proxy for SES arrest differences. Harris and Shaw (2000:136) claim that the correlation between race and SES is "so strong that any relation observed between race and crime might be nothing more than a cloaked relation between class and crime."

When all we had in terms of nationwide official statistics was UCR data on which to base our conclusions, it was difficult to determine if the highly disproportionate number of African Americans arrested for the index offenses represented disproportionate black involvement with crime or if it represented police bias in making arrests. Those who claim police bias in this regard rarely ask if the overrepresentation of whites relative to Asians in arrests is the result of anti-white bias, or if the overrepresentation of young males relative to older males, and males relative to females, is the result of ageism and sexism, respectively. In these cases, probably all criminologists would correctly put the discrepancies down to whites, young males, and males in general offending more frequently than Asians, older males, and females, respectively.

The advent of the NCVS gave researchers a better epistemology. Researchers are now able to compare arrest data from the UCR with NCVS data because victims of personal attacks identify the race of their assailants to NCVS interviewers. These comparisons yield essentially the same racial differentials in both data sets. For example, approximately 60% of robbery victims describe their assailants as black, and approximately 60% of the suspects arrested for robbery are black (O'Brien, 2001). The NCVS uses probability sampling of the entire United States (thus encompassing all SES levels) and interviews far more people bi-annually than all of the 35 studies examined by Tittle et al. (1978) combined.

D'Alessio and Stolzenberg (2003) brought National Incident-Based Reporting System (NIBRS) data, which combines the best features of the UCR and NCVS, to bear on the issue of differential racial arrest rates. Using NIBRS data from 17 states and 335,619 arrests for rape, robbery, and aggravated and simple assault, they found results directly opposite to the police bias hypothesis. African Americans were indeed arrested in far greater numbers than their proportion in the population led us to expect, but less often than the proportion of *offenses* they commit led us to expect. For crimes in which the race of the perpetrator was known, 30.8% of the white robbers were arrested versus 21.4% of black robbers, for aggravated assault the rates were 53.1 versus 42.5%, and for simple assault they were 46.8 versus 36.8%, respectively; however, no significant race difference was found for rape (27.2 vs. 28.1%). D'Alessio and Stolzenberg conclude that the disproportionately high black arrest rate is attributable to their disproportionately greater involvement in crime. They also speculate that blacks are less likely to be arrested than whites because there is less trust in the police in black communities and thus less willingness to aid them in their inquiries.

Pope and Snyder (2003), also using NIBRS data, analyzed 102,905 incidents of violent crime committed by juveniles and found essentially the same result; that is, white youths were more likely to be arrested than black youths despite the greater overall frequency and seriousness of the crimes committed by black youths. If it is true that race is a good proxy for social class, we should also draw the same conclusion for class differentials in arrest rates; that is, the claim that they reflect police bias rather than actual class differences in offending is bogus. Indeed, because most crime is intraracial, not to arrest black criminal perpetrators would result in charges of racism with respect to a disregard for black victims.

Conclusion

We have examined certain ideas about the reality of crime and how we go about uncovering facts about it. The most basic data of any discipline are the things it accepts as "real" and the assumptions is has about how its practitioners go about uncovering facts about those things it considers real. Ontology clarifies the structure of the knowledge we claim to hold and provides a vocabulary for representing that knowledge. It is thus imperative that we examine ontology underlying our theories because almost all of the categories of social science may be considered not "really real" by nominalists. Faulty ontology can lead us to taking positions that we really do not want to take as criminologists. Certainly "crime" is something humans have witnessed, named, and categorized, but some criminologists have taken this obvious fact and concluded that a criminal act is *defined* into existence—a social construction that need not be. I have previously noted that everything is socially constructed in a vacuous sense that humans see something, name it, and categorize it.

The epistemological question of the reliability of knowledge was addressed by illustrating the weaknesses of the self-report data that in the 1960s and 1970s labeling theorists (and others) considered as providing superior understanding of the crime problem than official statistics. They looked in the wrong places, asked about venial sins instead of crimes, and came to conclusions that few outside of academia would grant the time of day. Almost all of our community studies do not capture the "real" criminal who is of most concern to us.

Labeling theorists concluded that by and large, the overrepresentation of the lower classes and racial minorities in official arrest statistics was the result of police bias. Using race as a proxy for social class, we see that evidence supplied by the NCVS and NIBRS data show that labeling theory was off base on this question. Perhaps something as blemished as labeling theory would never have seen the light of day in criminology, or at least not have been taken to the extremes that is was, had its adherents been required to explore the ontological and epistemological foundations of their assumptions.

6

Materialism and Idealism
Structure Versus Culture

Mind and Matter

Among the many philosophical dichotomies is the one between materialism and idealism. It is of importance to philosophers because it is a battle between two contending images of what is "really real" and of the origins of that reality (mind from matter, or matter from mind?). Materialism is a realist position asserting that the world exists independently of our thoughts about it. Extreme materialism holds that the *only* thing that exists is matter, and that the human mind is the result of the complex interaction of things physical. Psychological phenomena depend on physical phenomena, but they occur as something additional to the electrochemical activity of the brain, and although they are emergent and epiphenomenal, they cannot exist without their physical substrates. Most materialists simply assert the primacy of matter and do not deny the reality of abstract entities such as societies and institutions, because at bottom they are composed of individual material people.

The opposite of materialism is idealism, which in its most extreme form posits that the human mind and spirit are fundamental and that the universe is made of "mind stuff." Plato's transcendental Forms are the quintessence of idealism. Before we dismiss idealism as the ramblings of mystics, we should note that many of the major proponents of idealism are physicists, the very people we think of as studying the material world. The great astrophysicist Sir James Jeans (1930:137) famously wrote that:

> the stream of knowledge is heading towards a non-mechanical reality; the Universe begins to look more like a great thought than like a great machine. Mind no longer appears to be an accidental intruder into the realm of matter ... we ought rather hail it as the creator and governor of the realm of matter.

Another great British astrophysicist, Arthur Eddington, wrote that "the universe is of the nature of a thought or sensation in a universal Mind" (in Schafer, 2006:509). When we think about the apparently infinite divisibility of matter, we have to wonder what it "ultimately" is: Is matter really only the gathering of the four nonmaterial fundamental forces of the universe? After all, ever since Einstein, matter and energy are equivalent, and no one has ever seen, heard, tasted, or smelled this abstraction we call energy—we only indirectly observe it through its effects.

As thoroughly fascinating as this topic is, we can safely leave it to the physicists and philosophers, who are better equipped to deal with it. We are only concerned with weak forms of materialism and idealism as they relate to pragmatic human activity. The argument in the social sciences is nothing as exotic and grand as the creation of the universe and the nature of ultimate reality but, rather, the comparatively mundane question of whether ideas create material conditions or material conditions create ideas. The issue is not exclusivity but, rather, the *primacy* of one or the other in guiding human affairs. It is quite obvious that ideas—what is in our heads at the moment—most directly and immediately determine how we will behave, but just as obviously, the material world of our existence strongly helped to plant those ideas in us.

Karl Marx Versus Max Weber

Karl Marx and Max Weber are the major exemplars of these two ontologies in social science. Both Marx and Weber are classified as conflict theorists, and because a significant proportion of criminologists are conflict theorists, an examination of their work as it relates to their respective ontologies is important. Marx was a materialist who saw the causes of social development and human action in material things such as economic factors. Society's intellectual superstructure—its law, religion, and values—is derived from these material things and represents the ideology of the ruling class. Weber was an idealist who posited the opposite: Ideas create reality, the structure of society, and determine how individuals and groups behave. Although both men adopted the position of the other when necessity intervened, their basic ontological positions led them to view, dissect, and evaluate a number of nominally identical concepts in different ways.

Marx and Weber were both influenced by the idealism of Georg Hegel, but they took different lessons from it. Marx took Hegel's dialectics, the notion of change through the dynamic interplay of opposites. Hegel asserted that opposites need one another to arrive at truth, and to arrive at truth, we state a thesis, engage an antithesis, and through rational discourse combine them into a coherent synthesis. Marx and Engels turned Hegel's dialectical idealism into dialectical materialism to explain the process of historical change by class conflict: "Freeman and slave, patrician and plebian, lord and serf, guildmaster and journeyman, in a word, oppressor and oppressed, stood in constant opposition to one another" (Marx & Engels, 1948:9). Marx and Engels describe history as a progression of economic struggles between classes, and mixing materialistic with historical dialectics, we get Marx's historical materialism in which capitalism is the thesis, its internal contradictions the antithesis, and communism the expected synthesis.

Weber was rankled by Marx's economic determinism and its corollary that ideas were just the reflection of material things. Very much influenced by Kant's view that the world could only be understood through the intellect that filtered and organized the buzzing confusion of sense perceptions, Weber preferred to think of ideas as autonomously affecting the economy. In his classic *The Protestant Ethic and the Spirit of Capitalism*, Weber (1930) asserted that capitalism was an unintended consequence of the ascetic protestant ethic. The protestant ethic originated in the Calvinistic idea of predestination—that is, the idea that one's postmortem destination is already known to an omniscient God. This created anxiety because nothing anyone could do, even living a totally exemplary life dedicated to good works, could change one's destiny. Given this, Calvinists began to look for signs of salvation by assessing their earthly status. To doubt one's salvation was an abnegation of faith and a sign of damnation, so ardent Calvinists developed a strong self-confidence, which led to worldly success. The protestant ethic developed into a set of principles favoring ambition, hard work, and asceticism, which led to the accumulation of wealth. Because piety and asceticism were in the forefront of the ethic, this wealth was not spent on conspicuous consumption but, rather, poured back into ever richer enterprises (Datetskaya, 2010). Thus, for Weber, a potent idea was inadvertently responsible for the development of capitalism.

Explaining Crime: Structure Versus Culture

Materialist and idealist ontologies touch on a variety of criminological issues. If material conditions "cause" people to behave the way they do and to possess the values they do, this leads us to different conclusions than if people's ideas "cause" the material conditions of their lives. Social structure is basically the organization of society consisting of its rules, institutions, and practices—that is, how established patterns among these things embodied in the interactions of individuals produce the particular configuration of society. Abstract though it is, structure reveals its reality by the impact it has on people because it is the setting in which they play out their lives. The structure of most concern to criminologists is the opportunity structure, the configuration of rules and practices that enable or constrain individuals in taking advantage of opportunities provided by society to advance their position through approved means.

This leads us to examine structural versus cultural explanations for criminal conduct. According to David Rubenstein (1992:9), structural explanations are the egalitarian imperative because "in structural sociology, there are no persons. That is, culture and personality, indeed everything that could distinguish one individual from another, either drop away entirely or are reduced to adaptive responses that have no autonomous power." This may be a little overstated, but structural theories do leave the impression that flesh and blood individuals are irrelevant to explaining crime. Such reasoning is derived from the assumption of human equipotentiality, with differences among people considered simply the result of their place in the social structural hierarchy (Guo, 2006). Those who adopt this position view it as a noble strategy to avoid holding what Richard Felson (2001) calls "protected groups" responsible for their condition or their behavior; in this view, only "structures of opportunity" must be held responsible.

People Versus Places: Where Does the "Blame" Lie?

Many social scientists view cultural explanations as "thinly veiled racist" (Almgren, 2005:220). Cultural arguments are considered racist by those who descend to name-calling because culture is embodied, carried, and expressed by people, and thus to invoke culture as a cause is to "blame the victim." In his discussion of "blame analysis," Felson (2001:231) writes that cultural arguments are acceptable when they celebrate "positive aspects of the protected groups' cultures and for explaining why certain groups such as Jews and Chinese Americans are economically well-off [and are] accepted when offending groups engage in discrimination." This contradiction may explain the long-term popularity of Merton's anomie theory despite its meager empirical support: It blames mainstream culture for advancing cultural goals and absolves individuals for their behavior by blaming structural impediments to achieving those goals. Cultural explanations are also acceptable when countering argument such as the genetic origins of racial differences in IQ (Patterson, 2000). Cultural explanations are thus conveniently useful in ideologically acceptable circumstances, but are racist when they are not.

Cultural explanations are not welcomed because individual people are carriers of culture, and the closer we get to flesh and blood, the less structuralists like it. If we start blaming culture, the next step might be blaming individual "victims" for their criminal behavior. Culture is linked to individuals because it is manifested in them. Culture provides them with a sense of reality, a Kantian information filtering system shared by similar others and transmitted across generations. As a worldview ordering cognitive reality, culture guides individual choices in ways that are presumably adaptive in their geographic, political, economic, and social environments. Like biological adaptations, cultural adaptations fit organisms into their environments as comfortably as possible given existing conditions. Also like biological adaptations, cultural adaptations can become maladaptive when environmental conditions change and the carriers of the culture do not change with them.

What qualifies as a structural versus a cultural variable is contested. According to Matsueda, Drakulich, and Kubrin (2006:335), among the factors said to qualify as "*structural* barriers to success" are concentrated poverty, joblessness, and drug use. Likewise, Rank, Yoon, and Hirschl (2003:6) list characteristics associated with poverty such as "birth outside of marriage, families with large numbers of children, and having children at an early age," and they blame these things on structural failure. Other factors listed by both or either of the previous studies as failures of the economic, social, or political systems include low educational attainment, divorce, poor work skills, and long-term welfare dependency.

But why are they considered structural rather than cultural, or indeed, the products of individual human choice? Poverty, joblessness, drug abuse, and illegitimacy rates are determined by aggregating the number of individuals who are in poverty, unemployed, abusing drugs, and so forth. Aggregate data are shaped by processes forged by numerous individual choices, each of which is shaped by many individual, cultural, and structural factors, but they are still choices. Once aggregate phenomena are formed from those choices, they serve as a cultural context in which further choices are made. Schwalbe and colleagues (2000:428) agree that these things are subculturally channeled choices that may be adaptive in a local context but maladaptive in the larger societal context: "Those who do well by the standards of the street acquire habits and create situations (drug addiction, lack of education, multiple dependents, criminal records) that are debilitating and risky, and diminish chances for mainstream success."

The most proximal context for these choices is the person's neighborhood. As understood by social ecologists, a neighborhood is a context in which culture is expressed. From an individualist perspective, a neighborhood is a macro mirror reflecting the combined micro images of all the individuals who live in it. John Wright (2009:148) employs this perspective to reduce putative ecological effects to the combined effects of individuals with similar characteristics. He writes:

> *It should be expected that individuals with similar traits and abilities, who have made many of the same choices over their life-course, should tend to cluster together within economic and social spheres. In other words, a degree of homogeneity should exist within neighborhoods, within networks within those neighborhoods, and within families within those neighborhoods.*

Yet, as I have said, choices people make are often constrained by factors beyond their power to control. None of us can do anything about the genes or rearing environment our parents provided us, neither can anyone do anything about the fact that factories have moved out of town or that the people around us sell drugs and are violent. What we can do—and here my existential streak comes to life—is decide to respond to the inevitable travails of life constructively or destructively.

Wright's comments echo those made by Ruth Kornhauser (1978:104) in challenging the ecological determinism of the Chicago School of human ecology more than 30 years ago: "How do we know that area differences in delinquency rates result from the aggregated characteristics of communities rather than the characteristics of individuals selectively aggregated into communities?" More recently, in an appeal to bring culture and the family back into analyses of poverty, sociologists Mario Small and Katherine Newman (2001:30) wrote the following: "People are not randomly distributed across neighborhoods. People live in neighborhoods as a result of both observable and unobservable characteristics that may themselves be independent of neighborhoods, affect life outcomes." This leads us to the question of whether people's traits, values, and attitudes or their physical environment best account for crime rates.

Longitudinal studies pitting neighborhood versus individual characteristics against each other invariably find greater explanatory power for individual factors. A German study conducted by Dietrich Oberwittler (2004:228) concluded that:

> *ecological contextual effects are likely to exist, and the neighborhood context appears to play an important role in these effects. However, as has been shown in previous*

research in U.S. cities, contextual effects on adolescents' behavior are generally very small compared with individual-level influences.

One large-scale United States example is Osgood and Chambers's (2003) study of 264 rural counties. This study found some ecological effects, but the greatest impact on crime and delinquency was the rate of female-headed households. Osgood and Chambers (2003:6) note that "a 10% increase in female-headed households was associated with a 73–100% higher rate of arrest for all offenses except homicide" (i.e., a 10% increase in female-headed households was associated with a 33% increase in homicide). One may want to transform the choices that led to a female-headed household into structural variables, but longitudinal behavioral genetic studies in the United States (Cleveland, Wiebe, van den Oord, & Rowe, 2000) and United Kingdom (Moffitt and the E-Risk Study Team, 2002) have shown that family structure is strongly conditioned by individual traits; that is, people create their family environments influenced by their genetic proclivities. None of these studies, of course, deny that individual proclivities are channeled by experience, culture, and social structure.

Class, Values, Structure, and Crime

There is a fundamental difference between the way subcultural–social process theorists such as Edwin Sutherland and Albert Cohen view the class–crime nexus and the way structural theorists view it. The key proposition in Sutherland's theory of differential association is "a person becomes delinquent because of an excess of definitions favorable to violations of law over definitions unfavorable to violations of law" (Sutherland & Cressey, 1974:77). "Definitions" refer to meanings that experiences have for us, how we see things, our attitudes, values, rationalizations, and habitual ways of viewing and responding to the world. In short, Sutherland asserts that how we think determines how we behave—cognition causes conduct.

Likewise, Albert Cohen's subcultural theory viewed crime and delinquency as expressions of short-term hedonism—the seeking of immediate gratification of desires without regard for long-term consequences. Cohen (1955:66) saw such behavior as nonutilitarian, malicious, and negative in the sense that it turns middle-class norms of behavior upside down by destroying rather than creating. Youths in run-down areas desire approval and status, but because they cannot (or will not) conform to what Cohen called "middle-class measuring rods," they establish "new norms, new criteria of status which defines as meritorious the characteristics they *do* possess, the kinds of conduct of which they *are* capable."

Walter Miller's (1958) seven-year multimillion dollar study of inner-city subcultures resulted in a picture of residents trapped by a set of "focal concerns." The hardcore lower-class lifestyle typified by focal concerns snares those engaged in it in a web of situations that virtually guarantee antisocial activities. The search for *excitement* leads to sexual adventures in which little preventive care is taken (*fate*), and the desire for personal freedom (*autonomy*) is likely to preclude marriage if pregnancy results. Miller was concerned about the fact that many lower-class males thus grow up in homes lacking a father or any other significant male role model. This leaves them with little supervision and leads them to seek their male identities in what Miller (1958:14) called "one-sex peer units" (male gangs).

Elijah Anderson's ethnographic work in African American neighborhoods in Philadelphia finds a hostile oppositional culture spurning most things valued by middle-class America, as in "rap music that encourages its young listeners to kill cops, to rape, and the like" (1999:107). He notes that although there are many "decent" families in these neighborhoods, the cultural ambiance is set by "street" families, which often makes it necessary for decent people to "code-switch" (adopt street values) to survive. Striving for education and upward mobility is viewed as "dissing" the neighborhood, and street people do what they can to prevent their "decent counterparts from … 'acting white'" (Anderson, 1999:65). Anderson is in agreement with Miller and many others who have studied African American subcultures; that is, the street code for young males is primarily a campaign for respect ("juice") achieved by exaggerated displays of manhood, defined in terms of toughness and sexuality.

For cultural theorists, then, crime and delinquency are motivated by conformity to lower-class values and beliefs: People commit crimes because they have learned that it is something almost demanded by their class heritage. It is crucial for Marxists to counter this view rooted in idealism, for if crime is really a valued social activity in some settings, it would mean that it is not an indicator of alienated social relationships, which is in turn viewed as a material consequence of their position in the capitalist mode of production.

Marxists accuse subcultural theorists of failing to identify the material origins of the values and beliefs said to generate crime, and they are skeptical of values and beliefs as behavioral motivators. All behavior must be viewed as generated by the concrete, material conditions of social life because people have the values they have because they occupy a particular place in the socioeconomic structure—they do not occupy that place because of the values they have. Values are simply a reflection of self-interest; therefore, we cannot stop crime by changing values. It is the *material* source of criminal values that must change, and this will only occur, as leftists used to be fond of saying, with the collapse of capitalism and the birth of socialist society. As Vold, Bernard, and Snipes (1998:267) write:

> *Marxist theories describe criminal behaviors as the rational response of individuals confronted with a situation structured by the social relations of capitalism. This view is consistent with the general view found in Marxist theory that, in general and in the long run, individuals act and think in ways that are consistent with their economic interests.*

Despite his idealism, Weber also believed that self-interest trumps ideas in the governance of human conduct: "Yet very frequently the 'world images' that have been created by 'ideas' have, like switchmen, determined the tracks along which action has been pushed by the dynamics of interest" (in Wallace, 1990:209).

Although Marx and Engels viewed crime and criminals as the products of an alienating social structure that denied productive labor to masses of unemployed—"the struggle of the isolated individual against the prevailing conditions"—unlike many modern structural theorists, they did not construe these conditions as a justification of criminal behavior. Unlike Durkheim, who viewed crime as a natural part of social life, and even functional in some ways, Marx and Engels saw it as a palpable indicator of social sickness that had to be cut out, and they made plain their profound disdain for criminals, viewing them as the lumpenproletariat ('rogue" or "rag" proletariat) and "social scum" incapable of developing class consciousness (Marx & Engels, 1948:11) and victimizing the honest laboring class.

The Dialectic Synthesis of Structure and Culture

Structure ("the material conditions of one's existence") necessarily precedes cultural adaptation to it. Culture emerges as a patterned strategy for survival in certain ecological, social, or political contexts—a set of adaptations that "worked" better than alternatives and was thus retained and passed down across the generations. Robert Sampson and Lydia Bean (2006:29), however, insist that interacting individuals create the conditions in which they live in real time, and that structure versus culture is a false dichotomy. Their position is that structure and culture are mutual creations pushing and pulling one another in a continuous dialectic spiral. They write:

> *Individuals are part of creating violent neighborhoods; put differently, without the cultural agency of neighborhood residents expressed in ongoing engagements in violent altercations, the neighborhood context would not be violent. The relational approach understands culture not as a simplistic adaptation to structure in a one-way causal flow, but an intrasubjective organizing mechanism that shapes unfolding social processes and that is constituent of social structure. From this perspective culture is simultaneously an emergent product and a producer of social organization, interaction, and hence structure.*

This appeal to human agency, and thus human responsibility for one's actions, as well as the mutuality of structure and culture, should carry some weight coming from Sampson, perhaps the preeminent social ecological criminologist of our time. The dialectic feedback loop between structure and agency is also central to Berger and Luckmann's (1966) *Social Construction of Reality* discussed in Chapter 2, but extreme structuralists may still view it as "victim" blaming.

Evoked and Transmitted Culture

Transmitted culture is an idealist view that culture is socially constructed and passed down the generations as mental representations of reality. The concept of evoked culture is a materialist concept more familiar to evolutionary ecologists than to social scientists.

It is a concept that maintains that humans have specialized domain-specific adaptation for responding to a range of environmental challenges (acquiring food, territory, and mates, avoiding disease, etc.) that had important fitness consequences over human phylogeny. Harsh ecological conditions, for instance, typically lead to cultural practices that emphasize parenting over mating effort, whereas people enjoying a rich ecology tend to develop cultures emphasizing the opposite (Buss, 2001). In other words, environmental conditions evoke certain patterns of behavior, which are then elevated to the level of transmitted values and norms guiding the expected behavior of all who belong to the culture. Cohen (2010:60) stated:

> *It is likely that many aspects of culture are synergistically evoked by the environment* and *ensconced in deeply felt and transmitted norms and values, and then transmitted by adherents of those cultures even after the groups no longer live in the same ecology.*

Gangestad, Haselton, and Buss (2006:79) describe the evocative nature of these design features as analogous to a jukebox designed to play different tunes according to the physical environment. This does not deny human learning in response to novel events or other forms of cultural variation. Rather: "[it shifts] the emphasis toward understanding how selection has shaped phenotypic sensitivities to environmental inputs."

It is little appreciated by social scientists that culture serves as a conduit for the selection of genetic variants, and that these variants then motivate their carriers to select cultural practices congenial to them over other cultural practices (Kitayama & Uskul, 2011). In addition to cultural transmission of practices across the generations, then, we will also see genetic transmission of traits favored by specific cultures. Members of a culture who enjoy a genetic advantage for the behaviors and values emphasized in it will enjoy greater fitness benefits, and thus those traits will then proliferate in the culture in a constant feedback loop. Consequently, the traits and behaviors will further differentiate between and among different cultures for genetic as well as culturally transmitted reasons due to gene–culture coevolution.

It is clear that a coherent explanation of cultural differences requires an understanding of human nature and the fitness imperatives imposed on it. Only such understanding can help us to appreciate the psychology underlying the social behavior of people in one culture in ways that would lead to predictions about the behaviors of other groups inhabiting similar ecological niches (Spiro, 1999). Transmitted culture suffices to explain transient modes of fashion, music, art, technology, science, culinary preferences, morality, and many other things, but when it comes to fundamental concerns about survival and reproductive success, we must not assume that culture is a realm ontologically distinct from biology. Walsh and Bolen (2012) provide many examples of gene–culture coevolution.

The concept of evoked culture may help us to understand that the culture–structure divide is no divide at all because they are born of one another and mutually reinforce one another. Race differences in income levels and crime rates are useful to explore the structure–culture relationship. According to the United States Census Bureau (2012) data, median family income for Asians/Pacific Islanders was $75,027 in 2009, for whites it was $62,545, for Hispanics it was $39,730, and for blacks it was $38,409. These figures produce a perfect inverse rank-order correlation with crime rates, which supports those who believe that poverty causes crime—or does it? Frank Schmalleger (2004:223) notes that the underlying assumption of all structural theories is that the "root causes" of crime are poverty and various social injustices. But as he also notes: "some now argue the inverse of the 'root causes' argument, saying that poverty and what appear to be social injustices are produced by crime, rather than the other way around." Likewise, Sampson (2000:711) writes:

> *Everyone believes that "poverty causes crime" it seems; in fact, I have heard many a senior sociologist express frustration as to why criminologists would waste time with theories outside the poverty paradigm. The reason we do … is that the facts demand it.*

On the other hand, crime rates have a perfect *positive* rank-order correlation with the rate of out-of-wedlock births across racial categories, and median income levels have a perfect *inverse* rank-order correlation with out-of-wedlock births. The United States Department of Health and Human Services (2011) lists illegitimacy rates of 73.5, 53.3, 29, and 17% for African, Hispanic, European, and Asian Americans, respectively. More than 20 years ago, Ellwood and Crane (1990:81) noted that the prevalence of single-parent families is so high in the black community that "a majority of black children are now virtually assured of growing up in poverty, in large part because of their family status." The United States Census Bureau's (McKinnon & Humes, 2000) breakdown of family types by race and income showed white single-parent households were more than twice as likely as black two-parent households to have an annual income of less than $25,000 in 1999 dollars (46 vs. 20.8%). To state it in reverse, *a black two-parent family is less than half as likely to be poor as a white single-parent family.* These figures constitute powerful evidence against the thesis that black poverty is the result of white racism. To be logically consistent with a racism argument, one would also have to claim that the Asian advantage in income and illegitimacy rates is the result of the white majority favoring Asians over themselves, which, of course, few would believe.

It is often argued that being poor and black does not equate with being poor and white because white poverty is more dispersed across different neighborhoods than black poverty, which is highly concentrated in single neighborhoods and termed "hyper-ghettoization" by Sampson and Wilson (2000). Hyper-ghettoization feeds ever higher concentrations of poverty and segregation because those who are able to do so flee the neighborhood and make room for more undesirables to move in to create even higher rates of antisocial behavior. However, Wilson and Herrnstein (1985:474) point out that hyper-ghettoization has been invoked as an explanation for *low* crime rates among Jews, Chinese, and Japanese: "What is striking is that the argument used … to explain *low* crime rates among Orientals—namely, being separate from the larger society—has been the same argument used to explain *high* rates among blacks."

We must not forget that historically the structural conditions African Americans have had to adapt to were real barriers—slavery, the Black Codes, disenfranchisement, racial stigma, Jim Crow laws, and any number of other things supported by the full force of law—to participation in mainstream society (Walsh & Hemmens, 2011). In response to these structural impediments, blacks evolved a subculture of opposition. As Richard Wright argued: "The Negro's conduct, his personality, his culture, his entire life flows naturally and inevitably out of the conditions imposed upon him by white America" (in Thernstrom & Thernstrom, 1997:51). Clarke (1998:50) traces high rates of crime, domestic violence, illegitimacy, and child neglect in the black community today to an evolved cultural system born out of slavery and that now "accounts for the social and sexual chaos that reigns in America's inner cities." Clarke points out that slaves did everything in their power to deceive their masters, and that stealing from whites was considered so "smart" that a black folklore emerged featuring stories and songs about slaves who outwitted their masters. Cultural norms developed that lauded thievery and deception and warned about the perfidious nature of whites. After emancipation, black lawbreakers came to be widely viewed as heroic figures among blacks, especially if they had been to prison. The outlaw tradition of the "bad nigger" was born from this form of hero worship (Milner & Milner, 1972). Even though the majority of victims of black crime were other blacks, black criminals still tended to be excused. The failure of blacks to condemn other blacks for their criminal behavior was viewed by the great African American scholar, W. E. B. Du Bois (1903/1969), as a major factor in the high rates of black-on-black crime in the late nineteenth and early twentieth centuries.

Choices people make are culturally channeled but are still choices for which they must bear responsibility. The relationships between crime, poverty, and the very personal choice of having children out of wedlock are strong. Condemning the practice of out-of-wedlock birth is not a condemnation made only by racists and moral entrepreneurs. A nationwide survey of public attitudes showed that almost as many blacks (68%) as whites (70%) agreed or strongly agreed that blacks should "stop having children out of wedlock" (Nunnally & Carter, 2012). This study also showed that most blacks are closer to mainstream whites than they are to white liberal academics on all moral and behavioral issues negatively impacting black communities.

Conclusion

The philosophical issues of idealism versus materialism in criminology involve attributing criminal behavior to either structural (materialism) or cultural (idealism) factors. Although cultural factors figure prominently in many of our criminological theories, structural theorists tend to view this as victim blaming because culture is embodied in people, whereas structure seems more distant and impersonal. We explored the structural/cultural issue in terms of black crime because it is important to structuralist egalitarians not to attribute black crime rates to black cultural practices, which, as I have argued, were evoked by the conditions of slavery and transmitted to the present. Many of the factors that structuralists claim as structural variables, however, are clearly in the domain of individual choices and choices "the system" spends multiple billions of dollars on every year trying to prevent, such as providing universal free education, family planning clinics, and job training schemes (Sawhill & Morton, 2007).

With Sampson and Bean (2006), I believe that the structure/culture division is flawed. Structure precedes transmitted culture, but once the ball is rolling, structure and culture are cause and effect of one another. Structure and culture represent a reciprocal interacting and ever-changing dialectic of objective material reality and subjective ideational meanings attached to that reality. This seems to me to be respectful of the dignity of human beings as autonomous creators rationally creating their environments rather than ragdoll victims. It is true, however, that black subcultures owe their origin to structures imposed on them by white society in the past over which they had no control at all. The case is not the same today because those conditions no longer exist. African Americans enjoy all the political, civil, and social rights that all races in the United States enjoy. Yet there are well-meaning academics who perpetuate this thinking as a sort of excusatory device for the behavior that is ironically partly generated by the cult of victimhood. If something else is the cause of one's plight, one has to wait for that something to change, which may never happen. What is needed is a change in one's self-image to an autonomous agent responsible for one's own fate.

7

Conflict and Cooperation: Alienation and Equality

The Interdependence of Conflict and Cooperation

Greek philosopher Empedocles viewed the universe as dictated by love and hate—opposites that only exist in relation to each other. Love produces concord and strife discord, each giving rise to the other in turn. The Chinese concept of the unity of opposites in yin and yang and Hegel's dialectic contain similar reasoning. Thus it is for conflict and cooperation. They are embedded in human nature because the material and symbolic resources needed for survival and reproductive success, the imperatives of all sexually reproducing species, are in short supply, and thus there is conflict over scarce resources among individuals and groups. But because resources are difficult to secure and interests are difficult to achieve, they are best secured and achieved in cooperation with others with whom we share a broad consensus about major issues. Without between-group competition, within-group cooperation would be weak. Conflict and cooperation thus serve vital interdependent social needs. Cooperation exists so we may better compete, and conflict exists as a vehicle whereby that which needs changing is changed.

Although critical about many things in society, most criminological theories are broadly consensus theories. I thus limit discussion in this chapter to conflict theories under which I subsume both Marxist and Weberian versions. I realize that there are multiple versions of critical/conflict theories, but I want to ignore the nuances and edit out all the qualifiers to converge on the common philosophical assumptions of a conflict view of society, focusing on philosophical concepts central to this tradition: Alienation and equality (Smith & Bohm, 2008).

A conflict view of society implies widespread discord, the seriousness of which ranges from minor disputes to wars and revolutions. When conflict is said to characterize a society, the claim is made that it is rife with hostility and held together only by a powerful state apparatus (e.g., Joseph Stalin's USSR, Marshal Tito's Yugoslavia, and Saddam Hussein's Iraq) and will fracture in its absence. Because of their distaste for capitalism, however, conflict theorists prefer to aim their barbs at Western democracies where they claim that stability and order are also maintained by coercion, albeit more subtly by the use of education, religion, and law to instill false consciousness: "The ideas of the ruling class are in every epoch the ruling ideas; i.e., the class, which is the ruling material force of society, is at the same time its ruling intellectual force" (Marx & Engels, 1965:136).

Conflict theorists consider the distribution of income and wealth to be the primary source of conflict within Western societies. Great wealth confers great privilege, and history is replete with class struggles. Plutarch wrote of the great disparity of wealth between classes and the conflict it generated in 594 BC. Athens (Durant & Durant, 1968:55), and United States President John Adams (1778/1971) wrote that American society in the eighteenth century was divided into a small group of rich people and a large mass of poor people engaged in a constant class struggle. The problem we face is how to confront disparities of wealth. On the one side are those who opt for wealth redistribution, and on the other side are those who consider unequal distribution to be necessary for economic growth and a natural consequence of free people with different abilities operating in a competitive free market that rewards talent and effort.

Marx believed that communism would eliminate conflict, a position viewed as pure fantasy by Max Weber. Weber (1978:39) wrote that:

even on the Utopian assumption that all competition were completely eliminated, conditions would still lead to a latent process of selection, biological or social, which would favor the types best adapted to the conditions, whether their relevant qualities were mainly determined by hereditary or environment.

Weber contended that conflict will always exist regardless of the social or economic nature of society, and that even though individuals and groups enjoying wealth, status, and power have the resources necessary to impose their values and vision for society on others with fewer resources, the various class divisions in society are normal, inevitable, and more acceptable relative to Marx's alternative (Gane, 2005).

Those who consider inequality of wealth and income to be natural and necessary tend to view society as held together by consensus and cooperation. They emphasize that society is an integrated network of institutions that function to maintain stability and order. For them, society is like an organism wherein each interdependent institution functions in its own way to maintain the whole. Social stability is maintained through cooperation, shared values, and the cohesion and solidarity that people feel by virtue of being part of a shared nation and culture. Consensus theorists are aware that conflicts often arise in social life, but they stress that most are temporary, and can be and are solved within the framework of shared fundamental values by a neutral legal system. Although consensus theorists value stability over change, they realize that change is often necessary for stability. Even the conservative British philosopher Edmund Burk viewed conflict as functional for social stability, writing that "a state without the means of some change is without means of its conservation" (in Walsh & Hemmens, 2011:288). The idea that conflict is often the foundation of consensus was also held by Durkheim (Rawls, 2003).

Conflict Criminology

A study of 770 American criminologists found that 35 of the 38 who favored critical/conflict-type theories were self-identified as liberal or radical (Cooper, Walsh, & Ellis, 2010). Liberals and radicals tend to hold a benign view of human nature, so why are they emphasizing conflict in social relations? For theorists with a Marxist bent, conflict is undesirable, but the blame for it resides in a capitalist mode of production, not in people, so all we have to do is change the mode of production to achieve lasting peace and harmony. Given such naive optimism, it is easy to see how William Perdue (1986:289) could write "conflict sociologists are routinely Utopian thinkers who believe in human and societal perfectibility."

The only conflict that mattered for Marx was between two monolithic economic classes headed toward an inevitable Armageddon and the victory of the proletariat. Weber's ideas of social stratification were quite different, and so were his ideas about conflict. For Weber, social life is at bottom all about the pursuit of social power. *Class* denotes economic power and is for Weber nonsocial or "barely social" because it is instrumental in orientation and lacks any sense of shared social belonging. *Status*, on the other hand, is fully social because status groups hold common values, express a common lifestyle, and possess a sense of belonging. *Party* represents political power and is based on associative social relationships to which people belong through free recruitment. Party-associative relationships are rational-legal in outlook rather than communal and traditional, and so they are less "social" than status groups (Gane, 2005).

Weber viewed society as composed of multiple temporary as well as semipermanent alliances of self-interested individuals that coalesce and dissolve as their interests wax and wane. The view that collective interests drive conflict is only true insofar as collective interests subsume individual interests was held by Marx also: "The separate individuals form a class only insofar as they have to carry on a common battle against another class; otherwise they are on hostile terms with each other as competitors" (in Coser, 1971:48). For Marx, then, class cooperation exists not to promote the well-being of the group as a whole but, rather, to promote each individual's interests that coincide at the time with the interests of others similarly situated.

Marxist criminologists reduce the explanation of crime to a single cause—capitalism—and it is often said that Marxist theory has very little that is unique to add to criminology theory "beyond simply attributing the causes of all crime to capitalism"(Akers, 1994:167). Likewise, Weber saw the law as a resource by which the powerful are able to impose their will on others by criminalizing acts that are contrary to their class interests, and he concluded that "criminality exists in all societies and is the result of the political struggle among different groups attempting to promote or enhance their life chances" (in Bartollas, 2005: 179). With this one sentence, Weber reduces criminal behavior to a single cause—conflict—prompting Adler, Mueller, and Laufer (2001:223) to conclude their analysis of non-Marxist conflict theorists on the same note as Akers: "Conflict theory does not attempt to explain crime; it simply identifies social conflict as a basic fact of life and a source of discriminatory treatment."

Alienation

The concept of alienation may mean different things to different people, but all meanings boil down to the idea of an individual's psychologically disturbing estrangement from something that he or she should "naturally" be involved with—God, the self, society, a spouse, and so forth. Although the concept has been pursued with philosophical vigor only for approximately the past two centuries, it was touched upon by a few earlier philosophers. Plato, for instance, believed that people could only achieve happiness and inner peace when the appetitive, emotional, and reasoned components of the self were in harmony, which could only be achieved by living connected to other people, the community at large, and God. Yet Kaufmann (1980:34) views Plato to be the epitome of an alienated being: "His *Republic* is the work of a man estranged from his society and from the politics and morals of his time." This sort of angst and disenchantment plagues many modern dreamers because the world as it exists is never good enough and ought to be better (Hanley, 2012).

Marx's idea of alienation is the opposite of that of Søren Kierkegaard, the philosopher who popularized the concept. Kierkegaard was an individualist who viewed alienation as the result of individuals being *too* engaged with the whole, *too* assimilated into the community, and *too* concerned with its conformity demands. According to Kierkegaard, this kind of herd mentality, integration, and conformity suppresses individuality and thwarts one's self-becoming (Matuštík, 1994). Marx was a holistic thinker and thus viewed alienation as individual estrangement from the whole. Kierkegaard's alienation was a spiritual condition, and the answer was spiritual renewal by living an authentic life and eschewing materialism, in both its philosophical and its acquisitive sense. Marx's alienation was a material condition that could only be alleviated by a socialist mode of production that would allow humans to realize their human essence.

For Marx, alienation is a human being's separation from his or her human nature. Because the essential being or nature of any species for Marx is the activity that distinguishes it from every other species, work is central to understanding his view of alienation. Since creative activity is the essence of what it is to be human: "man *qua* man only truly produces when he is free of physical need" (Nasser, 1975:487). Marx divorces work done out of the brute necessity for survival from "truly" productive work that only obtains when workers are their own masters and owe their existence only to themselves. If workers are not passionately involved with their work, they are estranged from their species being and reduced to working like animals—that is, as a means to an end (survival) rather than as a creative end in itself. Alienation is thus a state of incongruity between one's "species being" and one's behavior (e.g., mindlessly toiling to obtain life's necessities and becoming an appendage of the machine). Wage labor thus quite literally *de*-humanizes human beings by taking from them their creative advantage over other animals—robbing them of the species being and reducing them to the level of animals. As Tucker (2002:98) stated: "capitalism crushes our particularly human experience. It destroys the pleasure with labor, the distinctively human capacity to make and remake the world, the major distinguishing characteristic of humans from animals."

Under capitalism, humans are alienated from the products of their labor. This leads to alienation from one's self, which is experienced as malaise, powerlessness, and meaninglessness. When individuals become alienated from themselves, they become alienated from others and from their society in general. Alienated individuals may then treat others as mere objects to be exploited and victimized as they themselves are exploited and victimized by the "system" (Smith & Bohm, 2008). If one accepts this notion, perhaps one can view criminals as heroic rebels struggling to re-humanize themselves. Some Marxist criminologists do see it this way. William Chambliss (1976:6) viewed criminal behavior as "no more than the 'rightful' behavior of persons exploited by the extant economic relationships," and Ian Taylor (1999:151) saw the convict as "an additional victim of the routine operations of a capitalist system—a victim, that is of 'processes of reproduction' of social and racial inequality." David Greenberg (1981:28) even elevated Marx's despised lumpenproletariat to the status of revolutionary leaders: "Criminals, rather than the working class, might be the vanguard of the revolution." Marxist criminologists may even accuse non-Marxist criminologists of being parties to class oppression: "It is not too far-fetched to characterize many criminologists as domestic war criminals" (Siegel, 1986:276, quoting Tony Platt).

Contrast this excusatory sentimentality about criminal predators voiced by relatively modern Marxists with Marx and Engel's evaluation of them as "the dangerous class, the social scum, that rotting mass thrown off by the lowest layers of the old society" (1948:11). Their disdain and moral outrage is mirrored by Marxist statistician and eugenicist Karl Pearson in his essay *The Moral Basis of Socialism*, published in 1887:

> *The legislation or measures of police, to be taken against the immoral and antisocial minority, will form the political realization of Socialism. Socialists have to inculcate that spirit which would give offenders against the State short shrift and the nearest lamp-post. Every citizen must learn to say with Louis XIV,* L'etat c'est moi!
>
> *(in Paul, 1984:573)*

There is a real divide between Marxists who actually knew Marx and were much closer to his view of criminals and the maudlin sentimentality of more modern Marxists, most of whom have probably never had any dealings with criminals.

The origin of such illiberal attitudes on the part of the orthodox Marxist is that the concept of individual rights and procedural limitations on state power has purchase only as long as the state and the individual are distinct entities at odds with one another. In a socialist paradise, the state and the laws that support it would "wither away" and whatever would be construed as the "state" thereafter would become inseparable from the individual (*L'etat c'est moi!*). Consequently, individuals would not be in need of bourgeois procedural protections from themselves (Lovell, 2004). It is partly because of this that Gerhard Lenski wrote more than 30 years ago that "Marxism, like sociology, rests on much too naive, much too innocent, much too optimistic an assumption about human nature. Marxism, like sociology, still employs an eighteenth-century view of man"

(1978:380). What Lenski meant by this is that Marxists hold the blank slate view of human nature and that both human beings and their societies are almost infinitely malleable.

Capitalism: Alienation's Cause or Cure?

In the *Communist Manifesto*, Marx and Engels (1932:326) offer a paean to capitalism for unleashing the power of human productivity, stating that:

> the bourgeoisie during its rule of scarce one hundred years, has created more massive and more colossal productive forces than have all preceding generations together. Subjection of Nature's forces to man, machinery, application of chemistry to industry and agriculture, steam-navigation, railways, electric telegraphs, clearing of whole continents for cultivation, canalization of rivers, whole populations conjured out of the ground—what earlier century had even a presentiment that such productive forces slumbered in the lap of social labor?

Marx believed that the conditions of abundance created by capitalism also created the material means of its own destruction. That is, once capitalism created abundance, Marx thought we could slay the golden goose, change the division of labor, abolish class divisions and inequality, and still continue to enjoy economic and material progress. This kind of thinking was seen as monumentally naive by a number of Marx's contemporaries. Mikhail Bakunin (Marx's principal rival for leadership of the *First International*) wrote that if the proletariat were to gain control of the state, some of them would become rulers, and "from that time on they represent not the people but themselves and their own claims to govern the people. Those who can doubt this know nothing of human nature" (in Singer, 2000:4). Weber likewise chided Marx for his naiveté and noted, perhaps slightly unfairly, that "Marx was unique in the annals of social thought for his inability to ever make a correct prediction" (in Kahan, 2012:144).

Further evidence of Marx's naiveté is his belief that communism would magically transform specialist workers in his despised division of labor into self-actualized generalist creators, thus eliminating alienation as well as conflict:

> [In] communist society, where nobody has one exclusive sphere of activity but each man can become accomplished in any branch he wishes, society regulates the general production and thus makes it possible for me to do one thing today and another tomorrow, to hunt in the morning, fish in the afternoon, rear cattle in the evening, criticize at dinner, just as I have a mind, without ever becoming hunters, fisherman, shepherd, or critic.
>
> (Marx & Engels, 2004:53)

Perhaps in ancient tribal societies there was very little else to do but fish, hunt, and tell stories around the campfire, but transported to Marx's industrial London, it would either mean that everyone did everything remarkably badly or that everyone would somehow be transformed into Aristotelian polymaths. It could be argued that it is precisely the division of labor that allowed humans to realize their "species being." Surely our ancestors ensconced in primitive communism were far more like the other animals around them scratching out a day-to-day existence than modern humans who enjoy the marvels of science, technology, and medicine created by the division of labor. It is no wonder that Durkheim viewed socialist thought as a "cry of anguish" in the face of inequality that yearned for a return to communistic mechanical solidarity and warned that such a return could only be enforced by "external constraints to the detriment of the achievement of justice" (in Rawls, 2003:333).

Weber agreed that the capitalist mode of production generates alienation, but he denied that it was specific to capitalism, viewing it instead as a special case of a universal trend toward the rationalization and bureaucratization of the world necessary for modern economies (Sanderson, 2001). Weber's bureaucratization was seen as an "iron cage" that walled people off from each other and distorted individual autonomy—a central value for him and exemplified by charisma. Weber believed that capitalism provided opportunities to develop charisma because "it fosters entrepreneurship, the mother of charisma" (Kahan, 2012:147). Weber thus praised capitalism as a catalyst for the development of a characteristic that alleviates alienation. As a philosophical idealist, he saw alienation as a subjective appraisal of one's condition that can change, whereas for the materialist Marx, it is an objective appraisal of one's objective class position that can only be changed by changing the mode of production. Weber's individualistic conception of alienation as providing a catalyst for action may be the reason why there is rarely any mention of the concept in the work of conflict theorists for whom crime is about conflict and little else, which makes them as monocausal in their thinking as Marxist criminologists.

Equality and Relative Deprivation

Equality has been at the epicenter of so many struggles throughout history that its positive connotations make it enormously useful as a revolutionary slogan. We are all for it, but we differ on what it is exactly that we are for. The French philosopher Voltaire noted the contradictory nature of the concept when he wrote "equality is at once the most natural and the most chimerical thing in the world: Natural when it is limited to rights, unnatural when it attempts to level goods and power" (in Durant, 1952:245). In other words, the assumption of equal human value, equality before the law, and political equality are natural equalities due to us by virtue of our humanity. We do not have to earn those rights or even deserve them; they are simply our due and there is no justification for exceptions. No one of conscience denies the justice of equality in this sense. Equality of "goods and power," on the other hand, is "unnatural" because it defies the Aristotelian notion of treating equals equally and unequals unequally according to relevant differences, which has long been considered the essence of distributive justice by philosophers throughout the world.

The notion of equality in criminology is strongly tied to the notion of relative deprivation, which may be defined as "the judgment that one is worse off compared to some standard accompanied by feelings of anger and resentment" (Smith, Pettigrew, Pippin, & Bialosiewitz, 2012:203). Self-identified liberal and radical criminologists in Cooper *et al.*'s (2010) study considered "an unfair economic system" to be the most potent cause of crime rather than poverty, their old standby. Their opinion maps to that of nineteenth-century cartographer Lambert Quetelet, who opined that being poor amid riches produces more "misery" than being even poorer when others are perceived as just as poor (in Rennie, 1978). "Misery" is what we today call the relative deprivation that Smith and colleagues (2012) tell us leads to gnawing feelings of anger, envy, and resentment. Envy and resentment often lead to feelings of injustice and anger, and then by illegitimate attempts to obtain what is "owed" (Smith et al., 2012). However, envy and resentment only lead to criminal activity for those who believe that the world owes them a living and that people who have more than they have obtained it "unfairly." The essence of this kind of thinking is to hate those who are better off, to never admit that their success is due to their talents, efforts, and contributions they make to the community, and rather attribute their success to the exploitation and robbery of others. The cults of equality and entitlement have led us to the situation described by Joseph Sobran: "Today, wanting someone else's money is called 'need,' wanting to keep your own money is called 'greed,' and 'compassion' is when politicians arrange the transfer" (in Woods, 2004:231).

Since the implosion of the "hard" socialist countries of Eastern Europe and the current anemic state of the "soft" social–democratic nations of Western Europe, the focus of the left has shifted away from poverty (*objectively* deprived of basic necessities) to the inequalities of relative deprivation (*subjectively* deprived). Equality has become the overarching concern on the left, even if attaining it means reducing the resources of the least well-off as long as the resources of the more wealthy are reduced further, thus narrowing the gap. Economist Chris Snowdon (2011:40) comments on the logic of this relativistic thinking:

> *Since inequality can be alleviated by narrowing the gap without making anyone richer, their logic dictates that society would improve if the poor got 5% poorer so long as the rich got 20% poorer. A doubling of everyone's income, on the other hand, would make everyone's life worse.*

Inequality and Crime

We are all deprived of something relative to others to whom we compare ourselves and may feel envious, but how we choose to deal with such negative feelings is the important thing. Because some deal with relative deprivation negatively by engaging in crime, radical criminologists have a strong tendency to trace crime to inequality. In their institutional anomie theory, Messner and Rosenfeld point out that America's meritocracy *requires* inequality of outcomes because "winning and losing have meaning only when rewards are distributed unequally" (2001:9). They view this as both criminogenic and unfair, as do Sawhill and Morton (2007:4), who write that "people are born with different genetic endowments and are raised in different families over which they have no control, raising fundamental questions about the fairness of even a perfectly functioning meritocracy."

The assertion of those who think this way is that life should be fair, but the concept of fairness is saturated with divergent meanings. It is true that each of us finds ourselves existing with abilities and disabilities the *foundations* of which (the genes and environments our parents provided) we did nothing to deserve, but how does this engage the concept of fairness? We can nurture our abilities and combat our disabilities and develop what the radical egalitarian John Rawls calls a "superior character," but this is not enough to satisfy Rawls's egalitarian streak:

> *The assertion that a man deserves the superior character that enables him to make the effort to cultivate his abilities is equally problematic; for his character depends in large part upon fortunate family and social circumstance for which he can claim no credit.*
>
> *(1971:104)*

Marx also recognized that people have different abilities, but in his society they would not be granted license to benefit from them: "One man is superior physically or mentally and so supplies more labour in the same time…. This *equal* right is an unequal right for unequal labour. It is, *therefore, a right of inequality in its content, like every right*" (in Green, 1983:439; italics in original). For thinkers such as Marx and Rawls, meritocracy is unfair because under the principles of distributive justice the superior person will receive more benefits as a result of being blessed with a natural superiority. For them, rewards must be based on equal effort within the constraints of one's natural abilities. This notion is the basis for Marx's declaratory banner "From each according to his ability; to each according to his needs." Although this may be excellent advice for parents to apply to their children, it is not a recipe for just government. As biologist E. O. Wilson famously remarked about this slogan: "wonderful theory; wrong species" (in Walsh, 2009a:235).

Those who view unequal outcomes as not all unfair believe they are necessary to motivate healthy competition without which we would have economic stagnation and that the problems allegedly caused by inequality are unfortunate trade-offs. These individuals are not ogres who take pleasure in the misfortunes of the poor. They are people who view inequality as the natural outcome of a meritocratic system that ultimately benefits everyone, including its losers, by providing a dynamic economy and a free polity, and is certainly superior to command economies that have proved disastrous time and time again. Growing the economic pie rather than redistributing its pieces will do most for those at the bottom of the income distribution. Chandy and Gertz (2011:15) concluded a study on global poverty by stating that academics and policymakers debated the role of economic growth on poverty for years: "with some suggesting issues such as inequality and redistribution merited greater attention. Today, the developmental community has thankfully moved beyond this debate, with a broad consensus rightfully asserting the role of growth at the center of poverty alleviation." They are saying that baking larger pies rather than doling out ever smaller pieces of the existing pie equally has lifted untold millions out of abject poverty, as Marx acknowledged, and this is where our concern should be, not with "equality."

Ben Bernanke (in Sawhill & Morton, 2007:1) evaluates capitalism's requirement for unequal outcomes quite differently from Messner and Rosenfeld (2001). He states:

> Although we Americans strive to provide equality of economic opportunity, we do not guarantee equality of economic outcomes, nor should we. Indeed, without the possibility of unequal outcomes tied to differences in effort and skill, the economic incentives for productive behavior would be eliminated and our market-based economy—which encourages productive activity primarily through the promise of financial reward—would function far less effectively.

This is a position to which most people who work for a living subscribe. Studies in countries as diverse as Canada, China, Korea, Poland, and the United States (reviewed in Chan, 2005) show that ordinary people overwhelmingly reject John Rawls's difference principle (the principle that the most just distribution of wealth maximizes the wealth of the lowest income level). It is consistently found in these studies that subjects agree with Bernanke and "upheld a strong work ethic and gave little support for promoting equality of outcome, which, they believed, would dampen people's motivation" (Chan, 2005:460).

Historical Lessons on Equality Versus Freedom

Complaints about inequality come mostly from visionaries with dreams of how things should be. Although dreams of the possible are spurs to action, they can have horrible consequences if based on flawed images of human nature and on specious abstract principles. Aristotle rejected Plato's Utopianism contained in the *Republic* as too far removed from the reality of human nature. Aristotle knew enough about human nature that he would never trust an intellectual elite convinced that they alone have the truth and the right, indeed the obligation, to coerce the rest of us into conformity. This tension between dreamers of human and societal perfection and realists who fear the dangers of Utopian thinking has been played out in every historical period. Note, however, that in his last work (*Laws*), the mature Plato recognized that the state he had envisioned in the *Republic* was an impossibility given human nature, although he continued to view it as the ideal state. The *Laws* reflected a new psychology of human nature posited by a dreamer who had been mugged by reality (Laks, 1990).

In more modern times, contrast the French (1789) and Russian revolutions (1917) with the English (1688) and American (1776) revolutions. The first two were driven by abstract theories, appealed to the heart with stirring shibboleths of equality, and tried to wipe the slate clean of everything that went before. The latter two were driven by attempts to restore "an old order of things that had been violated by despotism" (Desai & Eckstein, 1990:455). The French revolution went from Rousseau to Robespierre to the guillotine; the Russian revolution drifted from Marx to Stalin to mass executions and gulags. The English and American revolutions went from Locke and Hobbes to Jefferson, Madison, and Blackstone and the English and American Bills of Rights. The French and Russian revolutions produced bloody reigns of terror driven by the belief that human nature and aspirations can be molded by force and fiat. The English and American revolutions were inspired by individuals with realistic visions of human nature and of the limits of social engineering. They brought stability and freedom, perhaps because their leaders believed that the idea that human nature and society are perfectible is dangerous Utopianism. Milton Friedman and Rose Friedman echo Bukunin and Durkheim when they remark that:

> *a society that puts equality—in the sense of equality of outcome—ahead of freedom will end up with neither equality nor freedom. The use of force to achieve equality will destroy freedom, and the force, introduced for good purposes, will end up in the hands of people who use it to promote their own interests.*
>
> *(1980:148)*

I believe that anyone who thinks otherwise has a dangerously naive view of human nature.

Conclusion

Conflict and cooperation are processes deeply embedded in human nature, and thus we should expect both to characterize human affairs. Criminologists who choose to emphasize one process over the other tend to have different views on alienation and inequality. Marx pounced on capitalism as the malevolent parent of both; Weber viewed capitalism as a cure for the former and was not overly concerned with the latter. Those who denigrate capitalism appear blind to the floods of people from all over the world who risk life and limb to partake of the "alienating" inequalities of life in Western capitalist societies. They do so because they know that it is in those societies where human rights are most respected and human wants and needs are most accessible, even if those wants and needs are not "equally distributed." Marxists compare the magnified problems of existing capitalist societies with an abstract communist society that exists only in their dream worlds, not with the actual nightmare spawned by Marxism. As Lewis Coser (1965:viii) aptly described such people: "They question the truth of the moment in terms of higher and wider truth; they counter appeals to factually by invoking the 'impractical ought.'" One of the ways of countering factuality is to claim that the societies that have fallen under the dark spell of communism were not "really" Marxist, and that "true"

Marxism has not been tried. How many times must we try the same thing and get the same result before we realize that poverty and oppression are inherent in any forced Utopian system? As many wise folks have pointed out, trying the same thing repeatedly and expecting different results is a pretty good definition of insanity.

This is not to say that the ideas of the left have nothing to offer. Many of the reforms of capitalism were forced on it by the threat posed by the specter of socialism. Friedman and Friedman (1980), strong adherents of capitalism, tell us that many items on the 1928 platform of the American Socialist Party have been adopted in the United States, including the 40-hour work week, unemployment benefits, social security, public works, and legal trade unions. These reforms were coopted by the Democratic and Republican parties because the American public demanded them, and they have been so integrated into American life that few other than the most reactionary of conservatives today would call them "socialist" or "un-American," or even imagine the whiff of Marx on them. In my opinion, there are still many faults in capitalism, but the problem with capitalism is the abuse of a good system by bad individuals, whereas the problem with socialism is the abuse of good individuals by a bad system. Capitalism has shown many times during the past 200 years that it can reform itself. If needed changes are to be made, they will come from the left, but to do so the left will need a more realistic view of what changes are possible and desirable, and thus a more realistic view of human nature (Singer, 2000).

8

Rationality and Emotion

Who Is in the Driver's Seat?

Because they both initiate behavior, the nature of the relationship between rationality and emotion has interested philosophers for centuries. But which one of these drivers is really in control of the train? The name Carl Linnaeus gave our species in 1735—*Homo sapiens* ("wise man" or "thinking man")—was happily accepted by the majority of Enlightenment philosophers and scientists, clearly showing that they opted for rationality. Many thought that if emotions took over, they would derail the train. The great philosopher of reason, Immanuel Kant, called emotions "pathological," and the eminent calculator Gottfried Leibniz called them "confused passions" (Solomon, 1977:41). Perhaps influenced by Descartes's mind/body dualism (mind = rationality; body = emotionality), for thinkers such as these, rationality is the exercise of reason, and emotions are feelings inimical to reason. The assumption of human rationality is explicit or implicit in almost all criminological theories, and if emotions are considered at all, they are treated negatively. It will be shown in this chapter that "the long-standing juxtaposition of emotion and rationality as polar opposites is simply wrong" (Turner & Stets, 2005:21).

Plato and Aristotle both believed that happiness is the ultimate goal of all human action. They viewed happiness not as a boundless hedonism but, rather, as a self-controlled and harmonious life governed by the Golden Mean, or what the ancient Greeks called *eudaimonia* ("good spirit"). All other life goals are only instrumentally desirable as means to the end of happiness. Jeremy Bentham's (1789/1948:125) famous dictum that "nature has placed mankind under the governance of two sovereign masters, pain and pleasure. It is for them alone to point out what we ought to do, as well as to determine what we shall do" is a relatively more modern version. But happiness is an *emotional* state of joy, satisfaction, and contentment; what then of rationality? The answer is that rationality is pressed into the service of happiness to calculate behavioral strategies most conducive to achieving it, and it is assumed that no one would knowingly reason a strategy that would reduce their happiness or increase their misery. This is Bentham's famous hedonistic calculus. Rational behavior is thus behavior with a logical "fit" between the goals striven for and means used to achieve them.

Rationality is not to be confused with morality. The goal of rationality is self-interest, and self-interest governs our behavior whether in conforming or deviant directions. Crime is rational (at least in the short term) if criminals employ reason and act purposely to gain desired ends. This is Max Weber's *zweckrationalitat*, or "instrumental rationality," which is a means–ends rationality that is self-serving and which Weber assumed to be innate in all people. Weber also posited a learned rationality called *wertrationalitat*. This type of rationality related to a value such as honor and duty to some respected entity that may appear to observers to be antithetical to instrumental rationality, such as a priest taking vows of poverty, obedience, and chastity. *Zweckrationalitat* thus points us to reasoned means of attaining a goal, and *wertrationalitat* helps to define those means and the goals in terms of norms and values with strong emotional valence.

Rational Choice Theory

The 1970s saw criminology swing somewhat away from the ideals of causal positivism toward a return to the classical notion that offenders are free actors responsible for their own actions. According to rational choice theory (RCT), rationality is the quality of thinking and behaving in accordance with logic and reason such that one's reality is an ordered and intelligible system. This does not mean that RCT contains an image of people as walking calculating machines, or that it is concerned about how people actually go about their subjective calculations. RCT posits that a person's choice to engage in crime, like any other choice, is made to benefit the chooser (Weber's *zweckrationalitat*). Criminal acts are specific examples of the general principle that all human behavior reflects the rational pursuit of maximizing pleasure and minimizing pain. People are conscious social actors free to choose crime, and they will do so if they perceive that its pleasures exceed the possible pains (formal or informal punishment) the actor may suffer if discovered. The theory does not assume that we are all equally at risk of committing criminal acts, or that we do or do not commit crimes simply because we do or do not "want to." It recognizes that personal factors such as temperament, intelligence, and cognitive style, as well as background factors such as family structure, class, and neighborhood impact our choices, but it largely ignores these factors in favor of concentrating on the conscious thought processes involved in making decisions to offend (Clarke & Cornish, 1985).

Rationality is both subjective and bounded, and unwanted outcomes can be produced by rational strategies (Boudon, 2003). We do not all make the same calculations or arrive at the same game plan when pursuing the same goals, for we contemplate our anticipated actions with less than perfect knowledge and with different mind-sets, values, and reasoning abilities. We do the best we can to order our decisions relating to our self-interest with the knowledge and understanding we have about the possible outcomes of an anticipated course of action. All people have mental models of the world and behave rationally with respect to them, even if others might consider one's behavior to be irrational. Criminals behave rationally from their private models of reality, but their rationality is constrained, as is everyone's, by ability, knowledge, emotional input, and time (Cornish & Clarke, 1986). If people miscalculate, as they frequently do, it is because they are ignorant of the full range of consequences of a given course of action, not because they are irrational. Of course, irrationality is subjective, but *intentional* irrationality—that is, making a decision based on a criterion that any sane and sober actor knows lacks rhyme or reason (e.g., tossing a coin to make a yes–no decision to commit a burglary or to get married)—is rare, to say the least.

From Rationality to Emotionality: Cultural/Anarchic Criminology

We are such children of the Enlightenment with its obsession with reason that we have seriously neglected the role of emotion in directing our behavior. But even in the midst of the Enlightenment's birth pangs, there were those, such as David Hume, who championed emotion over rationality. Hume's famous claim that "reason is, and ought only to be the slave of passions, and can never pretend to any other office than to serve and obey them" (1739/1969:462) makes that perfectly clear. Hume considered our species to be *Homo emovere* ("emoting man") rather than *Homo sapiens*, with our reason providing only *post hoc* rationales for doing what we feel like doing. For Hume, we perceive a situation, experience emotions, pass judgment on the event based on our emotions, and then provide reasons for our judgment. This is contrary to Kant, who believed that we perceive, reason, reach a judgment based on reason, and then emote. Given the battle between these two great philosophers, it seems that criminologists face an either/or dilemma: Is emotion or reason "really" driving the train? We shall see that this is a choice we do not have to make because, as is the case with free will and determinism and idealism and materialism, reason and emotion are team drivers indispensable to one another.

If criminologists analyze emotions at all, it is typically as toxic enemies of reason that instigate negative behavior. In Robert Agnew's (1992) general strain theory, for instance, strain (frustration and stress) leads to negative emotions such as anger, and these emotions then lead to criminal behavior—emotions intervene between perception and action. The emerging school of cultural criminology (sometimes called anarchic criminology), on the other hand, views emotions as primary causes of a great deal of antisocial behavior, rather than something that just happens to us when strained. Emotional satisfaction is seen as the goal often sought by one's behavior, and it is not simply an epiphenomenon of that behavior. Cultural criminologists view the rational calculator view of the criminal as offering us a flawed image of bloodless individuals devoid of passion (Ferrell, 2004). For them, crime's primary appeal is its intrinsic rewards—the thrills and the rush of taking risks and getting away with it, not the frequently negligible material rewards of most crimes. Studies of street criminals by researchers such as Jack Katz (1988) and De Haan and Vos (2003) paint a picture of "unreasonable" individuals seduced by a life of action who value their "badass" reputations more than monetary success. Their emphasis on emotions reminds us of Albert Cohen's (1955) view of delinquency as motivated by short-term hedonism, which is expressive, malicious, and destructive rather than instrumental.

When we survey the meager monetary gains and dismal long-term consequences of a criminal lifestyle, the claim made by such theories as Merton's anomie/strain theory that it is an alternative way to achieve monetary success does not cohere well with phenomenological accounts of crime presented to us by cultural criminologists. There must be something that makes crime appealing for its own sake, independent of any extrinsic rewards that may accrue from it. Chronic criminals are certainly motivated by the need for fast cash to feed their lifestyles, but interviews with criminals find that the internal rewards of committing expressive crimes are powerful motivators (Wood, Gove, Wilson, & Cochran, 1997). As Jock Young (2003:391) stated: "The sensual nature of crime, the adrenaline rushes of edgework—voluntary illicit risk-taking and the dialectic of fear and pleasure … all point to a wide swath of crime that is expressive rather than narrowly instrumental." The neurobiological details of this "dialectic of fear and pleasure" have been revealed in terms of a complex interplay of endogenous chemicals led by the exciting and reinforcing effects of dopamine and adrenaline, followed by the subsequent calming effects of the opioids (Gove & Wilmoth, 2003).

Nonetheless, emotional edgework is not devoid of cost–benefit considerations, and thus not devoid of rationality. For instance, the notorious Depression-era bank robber Willie Sutton plainly enjoyed the visceral rush of crime. When asked why he robbed banks, he replied: "Because I enjoyed it. I was more alive when I was inside a bank, robbing it, than at any other time in my life," but he would also sometimes answer "Because that's where the money is" (Sutton & Linn, 1976:120). The causes of behavior reside in the meaning it has for the person, the reasons he or she has for engaging in it. Behaviors that are noninstrumental from a material standpoint may be instrumental in terms of the expressive and "badass" status goals that the actor seeks. Reacting with anger and violence when others intrude on one's territory, resources, or mates is very useful in environments in which dialing 911 for the police to settle personal beefs is "just not done." Having a reputation for being quick to anger and for violence lets potential challengers know that it would be in their best interests to avoid you and your resources and look elsewhere. All this is why a badass reputation is so highly valued in some sub-cultures, why those with such a reputation are always looking for opportunities to validate it, and why it is craved to such an extent that "many inner-city young men … will risk their lives to attain it" (Anderson, 1994:89).

Cultural criminologists identify emotions as motivating antisocial behavior, and reading their research makes it easy to see why Kant called emotions pathological. One gets the impression that cultural criminologists romanticize criminals and their behavior as a kind of Nietzschean *ubermenschen* self-affirmation. But emotions should never be viewed only in a negative light; both Plato and Aristotle agreed that emotions are integral to our decision-making processes and that happiness cannot be separated from emo-tions. If this is the case, emotions *per se* cannot be pathological or irrational. As Freud (and Plato before him) reminded us, it is only when one dominates and excludes the other that problems arise. Negative emotions not reined in by studied reason can lead us to run amok. The emotions of anger, fear, jealousy, and hatred can lead to the worst kinds of violence, but so can Weber's *wertrationalitat* when it convinces vulnerable young minds, for instance, to become martyrs by blowing up busloads of innocent people in God's name. Then we have the psychopath's utilitarian *zweckrationalitat* calculations, which have no terms in their equations that contain the interests of others. The only mechanisms capable of reining in such rationality are the social emotions, because in addition to motivating some forms of crime, the emotions also function as powerful crime-prevention devices.

The Emotions and Their Functions

Biologists and psychologists distinguish between the primary and the secondary emotions. The primary emotions are those found in all animals to some extent, and the secondary (often called "social") emotions are composites of the primary emotions, much like the secondary colors are mixtures of the primary colors. Far from being pathological and maladaptive in all cases, the primary emotions have been enormously adaptive in the human phylogenic journey. Primary emotions such as fear, anger, and disgust focus our attention on an immediate problem and narrow responses toward some corrective strategy. Anger directed at injustice may prevent it, fear motivates escape and avoidance, and disgust urges expectoration and avoidance.

The social emotions, such as empathy, love, shame, embarrassment, and guilt, are retrofitted to the primary emotions as amalgams that broaden rather than narrow our focus. They counteract negativity and are integral to developing and strengthening social bonds (Fredrickson, 2003). They evolved as essential parts of our social intelligence and serve to provide clues about the kinds of relationships (cooperative vs. uncooperative) we are likely to have with others. They also serve as "commitment devices" and "guarantors of threats and promises" (Mealey, 1995:525). Barkow (1989:121) describes them as involuntary and invasive "limbic system overrides" that serve to adjust our behavior in social situations by animating, focusing, and modifying neural activity in ways that lead us to choose certain responses over other possible responses from the streams of information we receive. The social emotions move us to behave in ways that enhance our distant ancestors' reproductive success by overriding decisions suggesting alternatives to cooperation (i.e., cheating) that may have been more instrumentally rational in the short term by garnering us resources with little effort but that are ultimately fitness reducing. Short-term rewards are easier to appreciate than long-term consequences, and thus we often have the tendency to abandon consideration of the latter when confronted with temptation. It is the immediate warnings sounded by the social emotions, as well as the more distal cognitive appraisals, that lead us to attend to the long-term consequences of our social behavior.

Emotions and rational cognitions are not antagonists as so many thinkers have maintained; they are two inextricably linked components of all that we think and do. As Kant stated long ago, there can be no "pure reason." It has been well-known in neuroscience for some time that cognition is always suffused with emotions and rationality with emotion to various degrees (Nowak & Sigmund, 2005). Neural network research has shown that emotion and cognition are fully integrated in the lateral prefrontal cortex (LPFC). Pessoa (2008:154) tells us that "the convergence of both cognition and affective/motivational information enables the LPFC to dynamically weigh multiple lines of information in guiding action."

The social emotions cause positive and negative feelings when we survey the consequences of our actions, moving us to either repeat them or desist from them. Mutual cooperation evokes a deepened sense of friendship, a sense of pride, and a heightened sense of obligation and gratitude that enhances future cooperation. Because we find the emotions accompanying mutual cooperation rewarding and those accompanying defection punishing, the more intensely we feel the emotions, the less likely we are to cheat. Of course, this is rational because it increases pleasure and decreases pain, and thus produces happiness. Conversely, the less we feel the social emotions, the more likely we are to prefer the immediate fruits of cheating over concerns of prosocial reputation and its effects on future interactions with prosocial others. Emotions thus function to keep our temptations in check by overriding rational calculations of immediate gain. It is worth noting that one of the defining characteristics of psychopaths, the quintessential cheats, is their inability to "tie" the brain's cognitive and emotional networks together (Pitchford, 2001; Weibe, 2011). Psychopaths and chronic criminals have functioning cognitive systems in the sense that they are perfectly capable of reasoning; it is primarily (and sometimes exclusively) their emotional systems that are malfunctioning, and that is what causes them to discount their knowledge of moral norms (Walsh & Bolen, 2012). Emotionality adds reason to rationality.

Jean Jacques Rousseau was perhaps the first philosopher to put forth the modern notion that emotion precedes rationality in human phylogenic history (not just Hume's notion that it is more powerful than reason). He wrote of "two principles prior to reason," the first being an intense "interest in our own well-being" (Aristotle's happiness) and the second one that "inspires repugnance at the sight of the suffering of any sentient being." From these two principles: "all rules of natural right seem to flow" (in Velkley, 2002:38). Rousseau is saying that self-interest is original and that we come to be concerned with the interests of others when we can identify their suffering with our own through the emotions of empathy and sympathy. We revisit the idea that "all rules of natural right seem to flow" from these principles in Chapters 14 and 15 on justice and punishment, respectively.

Modern science supports Rousseau in multiple ways. Emotion is situated in the phylogenetically ancient limbic system, a set of brain structures that predated the arrival of the structures housing our vaunted reasoning powers by at least one million years (Suwa et al., 2009). The limbic system evolved in conjunction with the evolutionary switch from a reptilian to a mammalian lifestyle, which included the addition of nursing and parental care, audiovocal communication, and play (Buck, 1999). Two important structures relevant to our discussion are the amygdala and the hippocampus. The amygdala's primary function is the storage of memories associated with the full range of emotions, particularly fear. The hippocampus is specialized for storing and processing visual and spatial memories such as facts and events. Connections between the amygdala and the hippocampus help to focus the brain on what the organism has learned about responding to the kind of emotional stimuli that has aroused it, thus regulating it with memories of prior experiences ("Do I run, fight, scream, talk, ignore?").

If we ever doubted the intimate relationship between rationality and emotion, or perhaps the primacy of the latter over the former in understanding much of our behavior, neuroscience tells us that there are many more projections from the "emotional" amygdala to the "rational" hippocampus than *vice versa* (Richter-Levin, 2004). As a basis for social interaction, emotions preceded rationality in evolutionary time, with rationality being a later addition to the vitally important role of emotions in social life. As Massey (2002:15) stated: "Emotionality clearly preceded rationality in evolutionary sequence, and as rationality developed it did not replace emotionality as the basis for human inter-action. Rather, rational abilities were gradually added to preexisting and simultaneously developing emotional capacities." Jonathan Haidt (2001:819) stated it even more strongly: "It [emotion] comes first in phylogeny, it emerges first in ontogeny, it is triggered more quickly in real-time judgments, and it is more powerful and irrevocable [than rationality] when the two systems yield conflicting judgments."

Important Social Emotions: Empathy, Guilt, Embarrassment, and Shame

It hardly needs pointing out that empathy is important to social life. Empathy is an ancient phylogenic capacity predating the emergence of *Homo sapiens*, and it evolved rapidly in the context of mammalian parental care (de Waal, 2008). Empathy is the cognitive and emotional ability to understand the feelings and distress of others. The cognitive component allows us to understand why they are feeling distress, and the emotional component allows us to "feel" it with them. To the extent that we feel empathy, we have an evolved visceral motivation to take some action to alleviate the distress of others if we are able. Because we feel distress personally when witnessing the distress of others, we alleviate our own distress if we can help to alleviate the distress of others. Empathy thus has a selfish component, which is good because if we were lacking in emotional connectedness to others, we would be like psychopaths, callously indifferent to their needs and suffering (Walsh & Wu, 2008). Empathy channels altruism in social species because it moves us to rapidly assess a situation and respond to it without having to rely on cognitive ruminations to determine our response. It is an integral component of the nurturing of offspring because caregivers must quickly and automatically relate to the distress signals of their offspring. Parents who were not alerted to or were unaffected by their offspring's distress signals or by their smiles and cooing are surely not among our evolutionary ancestors.

The neural architecture that gives rise to shared representation of affective states such as empathy resides in so-called mirror neurons. Mirror neurons are brain cells that "mirror" in the brain of an observer by "firing" the identical neurons that are firing in the brain of the person being observed in emotional situations. This unconscious communication between neurons of one person and another reflects a correspondence between self and other that turns a perception into empathy. Mirror neurons provide us with a tangible substrate for philosopher and social scientist George Herbert Mead's notion of the process by which the self becomes both a subject and an object by taking the roles of others. It has been shown in functional magnetic resonance imaging (fMRI) studies that mirror neuron mechanisms are selectively recruited when attributing feelings to the self or to others in response to a variety of emotional facial expressions (angry, fearful, sad, etc.). Subjects who score high on a variety of empathy scales show stronger brain activation than those who score low, particularly in the various prefrontal cortices (Schulte-Ruther, Markowitsch, Fink, & Piefke, 2007).

Because individuals in social groups react toward others who violate social expectations, it is adaptive for humans to have evolved social emotions such as guilt, embarrassment, and shame to monitor and constrain negative impulses. When things under our control have a negative effect on ourselves or on others, it is useful to be aware of them and to be appropriately motivated to take some remedial action. Guilt involves anxiety, remorse, and concern about how one's actions have negatively impacted others. It is a socially adaptive form of moral affect that motivates both avoidance and approach behavior. Because guilt is psychologically punitive, it motivates one not to repeat the transgression (avoidance), and because it also moves one toward reparative behavior (apologies, restitution, etc.), it motivates approach behavior. As we might expect, guilt is positively related to empathy, because people are not likely to feel bad about offending others if they are indifferent to them (Silfver & Klaus, 2007).

Guilt is other-centered because it focuses our thoughts on recognizing the rights of others and how we have violated them. Shame and embarrassment, on the other hand, are much more self-centered. Shame involves an appraisal of self-worth in light of what the person has done to be ashamed of. Unlike guilt, shame can be very private, with only the person experiencing the emotion being aware of the origin of the emotion. The object of shame is thus the self ("I *am* a bad person") rather than an event, as is guilt ("I *did* a bad thing"). We will see in Chapter 9 how via certain neurohormonal routes the emotions function in conjunction with rationality to develop our consciences. Embarrassment is also a self-conscious emotion, although it is a more fleeting and less painful emotion than shame. Shame can be very private, but embarrassment can only occur as breaches of some sort of social etiquette such as committing an obvious faux pas during a professional presentation.

The importance of social emotions such as these can perhaps be best expressed in terms of their absence. The social emotions are notoriously absent or extremely weak in chronic criminals, especially psychopaths. Because psychopaths operate "below the emotional poverty line" (Hare, 1993:134), they do not reveal physical clues that would allow others to judge their intentions. Lacking an emotional basis for self-regulation, they make social decisions exclusively on the basis of rational calculations of immediate costs or benefits. Richard Wiebe (2004:33) summarizes the literature on emotional processing of psychopaths as follows:

> *Unlike non-psychopaths, psychopaths tend not to react autonomically to either faces or words that convey emotions. Further, they do not recognize fear and disgust as readily, although they can identify other basic emotions. These features allow the psychopath to cold-bloodedly pursue selfish interests, without being distracted by emotional signals, especially the fear and disgust of another person.*

Emotions and Gender Differences in Criminal Behavior

The huge universal gender difference in criminal behavior has long been a major issue in criminology and has been characterized as the "single most important fact that criminology theories must be able to explain" (Bernard, Snipes, & Gerould, 2010:299). "Most important" fact or not, it is certainly a very important one. Attempts to explain it have focused almost exclusively on the rational side of the rational–emotional whole in terms of learned attitudes, values, and social role practices. The fact that gender differences with regard to antisocial behavior are universal makes it problematic to limit the analysis to variable cultural practices such as appeals to gender socialization; we all know that we cannot explain a universal constant with a variable, even if we tend to forget it when attempting to be good Durkheimian social factists. Gottfredson and Hirschi (1990:149) agree in concluding that an explanation of gender differences in criminal behavior from the dominant social learning perspective is "beyond the scope of any available set of empirical data." I am certainly not offering my own theory of why the gender gap exists, but in terms of emotions, a starting point may be sex differences in empathy and fear. I have written elsewhere that:

> *empathy and fear are the natural enemies of crime for fairly obvious reasons. Empathy is other oriented and prevents one from committing acts injurious to others because one has an emotional and cognitive investment in the well-being of others. Fear is self-oriented and prevents one from committing acts injurious to others out of fear of the consequences to one's self. Many other prosocial tendencies flow from these two basic foundations, such as a strong conscience, altruism, self-control, and agreeableness.*
>
> (Walsh, 2011a:124)

Reviews of the literature show that females are invariably found to be more empathetic than males, regardless of the tools and methods used to assess it (Campbell, 2006b). This may be traced to the effects of higher testosterone levels in males (Knickmeyer, Baron-Cohen, Raggatt, Taylor, & Hackett, 2006) and/or to higher oxytocin functioning in females (Taylor, 2006), and ultimately to Darwinian sexual selection for empathy and nurturing behavior in human females. Testosterone and oxytocin act antagonistically to one another, which supports the notion that the evolution of empathy was driven by caregiving—that is, a strong focus on parenting effort (oxytocin) at the expense of mating effort (testosterone) (Herman, Putman, & van Honk, 2006). A number of neuroimaging studies have found that administering small doses of testosterone to females reduces empathy (Herman et al., 2006), and that administering oxytocin to males increases empathy (Domes, Heinrichs, Michel, Berger, & Herpertz, 2007). Furthermore, fMRI studies comparing neural correlates of empathy and gender differences have found that females recruit far more emotion-related brain areas than males when processing empathy-related stimuli (Derntl et al., 2010). It is important to note that these responses take place outside conscious awareness because the target sites for both testosterone and oxytocin are located in the limbic system.

Similarly, the fact that females experience fear more readily and more strongly than males, whether assessed in early childhood (Kochanska & Knaack, 2003), the middle-school years (Terranova, Morris, & Boxer, 2008), or among adults, appears to be a universal (Brebner, 2003). There do not appear to be sex differences in fearfulness *unless* a situation contains a significant risk of physical injury. A meta-analysis of 150 risk experiment studies found that sex differences were greater when the risk involved meant actually carrying out a behavioral response rather than simply responding to hypothetical scenarios requiring only cognitive appraisals of possible risk (Brynes, Miller, & Schafer, 1999). It has also long been noted that females consistently report being more fearful of crime than males and assess their chances of victimization higher despite objectively being less at risk for criminal victimization (Fetchenhauer & Buunk, 2005).

Whatever else contributes to universal sex differences in criminal behavior, sex differences in fear and empathy are surely central. Anne Campbell's (1999) "staying alive" hypothesis addresses fear as a proximate mechanism explaining gender differences in criminal behavior. Campbell argues that because the *obligatory* parental investment of females is greater than that of males, and because of the infant's greater dependence on the mother, a mother's presence is more critical to offspring survival than is a father's presence. She notes that offspring survival is more critical to female reproductive success than to male reproductive success. Because of the limits placed on female reproductive success by long periods of gestation and lactation, females have more investment tied up in children they already have than do males, whose reproductive success is only limited by access to willing females. Let us remind ourselves here that we are adapted to seek sexual pleasure, not reproductive success *per se*. Reproduction was simply a more common outcome of sexual activity in precontraceptive times.

Campbell (1999) argues that because offspring survival is so enormously important to their reproductive success, females have evolved a propensity to avoid engaging in behaviors that pose survival risks. The practice of keeping nursing children in close proximity in ancestral environments posed an elevated risk of injuring the children as well as the mother if she placed herself in risky situations. Thus, it became adaptive for females to experience many different situations as fearful. Females do engage in competition with one another for resources and mates, but it is rarely violent competition.

Most of it is decidedly low-key, low-risk, and chronic as opposed to high-key, high-risk, and acute male competition.

Campbell's (1999) theory also focuses on gender differences in status-striving. Campbell shows that when females engage in crime, they almost always do so for instrumental reasons, and their crimes rarely involve risk of physical injury. There is no evidence, for instance, that female robbers crave the additional payoffs of dominance that male robbers crave, or seek reputations as "hardasses." Campbell (1999:210) notes that although women aggress and do steal: "they rarely do both at the same time because the equation of resources and status reflects a particularly masculine logic."

Campbell's (1999) work is a well-thought-out piece of theorizing that encompasses all levels of analysis from the biological to the social. It appeared in the prestigious journal *Behavioral and Brain Sciences* and elicited comments from 27 scientists from various disciplines. Yet it is rare to see her work cited in feminist criminology, perhaps because is abjures discipline parochialism and only briefly touches on the old standby that is often used to explain gender difference—socialization.

Conclusion

I do not think anyone would deny that we are all ultimately concerned with happiness— that is, in increasing our pleasures and decreasing our pains. Happiness is an emotional feeling of deep satisfaction and joy, and we press rationality into service to seek ways in which we can increase it. If the search for happiness is the prime motivator of our behavior, we need to gain a deeper appreciation of its role in criminal activity. The role of emotion in social life has been vastly underappreciated by criminologists until relatively recently. We have attempted to understand criminal behavior only from the standpoint of rational actors. No one denies criminals their rational faculties, but rationality goes beyond serving only material needs. It is pressed into service to calculate whatever we consider, for good or ill, is conducive to greater happiness.

Along with most other social scientists and philosophers, criminologists have tended to pose rationality and emotions as opposites, with rationality being privileged over emotion. This leads to a fundamental misunderstanding of the driving forces of human behavior. We have seen that emotion is more evolutionarily relevant, and that this fact is underscored by the ratio of neural fibers running from "emotional" to "rational" brain regions than *vice versa*. Cultural criminology is an exciting addition to the literature because of its emphasis on emotion, but it unfortunately focuses on emotion as a motivator of crime rather than as a powerful source of crime prevention. Fear, disgust, empathy, guilt, shame, and so forth are all viscerally felt before they can be cognitively articulated, and they are vital to social life because they are component parts of our consciences. Criminology would do well to pay closer attention to the role of emotion as both a stimulator and an inhibitor of criminal behavior.

9

Right and Wrong Conscience

What Is Conscience?

In *The Descent of Man*, Charles Darwin wrote that he "fully subscribe[s] to the judgment of those who maintain that of all the differences between man and the lower animals the moral sense of conscience is by far the most important" (in Ayala, 2010:9015). Darwin viewed the conscience as he viewed every other human characteristic—as an evolved adaptation. It hardly needs belaboring how possessing what the theologians like to think of as "the voice of God" would have strong fitness benefits. It marks one as a person of good character who desires to do the right thing and who is cognizant of the rights and concerns of others. Individuals who demonstrate a sturdy conscience mark themselves off as people who would make conscientious and agreeable mates, employees, colleagues, and friends.

The concept of conscience is surely central to criminology because it is the primary characteristic lacking or greatly weakened in criminals. But perhaps because of its religious and moral overtones, it is rarely addressed in criminology apart from defining it simply as the "internalization of norms," nor are its origins addressed except to invoke a disembodied "socialization" (Grasmick & Bursik, 1990). Jeffrey Arnett's influential model of socialization in sociology speaks to the goals of socialization, and it claims that the most important goal is "impulse control, including the development of a conscience" (1995:618). Yet nowhere does Arnett venture past repeating that children must learn to control their natural egoistic impulses and must do so by "internalizing" the messages of their parents, teachers, and peers. For him, as for many others in his discipline, socialization is simply a cognitive process whereby others pour prescriptions and proscriptions into empty heads. The process is much more complicated than that, and if we are to understand how people acquire a conscience, we must engage neuroscience, genetics, and, yes, philosophy. There is a large literature in the psychological and biological sciences relating to conscience that could enrich our understanding of moral behavior if we would access it.

As unwelcome as pain is, it is vital to keeping us alive because it alerts us to the fact that a bodily system has reached unacceptable levels of what it will tolerate. Pain is an adaptation warning us when we are vulnerable to injury and death and that something requires attention. Individuals born with insensitivity to pain (congenital analgesia) often do serious damage to themselves and suffer serious illnesses simply because their pain insensitivity renders them unaware of any danger (Mogil, 1999).

The psychological analogue of physical pain is the bite of conscience. This too is unpleasant because it engages the primary emotion of fear and social emotions of guilt, shame, and embarrassment. The bite of conscience alerts us to the fact that our social relationships are in danger because of something we have done or contemplate doing. The bite of conscience is just as self-centered as physical pain, because it warns us not to damage our relationships since the consequences of doing so are detrimental to the self. It is also other-centered because it warns us not to damage our social relationships or to repair them if we have already done so. Because group living requires cooperative relationships, without conscience there can be no civilization, for as Freud (2002) stated long ago, civilization is bought at the cost of our inability to do what we damn well please.

Is there a psychological equivalent of congenital analgesia? Conscience is something that is developed over time in interaction with others, rather than a set of autonomous processes confined to individual physiology. There are individuals with consciences so severely compromised that we might call the condition "acquired moral analgesia," although we already have other names for it, such as chronic criminal, psychopath, or sociopath. Just as those suffering from congenital analgesia have genetic mutations that compromise the physiological regulatory systems that engage pain receptors, chronic criminals also have identifiable physiological processes that compromise the systems that engage the social emotions.

Early Models of Approach–Avoidance Behavior

If social animals are to function peacefully and predictably in their social groups, they must possess the ability to respond to signals of reward and punishment with socially appropriate approach and avoidance behavior. Numerous philosophers have written about the hedonic tug-of-war that humans play with themselves as they struggle to meet their wants and needs while being aware of the wants and needs of others in their social worlds. Plato's (1960) tripartite model of the soul (human nature) is the classical model of approach–avoidance motivation and behavior. The soul in Plato's model is composed of the appetitive, rational, and spirited parts. The appetitive part motivates us to seek the pleasures necessary to sustain individual life and the continuation of the species (food, water, and sex). The rational soul thinks and urges us to make wise decisions when seeking our goals, and the spirited soul values virtue and emotionally enforces the dictates of the rational soul. In his famous chariot allegory, the charioteer is the rational soul fighting to control the spirited noble white horse (emotion) and the ugly black horse (appetitive). Both horses and charioteer are necessary to move the chariot forward, so none of the parts are bad *per se*. The traits represented by both horses, especially the black horse, can be detrimental if not reigned in and dominate the direction of the chariot, and the just and moral person is dominated by the reasoned soul holding the reigns.

Similar to Plato, Freud (1965) believed that a harmonious relationship must exist among the constituents of his tripartite model of personality (the id, ego, and superego) to ensure individual well-being. The basic biological instincts that constitute Freud's id are analogous to Plato's appetitive soul, the superego is analogous to the spirited soul, and the ego is the rational or reasoned soul. We are born with the id, the norms and values of our socializing agents provide the superego, and our capacity for reason provides the necessary balance between the two. There are certain differences between the approach–avoidance models of Plato and Freud, but the underlying concept is the same; that is, we are in a perpetual war with ourselves as the three components vie for supremacy when we are confronted with temptations both licit and illicit.

Criminal behavior reflects a failure of the spirited soul to enforce what the reasoned soul knows to be right or, as more modern folks would put it, a failure of our prosocial socialization agents to mold us into the kind of moral beings our cultures expect. A large part of successful prosocial socialization revolves around individuals' relative sensitivity to reward and punishment as they contemplate the approval or disapproval of their behavior by others. The person must learn cognitively what is expected of him or her, but how well the lesson is learned is more a function of how the lessons engage limbic system emotions than how they engage rational reflection (Muñoz & Anastassiou-Hadjicharalambous, 2011).

Reward Dominance Theory and Conscience

Conscience can be viewed as the sum of the social emotions coupled with the moral learning that evokes them. It is the term we apply to a series of processes that regulate our approach and avoidance behavior in ways that are functional for us and our fellow citizens. Reinforcement sensitivity theory is the major neurobiological personality theory focusing on the conditioned suppression or expression of behavior (Cooper, Perkins, & Corr, 2007). This theory is more familiar to criminologists and addiction theorists as reward dominance theory (RDT). Similar to the Platonic and Freudian models, RDT posits three interacting systems of behavioral regulation located within separate brain circuits and governed by separate neurotransmitter systems. These self-regulating feedback systems are the *behavioral activating (or approach) system* (BAS), the *behavioral inhibition system* (BIS), and the *fight–flight–freeze system* (FFFS). The BAS and BIS are part of the central nervous system's limbic system and prefrontal cortex (PFC), and the FFFS is part of the autonomic nervous system (ANS) of the peripheral nervous system.

The BAS is sensitive to signals of reward from both conditioned (alcohol and other drugs, gambling, etc.) and unconditioned (food, sex, affiliation, etc.) appetitive stimuli. The BAS is important to us because it motivates us to seek things vital to survival and reproductive success; it is Mother Nature's built-in reward system. Of course, seeking other appetitive goals such as alcohol and other drugs was probably not part of Mother Nature's plan; these evolutionary novel stimulants hijack the natural reward system and use it for unnatural purposes. The BAS is reminiscent of the Freudian id in that it obeys the pleasure principle, craves instant gratification of its desires, and unless governed by a watchful avoidance system, cares not (or is oblivious to) whether the means used to satisfy them are appropriate or injurious to self or to others.

The BIS is activated when the search for reward stimuli exceeds reasonable limits, and it is sensitive to conditioned (e.g., violations of social rules) and unconditioned (e.g., heights and snarling creatures) threats of punishment (Corr, 2004). It inhibits approach behavior by inducing feelings of fear and anxiety when negative consequences are anticipated. The BIS can be likened to the Freudian superego striving for the ideal and representing all the moral "brakes" (the dos and don'ts) internalized during the process of socialization. An overly strong BIS is related to anxiety-related disorders such as obsessive–compulsive disorder and agoraphobia, and a weak BIS is correlated with attention deficit hyperactivity disorder and psychopathy (Amodio, Masters, Lee, & Taylor, 2007).

The Platonic and Freudian models of approach–avoidance once again illustrate the debt modern scientists owe to astute observers of human nature of the past. But unlike these earlier models, the biological substrates of approach and inhibition have been neurologically and genetically mapped out. The BAS is primarily associated with the neurotransmitter dopamine and with mesolimbic system structures such as the ventral tegmental area (an area rich in neurons that synthesize dopamine), and also the nucleus accumbens (the "pleasure center"), which is the major target of dopamine (Day & Carelli, 2007). The BIS is associated with the neurotransmitter serotonin and with limbic system structures such as the hippocampus and the amygdala that feed their memory circuits into the PFC, where judgments and decisions are supposed to be made in accordance with rationality (Blair, 2007).

The PFC does not have to resolve BAS/BIS conflicts on its own. Much of the conflict has been emotionally resolved by the anterior cingulate cortex (ACC), a structure that curves around the limbic system and provides a connection between the limbic system and the cerebral cortex. The ACC has a number of functions, including mediating between possible responses "suggested" by the "cold" memories of the hippocampus and the "hot" memories of the amygdala, and also in aiding self-control by assisting the hippocampus to reign in negative emotions (Davidson, Putnam, & Larson, 2000). According to Tancredi (2005:36), the ACC "provides for civilized discourse, conflict resolution, and fundamental human socialization." A number of neuroimaging studies have shown that the ACC actively monitors the conflicts between the BIS and the BAS (Amodio et al., 2007; Spielberg et al., 2011). It might not be too far-fetched to physically situate Freud's hypothetical ego or Plato's metaphorical charioteer in the ACC, emotionally enforcing what the PFC (the "reasoning soul") knows is right.

An unbalanced approach–avoidance system may produce a "craving brain" that leads the person into all sorts of physical, social, moral, and legal difficulties, such as addiction to gambling, food, sex, and drugs (Walsh, Johnson, & Bolen, 2012). A faulty BAS may be seen as a brain less efficient in binding dopamine, overly efficient in transporting it back into the presynaptic knob, and/or overly efficient in clearing it from the synaptic gap. Defective brakes, on the other hand, are associated with similar deficiencies of the serotonergic system (Propper & Moore, 2006). Carriers of any or all of these genetic variants will be led on an incessant search for more pleasure-inducing experiences to increase dopamine levels (DeLisi, Beaver, Vaughn, & Wright, 2009). A balanced BAS/BIS system obeys the Freudian reality principle; it does not deny the pleasure principle but, rather, simply adjusts it to the demands of social reality.

The Autonomic Nervous System and Conscience

Jeffrey Gray (1994), one of the pioneers of reward dominance theory, added the FFFS to the BAS/BIS model to account for additional data related to avoidance behavior. The FFFS is a generalized response system sensitive to *unconditioned* aversive stimuli, such as pain and extreme frustration, whereas the BIS responds to stimuli associated in the past with aversive consequences—that is, *conditioned* aversive stimuli. The FFFS also includes the amygdala and hippocampus in Gray's model, which suggests that in many ways the BIS and the FFFS may be thought of as a single integrated inhibition system. Although most researchers interested in the behavioral biology of arousal refer to the whole ANS, the FFFS terminology was coined by Gray to distinguish the ANS's fight/flight function from its "housekeeping" functions such as automatically maintaining homeostasis in the visceral parts of the body (heart, lungs, kidneys, etc.).

The ANS has two complementary branches: The sympathetic and parasympathetic systems. When an organism perceives a threat, its amygdala-associated neural networks send signals to the sympathetic branch to mobilize the body for vigorous action (the "fight-or-flight" reaction). Pupils dilate for better vision, the heart and lungs accelerate their activity, and digestion stops, among other things, all of which is aided by pumping out epinephrine (adrenaline). The parasympathetic system restores the body to homeostasis after the organism perceives the threat to be over.

Because BIS and FFFS components are engaged simultaneously in approach–avoidance situations, the reactivity or response level of the ANS is considered a major determinant of the development of a conscience (Gao, Raine, Venerables, Dawson, & Mednick, 2010; Kochanska & Aksan, 2004). The conscience is the basis for forming moral judgments and for moving one's behavior into conformity with those judgments, but it is more than a reasoning mechanism because it typically moves us in one direction or another before we have had an opportunity to consciously contemplate options. This is the emotional component of the conscience that precedes cognition that Barkow (1989:121), as noted in Chapter 8, describes as an involuntary and invasive "limbic system override" that serves to adjust our behavior in social situations. We have previously described how the social emotions animate, focus, and modify neural activity in ways that lead us to choose moral responses over other possible responses in approach–avoidance situations. It is thus easy to understand how the social emotions would have enhanced reproductive success by overriding temptations to avoid group cooperation, thus marking individuals strongly influenced by them highly trustworthy candidates for friendship, marriage, and employment.

The Autonomic Nervous System, Conscience, and Antisocial Behavior

Conscience is the cooperative output of limbic emotional and rational cognitive mechanisms that enables individuals to internalize the moral rules of their social groups. Individuals with a strong conscience will feel guilt, shame, and anxiety when they violate these rules; those with an impaired conscience will experience none of these emotions. As Kochanska and Aksan (2004:304) stated: "An impaired conscience is the core aspect of conduct disorders, antisocial development, and psychopathy. Conversely, the capacity for remorse and empathy, an appreciation of right and wrong, and engaging in behavior compatible with rules all mark successful adaptation."

We have noted that psychopaths have been neurobiologically defined by their reduced ability to connect the brain's cognitive and emotional networks together (cortical–subcortical decoupling). It has also been found that they have significantly reduced ANS responses to fear-inducing stimuli (Blair, 2007; Gao et al., 2010). Studies (e.g., Soderstrom, Blennow, Sjodin, & Forsman, 2003) have found the ratio of the metabolites of dopamine and serotonin to be robustly related to scores on the Hare's Psychopathy Check List–Revised (PCL-R) instrument used to asses psychopathy throughout the world. The PCL-R has two primary components—personality and behavior. The metabolite ratio related $r = 0.50$ ($p < 0.01$) with PCL-R personality $r = 0.523$ ($p < 0.004$) behavioral traits. A high ratio between these metabolites implies high dopamine turnover and/or deficient serotonergic regulation of the dopamine system—in other words, a reward-dominant brain with poor behavioral controls due to deficient serotonergic activity.

Differences in the emotional component of conscience are observed in infancy and toddlerhood, long before children are able to reflect cognitively on their behavior as morally right or wrong. Variations in ANS arousal patterns lead to significant variation in how well the prescriptions and proscriptions of moral behavior are learned via classical conditioning (Kochanska & Aksan, 2004). Unlike operant conditioning, which is active and cognitive in that it forms a mental association between a person's behavior and its rewarding or punishing consequences, classical conditioning is mostly passive and is visceral in nature. Classical conditioning simply forms a subconscious association between two paired stimuli, the strength of which depends on the level of ANS arousal more than on conscious deliberation. In terms of acquiring morality, it seems that modern science is coming down more in favor of Hume than of Kant—emotion is in the driver's seat taking us to our prosocial destinations.

ANS arousal thresholds (as measured by heart rate, blood pressure, and electro-dermal activity) are normally distributed, with most individuals by definition clustered around the mean and a small minority on each tail. Individuals with a *hyper*arousable ANS are easily aroused by situations they perceive as threatening, and thus they condition easily because arousal produces punishing visceral feelings. When hyperarousable individuals contemplate behaving in a way they might want to but that is contrary to the expectations of others, memories of previous responses to their behavior flood their amygdala. The amygdala then engages the sympathetic system producing anxiety or fear. When such individuals subconsciously decide not to act on the antisocial impulse (the "limbic system override"), the parasympathetic system engages to restore the ANS to homeostasis, which constitutes physiological reinforcement for conforming behavior.

The visceral associations between behavior and the responses of others is the mechanism by which we develop the "gut-level" social emotions that make up the "feeling" superstructure of our consciences. These social emotions are retrofitted to the same machinery that drives the hardwired primary emotions of fear, anger, sadness, and joy (Tibetts, 2003). Retrofitting the primary emotions involves elaboration and refinement by cognition during the socialization process. This is the "knowledge" part of conscience—the lessons we learn relating to what things we should feel guilty, ashamed, and embarrassed about, and what things we should feel happy and proud about. Properly socialized individuals with a well-developed conscience will fear the visceral pain of punishment and the shame of rejection when they transgress, and they will welcome the joy of acceptance and affection when they behave well.

A hyperarousable ANS is a powerful protective factor against criminal behavior. A review of 40 studies of ANS activity and criminal and other antisocial behaviors found 38 studies that supported the link and 2 that had nonsignificant results (Ellis & Walsh, 2000). A number of subsequent studies have shown that young males living in criminogenic environments who remain free of their influences (i.e., they do not become delinquent) show hyperactive ANS arousal under conditions of threat (Lacourse et al., 2006). Youths whose ANSs are highly reactive and who are reared in criminogenic environments are actually less likely to commit antisocial acts than youths with hyporeactive ANS arousal reared in noncriminogenic environments (Brennan et al., 1997). A longitudinal study of a birth cohort found that measures of poor ANS conditioning (measured electrodermally) at age 3 years successfully predicted criminal offending (official records) at age 23 years, independent of controls for a variety of social adversities (Gao et al., 2010). Finally, Moffitt and Walsh (2003) aver that among those rare individuals who abstained from antisocial behavior altogether during adolescence, a good deal of credit must be given to hyperactive ANS functioning.

Thus, individuals with a hyperactive ANS are easily socialized. They learn their moral lessons well because sympathetic ANS arousal is subjectively experienced as fear and anxiety. Children learn that when they behave well, they do not incur the wrath of others and fear and anxiety do not occur. Individuals with relatively unresponsive ANSs are difficult to condition because they experience little anxiety, fear, or guilt when they transgress, even when discovered and punished, and thus have no visceral restraints against further transgressions. They are not viscerally reinforced for conforming behavior because they are not aroused to fear in the first place, and thus cannot receive positive reinforcement for conforming behavior by way of a return to ANS homeostasis (Bell & Deater-Deckard, 2007). Having knowledge of what is right or wrong without that knowledge being paired with emotional arousal is like knowing the words to a song but not the music—not much good for singing in the social choir.

Criminality, Empathy, and Fear

I noted in Chapter 8 that empathy and fear are the natural enemies of crime; thus, it follows that the low levels of empathy and fear are its natural allies. If the social emotions are foreign to psychopaths, it is not surprising that they cannot vicariously experience the emotions of others. If the fine-tuning of the social emotions is realized through fear of punishment, it is again not surprising that psychopaths have very little appreciation of them. Psychopaths and chronic criminals are thus granted permission to prey on others by their lack of concern for the feelings of others, and by the lack of fear about the possible punitive consequences to themselves. According to some, psychopathy is rooted in and nourished by low fear. As Syngelaki and colleagues (2013:1) stated: "Poor fear conditioning is a predisposing factor to crime because individuals who lack fear are less likely to avoid situations, contexts, and events that are associated with future punishment—resulting in a lack of conscience." Lykken writes of the usefulness of fear in guiding behavior in early life: "Like the ability to experience pain, the fear mechanism is especially useful early in life before the individual's judgment and reason are sufficiently dependable guides to behavior" (1995:144). Fear and anxiety are emotional components of the conscience, the strength of which has much to do with levels of amygdala and ANS arousal levels. Lykken's premise is that psychopaths are difficult to condition because they are relatively fearless, and that they are relatively fearless because they are autonomically hypoarousable.

Although ANS responsiveness predicts antisocial behavior independent of other factors, we certainly cannot dismiss the role of these other factors. It is reasonable to assume that the rational cognitive components of conscience are strongly stressed in the socialization process of children from advantaged environments with warm attachments to parents. As Travis Hirschi (1969:18) stated: "The essence of internalized norms, conscience, or superego, thus lies in the attachment of individuals to others." If children in advantaged environments become antisocial, because they lack the environmental instigation to such behavior, they may be less conditionable than their peers. Variance in physiological measures will therefore be more salient in accounting for antisocial behavior in higher socioeconomic status (SES) individuals than it will be in lower SES individuals whose physiological risks are masked by psychosocial risk factors. This is consistently found and has been called the "social push hypothesis" (Raine, 2002). Scarpa and Raine (2003:213) define the social push hypothesis thusly: "If an individual lacks psychosocial risk factors that predispose toward antisocial behavior yet still exhibits antisocial behavior, then the causes of this behavior are more likely to be biologically than socially based." Children from lower SES environments who are difficult to condition because of a hyperactive ANS are at greatest risk for antisocial behavior because they are also more likely, on average, to lack the cognitive conditioning necessary for acquiring a conscience.

The Cognitive Conscience

In *The Descent of Man*, Darwin concluded that conscience, or the Golden Rule, is based on the social instincts plus cognition and habit: "The social instincts—the prime principle of man's moral constitution—with the aid of active intellectual powers and the effects of habit, naturally lead to the golden rule" (1981:106). Thus, the limbic substructures are not sufficient by themselves to engage the conscience; they require input from the higher cortical regions. The other side of the conscience coin is the cognitive appraisals of our behavior, which are carried out by the PFC—"the most uniquely human of all brain structures" (Goldberg, 2001:2). The PFC occupies approximately one-third of the human cerebral cortex, a proportion greater by far than in any other species, and is the last brain area to fully mature (Romine & Reynolds, 2005). This vital part of the human cortex has extensive connections with other cortical regions, as well as with deeper structures in the limbic system. Because of its many connections with other brain structures, and because it is involved in so many neuropsychological disorders, it is generally considered to play the major integrative role, as well as a major supervisory role, in the brain, and it is vital to the forming of moral judgments, mediating affect, and for social cognition (Romine & Reynolds, 2005; Sowell, Thompson, & Toga, 2004). It can perform all of these tasks because it is the only part of the neocortex free of the burden of sensory processing (Massey, 2002) and can thus concentrate on sorting out input from other brain areas and making sense of them. If any of the various parts of the PFC are compromised in any way, emotional messages may not be recognized and properly acted upon, and planning strategies may be ultimately dysfunctional.

Neuroscientists have gone beyond examining the limbic system or the prefrontal cortex in isolation to consider dysfunctions in the pathways linking these systems. Craig and colleagues (2009) used diffusion tensor imaging (a magnetic resonance imaging-based system allowing for the assessment of the integrity of connections between various brain systems) at a micro-architectural level by viewing the diffusion of water molecules along axon pathways (axons are protrusions from neurons) in British violent criminals with PCL-R scores ranging between 25 and 34 (25 is the cutoff point for psychopathy in the United Kingdom, whereas it is 30 in the United States). They examined the uncinate fasciculus (UF), which is the white matter tract connecting the anterior temporal lobe (where the amygdala resides) with the brain's frontal lobes, to analyze its volume and structural integrity. Highly significant correlations (in the high 0.80s) between PCL-R factor 2 (behavioral aspects of psychopathy) scores and tract volume in both the left and the right UF, and significantly reduced fractional anisotropy in the right but not the left UF were found.[1] Craig and colleagues conclude that "taken together, our findings suggest that abnormal connectivity in the amygdala–OFC [orbitofrontal cortex] limbic network may contribute to the neurobiological mechanisms underpinning the impulsive, antisocial behavior and emotional detachment associated with psychopathy."

A theory of criminal behavior tightly linked to approach–avoidance behavior, and thus to the acquisition of a conscience, is prefrontal dysfunction theory (PDT) (Boots, 2011). The PFC provides us with knowledge about how other people see and think about us, thus moving us to adjust our behavior to consider their needs, concerns, and expectations of us. These PFC functions are collectively referred to as executive functions (Fishbein, 2001). Executive function refers to a set of cognitive abilities that are necessary for goal-directed behavior by anticipating possible outcomes and our ability to think abstractly. These properties of the PFC are major rational components of the conscience, and in a normally functioning PFC, they are clearly involved in funneling us in prosocial directions.

The association between the frontal lobes and pro- and antisocial behavior is often illustrated by the dramatic case of Phineas Gage, whose skull had a tamping iron blasted through it at the PFC. This case gave early neuroscientists their first clues about the functions of the PFC, although it is an extreme example; the damage does not have to be massive or even anatomically discernible to impact behavior negatively. PFC damage could be at the cellular level and be the result of genetic factors that affect neuron migration during the earliest stages of frontal lobe development, or by such things as maternal substance abuse during pregnancy (Perry, 2002). Individuals with deficits in the ventromedial PFC are particularly impaired in the decision-making process because this area plays a vital role in evaluating past emotional associations and regulating them through its abundant connections with the amygdala (Alves, Fukushima, & Aznar-Casanova, 2008).

Cauffman, Steinberg, and Piquero (2005) combined reward dominance and prefrontal dysfunction theories in a large-scale study of incarcerated youths in California and found that seriously delinquent offenders had slower resting heart rates (indicative of low fear and low ANS arousal) and performed poorly relative to nondelinquents on various cognitive functions performed by the PFC. In another study combining both theories, Yacubian (2007) and colleagues monitored activity in the PFC and the ventral striatum areas (areas that are strongly innervated by dopaminergic fibers) via functional magnetic resonance imaging scans among 105 healthy male volunteers. Some subjects showed

---

[1]Fractional anisotropy (FA) is a measure ranging from 0 (isotropy) to 1 (anisotropy) that provides information about water diffusion along white matter fibers (myelinated axons). It is measured by a technique called diffusor tensor imaging, which assesses the integrity of connections between various brain systems at a micro-architectural level. Isotropy implies random movement in all directions, much like an ink drip spreading out on blotting paper, and anisotropy is directional and non-random, like rain water flowing one way in gutters. White matter fibers are the brain's rain gutters acting as barriers to free diffusion and guiding movement in one direction (i.e., parallel to them). Thus, the greater the FA value, the better the integrity of the axonal connection between brain areas (Mori & Zhang, 2006). We may think metaphorically about this relative lack of limbic–PFC connectivity in psychopaths as leaky gutters rotting the foundations of conscience.

high levels of activity, and some showed blunted activity in anticipation of similar rewards. Examining subjects' genotypes, the researchers found that variation in neural activity was mediated by variation in the dopamine transporter gene DAT1 and in catechol-*O*-methyltransferase (COMT)—an enzyme that degrades dopamine in the synaptic gap.

If dopamine is transported back into the presynaptic knob by one allele of the gene faster than by another, persons possessing the fast variant will find themselves less rewarded by the same amount of dopamine released into the synaptic gap than persons not possessing this variant. This is the case in the so-called 10-repeat version of the DAT1 (Beaver, Wright, & Walsh, 2008). The same applies if dopamine is degraded faster by one variant of COMT than by another, as it is in the case of valine as opposed to the methionine version (Miller-Butterworth et al., 2008). Those who have such deficiencies in their dopaminergic functioning are prompted to seek out more substances (alcohol or other drugs, etc.) or experiences (sex, gambling, etc.) that lead to the further release of rewarding dopamine. This is the basis of a reward-dominant craving brain that leads to addiction (Walsh et al., 2012). Because a functioning conscience is guided by an appropriately balanced approach–avoidance system, an addicted brain's overwhelming concern for obtaining what it is addicted to severely compromises concerns about behaving in accordance with social norms.

Conclusion

The acquisition of a moral conscience is a complex process that involves the coming together of cognitive and emotional mechanisms. Conscience is the name we give to a series of neurohormonal processes that have evolved to help us navigate our way through social life. Our natural and necessary selfish proclivities have to be tamed, as philosophers have told us for millennia. Nature rewards us with a dopamine surge when we do things that contribute to our survival and reproductive goals, and it is this unassailable fact that provides all living things with the strong tendency to put the self before others. This "go for it" feature is what Plato called the appetitive soul, what Freud called the pleasure principle, and what modern neuroscientists call the behavioral activating system. This necessary system is balanced by the behavioral inhibition system, which urges us to seek our rewards and interests with caution, and with the rights and needs of others in mind.

Conscience is the internal police officer we carry with us from situation to situation that helps to monitor our behavior. It is the abstraction composed of the social emotions and the knowledge of what is expected of us that motivates us to want to conform with the expectations of others, and it is thus very useful to possess. Learning the social emotions takes place largely through the process of classical conditioning, whereby the prescriptions and proscriptions provided by socialization agents are reinforced and punished. Among normally functioning individuals, how well they learn these lessons depends primarily on the reactivity of the autonomic nervous system that stamps the "avoidance" social emotions of guilt, shame, and embarrassment on our viscera. We have seen that psychopaths condition poorly. They are perfectly capable of understanding the rules of social life, but as numerous experiments have shown, they lack the emotional component of conscience. Understanding the nature and origin of conscience would seem to be of the utmost importance on the agenda of a criminological education because it is each person's crime-prevention device. However, I have yet to see it discussed in our textbooks, which is a deep mystery to me. Perhaps it is because to include it necessitates the discussion of neurological and physiological mechanisms and processes with which we are uncomfortable. If this is the case, it is reason enough to spend the time to become comfortable with them.

10

The Science Wars and Ideology in Criminology

Wars over Science

Science is the greatest intellectual achievement of humankind and the only source of reliable knowledge about anything natural in the universe. It is superior to other ways of knowing because it yields justified beliefs—that is, beliefs that are verifiably true across all cultures. It is thus little wonder that people involved in many areas of inquiry that deal with "softer" material than that found in the nonhuman world want these to be viewed as sciences. Despite some fleeing to such anti-science schools of thought as postmodernism and social constructionism where nothing passes for objectively justified belief, I think that most criminologists want to claim scientific status for their discipline.

There are arguments about whether criminology (or any other branch of social inquiry) can be considered a science in the same way that physics, chemistry, and biology are sciences. After more than a century of claiming scientific status, no area of social inquiry has an established body of general laws or elegant theories with broad explanatory scope with the capacity to yield reliable and robust predictions. Multiple theories compete in the marketplace and then disappear, not falsified or replaced by something demonstrably more encompassing and robust, but simply pushed to the side as stale. Neither is there anything like the broad unanimity about what counts as established fact and what constitutes reasonable explanations in the social sciences. Unlike in the social sciences, students in the physical and natural sciences encounter no subject matter disputes until they reach the back end of graduate school. Even then, there is a strong belief that any dispute will eventually be resolved to almost everyone's satisfaction when the right observations are made and when the right technology for making them is designed and manufactured.

There is no definitive observation that I can imagine that would lay to rest any of the disputes that exist in criminology. This is not necessarily a bad thing because it affirms that human beings are of a quite different constitution from the phenomena of the hard sciences. Unlike chemical elements, for instance, humans act purposefully and with agency. There are just 92 naturally occurring elements (different types of atoms determined by the number of protons in their nucleus), and chemists know precisely how each one will (or will not) react with other elements when subjected to certain conditions. On the other hand, all of the billions of human beings are in many ways unique given the almost unlimited permutation of their genes and of their genes with their environments.

Criminological Theory

Thus, we will never achieve the explanatory and predictive power of the hard sciences; if we could, we would be no better than automatons.

It is true that each individual is unique, as the nominalists insist, but each individual is also like every other individual in the most important ways, as the Darwinists insist. Regardless of human variation, we all share the same genes, brains, hormones, and evolutionary history, so explaining and predicting human behavior with more precision than is now the case is certainly not a lost cause. Because we are biological as well as cultural beings, there are criminologists who have observed biology develop coherent and florescent theories from which have sprung a cascade of testable propositions and hypotheses resulting in robust explanations of biological phenomena, and they see no reason why criminology, in principle, cannot follow suit. These individuals see no defensible *scientific* reason why criminology should not be continuous with biology in the same way that biology is continuous with chemistry, and chemistry with physics (Beaver & Walsh, 2011; Cullen, 2009; Wright & Boisvert, 2009). People in the human sciences who believe that it is both possible and desirable to adapt the objectives and methods of the biological sciences to study human behavior operate from a philosophical position called *naturalism*.

On the other hand, we have seen that there are scholars in the social sciences who are hostile to both the practice and products of science and who have built careers around flagellating it (Hacking, 1999). These latter-day children of romanticism see naturalism in the social sciences as thoroughly misconceived, and they see ugliness and destruction in what is from their perspective the soulless reductionism of science. Scholars of this bent gravitate to alternative ways of seeking to understand humans, such as social constructionism and postmodernism, and elevate subjectivity and relativism over the hard methods of science. Many of them seem to view science as little more than a smokescreen hiding power relations in society and which is often used to further sexist, racist, or classist goals. As Williams and Ariggo (2006:13) write: "Assertions of impartiality and neutral knowledge merely endeavor to disguise the reality (the power and authority) underlying claims to knowledge, truth, and progress." Cordelia Fine (2010), for example, characterized neuroscience's use of brain scans to discover brain structures and functions that putatively explain sex differences in behavior and personality as "neurosexism," and Ash Amin (2010) charges that the use of new genetic techniques to claim that race is a biological reality means that "biological racism" has replaced "phenotypic racism."

Ideology in Criminology

The science wars are not just fought between pro- and anti-science scholars. Different criminologists who hold science in high esteem have waged seemingly intractable disputes about their subject matter, even when looking at the same data. Where ostensibly reasonable and intelligent people continue to disagree when in principle the matter should be settled, we are leaving the world of rational discourse and entering the muddy world of ideology. Ideology is a more or less coherent pattern of ideas, beliefs, and attitudes; a way of looking at the world—a general emotional picture of how things are or should be, and are a "central component of an individual's general life orientation" (Smith, Oxley, Hibbing, Alford, & Hibbing, 2011:378). Ideologies thus provide individuals with a shorthand guide to organizing their intellectual world, which is compact and can be carried with them from issue to issue. It is not necessarily a particular "ism" such as Marxism, and it may not be explicitly formulated. Indeed, persons may not know that they are expounding a particular ideology, and they may even deny that they are doing so, claiming that they have the values and attitudes they have for pragmatic reasons or because their position is simply "common sense." Nevertheless, the same people consistently line up on opposite sides of the barricade on a whole host of different issues—the death penalty, abortion, immigration, gay marriage, school prayer, school vouchers, the free market, and so on. Contrasting positions on these and many other issues define the liberal–conservative divide.

Orlando Patterson (1998:ix) views the ideological conservative–liberal polarities as major barriers to advancement in social science. He complains that conservatives believe that only "the proximate internal cultural and behavioral factors are important ('So stop whining and pull up your socks, man!')" and that "liberals and mechanistic radicals" believe that "only the proximate and external factors are worth considering ('Stop blaming the victim, racist!')." Patterson's observation is reminiscent of the ancient Indian parable of the six blind men feeling different parts of an elephant. Each man described the elephant according to the part of its anatomy he had felt, but each failed to appreciate the descriptions of the others who felt different parts. The men fell into dispute and departed in anger, each convinced of the utter stupidity, and perhaps the malevolence, of the others. The point is that ideology often leads criminologists to "feel" only one part of the criminological elephant and then to confuse the parts with the whole and to prate about the whole elephant, which none of them have seen. As with the blind men, criminologists sometimes question the intelligence and motives (e.g., having some kind of political agenda) of other criminologists who have examined different parts of the criminological elephant. Needless to say, such *ad hominem* attacks have no place in scientific criminology.

Writing about social science in general, anthropologist Charles Leslie (1990:896) tells us that "non-social scientists generally recognize the fact that the social sciences are mostly ideological.... Our claim to be scientific is one of the main academic scandals." Few scholars in criminology would deny that their discipline is plagued with ideology and with theories and models that feel only one part of the elephant. Walsh and Ellis (2004) have called ideology criminology's "Achilles' heel" because few things prevent the accumulation of reliable knowledge more surely than ideological intransigence. Unfortunately, ideology is not often enough discussed in criminology textbooks, leading some students to believe that criminological issues are settled with data as they are in the hard sciences, but this is rarely the case. By definition, ideology implies a selective interpretation of evidence that comes to our senses rather than an objective and rational evaluation of it (Barak, 1998). Ideology forms, shapes, and colors our concepts of crime and its causes in ways that lead to a tendency to accept or reject new evidence according to how well or poorly it fits our ideology.

As an example, let us take liberal and conservative criminologists' interpretation of the effects of imprisonment rates on families. Noting that a highly disproportionate number of offenders come from the same neighborhoods, some criminologists (mostly liberals) believe that imprisonment provides only a temporary respite from crime, that it eventually leads to more crime by weakening families and communities, and by imprisoning fathers it reduces supervision of children, which at least must be occasionally true (DeFina & Arvanites, 2002). Conservatives on the other end of the ideological pole might reply that the very same data show that there were few families in the traditional sense in criminal populations to begin with (Mumola, 2000). They may further point out that longitudinal studies show that the presence of criminal fathers in the home increases children's antisocial behavior, the risk increases the longer the father is in the home, and thus removing the rotten apples from the barrel is a positive thing (Moffitt & E-Risk Study Team, 2002). The only reason why these different folks came to opposite conclusions regarding the question of the net result of America's "imprisonment" binge is selective perception, and thus their positions are incommensurable.

Plato, Aristotle, and Visions

Given the centrality of ideology in our disciplines, it behooves us to understand what it is, how it moves us, and how we come to be on one side or the other in ideological debates. Why do we see people of such radically different dispositions being attracted to grassroots movements such as the Tea Party and Occupy Wall Street with two totally opposite agendas, the first wanting to radically limit government influence on the economy and the other wanting to radically expand it? As Sniderman and Bullock (2004:353) ask: "Why are some disposed to a liberal or broadly left political outlook while others are disposed to a conservative or broadly right orientation?" To explore these questions, it is a good idea to point out the polarity of thought that philosophers have had and have commented on since at least the time of Plato and Aristotle. In his analysis of the philosophies of these two great pillars of Western philosophical thought, A. T. D. Porteous (1934:97) begins by quoting poet and philosopher Samuel Taylor Coleridge:

> *Every man is born an Aristotelian or a Platonist. I do not think it possible that anyone born an Aristotelian can become a Platonist; and I am sure that no born Platonist can ever change into an Aristotelian. They are two classes of man, beside which it is next to impossible to conceive a third.*

The central aspects of the respective philosophies and temperaments of these two ancient geniuses were allegorized in Raphael's famous fresco *School of Athens* on the wall of the Stanza in the Vatican. Plato was a dreamer who points skyward in his search for a reality more profound and lasting than that which was immediately apprehended by the senses. He did not deny the reality of the phenomenal world where humans exist, but this world is as ephemeral as the flickering shadows of appearance on the walls in his famous allegory of the cave. Plato believed that the task of philosophy is to lead humans imprisoned in the cave (essentially all humans, save the enlightened philosophers) up into the sunlight of the "really real." This ultimate reality consisted of eternal and immutable "Forms" that existed in some transcendental realm "beyond the heavens." Analogous to Kant's noumenal–phenomenal distinction, for Plato, the things we experience in the phenomenal world participate in the Forms but are corrupt, ever-changing, and imperfect copies of their perfect and unchanging Forms. Thus, it is more desirable in the pursuit of knowledge to think analytically about the world from *a priori* truths than to trust our sense perceptions, derived as they are from these corruptions.

Analytic thinkers such as Plato rely on deductions from what they take as *a priori* truths; synthetic thinkers such as Aristotle, who gestures toward the ground in Raphael's painting, aver that the truth of a statement or proposition can only be determined by observation and experience. Contrary to Plato, synthetic thinkers maintain that it is our reasoning that leads us astray more than the sense data of experiences, and that we can think ourselves into all sorts of implausible messes. Two such particularly egregious postmodernist examples of this come to mind. First is Luce Irigary's claim that Einstein's $E = mc^2$ is a "sexed equation" because it "privileges the speed of light over other speeds that are vitally necessary to us" (Sokal & Bricmont, 1998:109). For folks such as Irigary, the equation does not describe the speed of light; it creates it. How 186,000 miles per second is "sexed" is a mystery to me, as is what the other speeds are that are "vitally necessary" to us. Second is Jacques Lacan's effort to prove that $\sqrt{-1} =$ the human penis (Dawkins, 1998). Perhaps the "minus one" is a sly dig mathematicians dreamed up to quantify Freud's concept of penis envy (women are minus one), or perhaps because $\sqrt{-1}$ is an irrational number, Lacan is commenting on the irrationality of the penis, in which case he may have something. Despite howlers such as these, it remains true that both Plato's analytic and Aristotle's synthetic path to knowledge have their place in responsible hands. Porteous's summation of the contributions of Plato and Aristotle makes this clear. He describes Plato's work as "challenging and revolutionary" and possessing an "emotional quality" that he finds lacking in "Aristotle's dispassionate analysis": "Aristotle is the master of those who know, as Plato is of those who dream" (1934:105).

Economist and philosopher Thomas Sowell (1987) brings Coleridge's dichotomy to life in the modern world. Sowell claims that two conflicting visions have shaped thoughts about important issues throughout history that mirror the Plato/Aristotle divide. The first of these visions is the constrained vision, a hard-headed vision that Aristotle would call home. Constrained visionaries believe that human activities are constrained by an innate human nature that is self-centered and largely unalterable. The contrasting vision is the unconstrained vision, the home of dreamers such as Plato. Most unconstrained visionaries deny an innate human nature, viewing it as formed anew in each different culture. The unconstrained vision also believes that human nature is perfectible, which is why thinkers from Plato to Marx offer Utopian visions of secular salvation. This view is scoffed at by those who profess the constrained vision. Thus, constrained visionaries say "This is how the world *is*," and unconstrained visionaries say "This is how the world *should be*." Sowell's visions are purposely presented as Weberian ideal types to accentuate and polarize differences between competing positions for purposes of guiding exploration of them.

Given these contrasting ideological visions, it is surprising that there are contrasting ways of approaching a social problem such as crime. Sowell (1987:31) writes that "while believers in the unconstrained vision seek the special causes of war, poverty, and crime, believers in the constrained vision seek the special causes of peace, wealth, or a law-abiding society." Note that this implies that unconstrained visionaries believe that war, poverty, and crime are abnormalities to be explained, whereas constrained visionaries view these things as historically normal, although regrettable, and believe that what has to be understood are the conditions that prevent them. Given their pessimistic view of human nature, constrained visionaries are saying that without due care and diligence, the default conditions will always be negative. Unconstrained visionaries are saying, given their optimism and lack of an articulated view of human nature, that negative events occur because of the actions of a few evildoers in powerful places who have been corrupted by evil institutions. This is Hobbes and Rousseau battling it out all over again.

Constrained visionaries tend to identify themselves as conservatives, and unconstrained visionaries tend to identify themselves as liberals. *Conservative* and *liberal* are terms that can be confusing, however. The Russians who opposed Mikhail Gorbachev's efforts toward a free market (perestroika) and social openness (glasnost) were conservatives supporting their vision of stability, tradition, and cultural continuity, which, of course, for them meant socialism. Anyone favoring socialism over capitalism in the West would be a liberal or radical and certainly not a conservative. On the other hand, classical Western liberalism was defined primarily by support for a free-market economy and limited government, which is a conservative position in the Western world today. Modern American conservatism and liberalism are not the throne-and-altar conservatism or the gun-and-guillotine liberalism of our European ancestors. It is therefore difficult to cluster together a set of attitudes and values that can be labeled "conservative" or "liberal" across time and place. Liberal and conservative are thus terms that have to be defined in cultural and historical context, which is why I prefer Sowell's "unconstrained" and "constrained" visions as more neutral terms that are much less context-dependent. The American Founding Fathers, for instance, were in the most obvious of senses overtly constrained visionaries even as they bore the liberal label with pride (Dupre, 2009). Visions are more like intellectual and emotional paradigms (in the Kuhnian sense) within which people in diverse times and places do the kinds of "normal thinking" dictated by their cognitive paradigms.

The unconstrained vision dominates the social sciences, and its adherents are reluctant to admit constrained visionaries into their discourse. Noteworthy of considerable ideological bias in academia is a survey of 800 social and personality psychologists by

Inbar and Lammers (2012). These researchers found that one-third of respondents admitted that they, as well as their colleagues, would discriminate against known conservatives in faculty hiring, and a slightly lower number would discriminate in other areas, such as turning down grant applications and invitations to symposiums. Furthermore, the more liberal the respondent, the more he or she was willing to discriminate on paper reviews ($r = -0.31$), grant reviews (-0.34), symposium invitations (-0.20), and particularly on hiring decisions (-0.44) (Inbar & Lammers, 2012:500). These are just the ones who admitted their prejudices.

Richard Redding (2012) supplies copious evidence from other similar studies that a single voice dominates the idea marketplace in the social sciences and makes it perfectly clear that this kind of tribal groupthink places no high priority on diversity of ideas. The praise of diversity includes only race, gender, and sexual orientation, and it hits a solid brick wall when it comes to diversity of thought. This is tragic for scientific advancement because as the sagacious Benjamin Franklin is reported to have said: "If everyone is thinking alike, then no one is thinking." Progress demands the Hegelian dialectic of opposing ideas, but this can rarely happen when contrary ideas are summarily trashed by partisans of the ideal locked into a tribal morality and countered only with inbred notions of the politically correct.

Ideology among Contemporary American Criminologists

Given our discussion of ideology and visions, it is no surprise to discover that criminological theories differ radically on how they approach explanations of the crime problem. It is difficult to disagree with the assumption that a theory of criminal behavior is in large part shaped by the ideological vision of the person who formulated it. Sowell avers that a vision "is what we sense or feel *before* we have constructed any systematic reasoning that could be called a theory, much less deduced any specific consequences as hypotheses to be tested against evidence" (1987:14). Those who feel drawn to a particular theory owe a great deal of their attraction to it to the fact that they share the same vision as its formulator (an example of Bacon's idols of the theater). The upshot of this is that "visions" more so than hard evidence often lead criminologists to favor one theory over another more strongly than most would care to acknowledge (Cullen, 2005).

In a 1997 survey of American criminologists, Walsh and Ellis (2004) asked respondents to self-report their basic ideological perspective (conservative, moderate, liberal, or radical) and found that it strongly predicted a person's favored theory ($\chi^2 = 177.23$; Cramer's $V = 0.65$). This study was repeated in 2007 by Cooper, Walsh, and Ellis (2010) with basically the same results. Both 1997 and 2007 surveys asked: "Overall, which theory do you consider the most viable with respect to explaining variations in serious and persistent criminal behavior?" A total of 24 theories were checked as being "most viable" in the 2007 survey (23 in the 1997 survey). It seems that we have a Baskin–Robbins discipline with so many theoretical flavors that we are both spoiled and confused by the choices available. The sheer numbers of theories listed (as well as the many that were not) are indicative of our theoretical fragmentation and a tunneled reading of the literature, because by definition there can only be one theory that is *most* viable. Among respondents checking a theory (only 49% of the sample of 770 did, which itself says a lot between the lines), the choice of theories varied predictably by ideology, although its effect ($\chi^2 = 134.6$; Cramer's $V = 0.34$) was not as strong as in the 1997 sample. These results hint at a positive weakening of the grip of ideology in criminology, but this trend could be reversed in future iterations of the study.

In both 1997 and 2007 samples, liberals and radicals favored theories that posit crime as an aberration to be explained (i.e., crime is positively caused), such as social learning, differential association, and critical theories. Conservatives tended to favor more individualistic theories (biosocial and rational choice) and those theories that posit that crime is a default option of poorly socialized and unmonitored individuals (i.e., crime is negatively caused), such as social bonding and self-control theories. Moderates were more eclectic, favoring social learning- and control-type theories almost equally. These findings support Paterson's "stop whining"/"stop blaming the victim" dichotomy mentioned previously. Theories favored by conservatives often fail to address distal variables that mediate proximate causes (thus absolving society from any blame), and theories favored by liberals and radicals tend to avoid addressing variables in direct proportion to their closeness to individuals (thus absolving individuals from blame). It is thus difficult not to agree with Richard Felson's (1991, 2001) claim that much of social science research focusing on negative practices such as crime or conditions such as poverty involves "blame analysis" rather than causal analysis.

"Ideology" is used mostly pejoratively as denoting a set of dogmas having little or no basis in reality, whereas a theory is supposed to rest on empirical data and be open to falsification. Given the previously discussed data, it is reasonable to propose that in many ways contemporary criminology blurs the line between theory and ideology. Whatever theory we are talking about, when we derive hypotheses from it and make our observations, we think of these observations as being objective, and in a sense they are objective. We may find that the proposed model explains a fair amount of the variance in the criterion variable, and that the effect is statistically significant at, for example, the 0.001 level. If this is the case, we have ruled out chance with a low probability that we are wrong and can claim that what we observe has an objective reality. What we tend to forget, however, is that what we observe is very much a consequence of the models we propose, and those models are what Thomas Kuhn (1970) called theory-laden. As discussed in Chapter 3, theory ladenness is the idea that models, concepts, and observations make sense only in light of that particular theory. We should not take this too far into subjectivity; let us just say that our observations come with theoretical baggage, and hence they cannot be entirely objective. We can be objective, however, about which theory or theories consistently account for the most variance in serious criminal offending. If our theories are contaminated with ideological notions of which we may only be dimly aware, then it is a good idea to explore the origins of our ideological visions.

The Temperamental Origins of Ideological Visions

We all like to believe that we form our attitudes, values, and beliefs about various things from long and rational thought and discussion about them. If this is so, would not almost all rational people engaging in this process arrive at roughly similar conclusions when examining the same data? It is doubtless true that criminologists do think long and hard about their subject matter, but Jost, Federico, and Napier (2009) aver that ideological stances reflect the influence of hereditary, temperament, and personality on our thought processes. Constrained and unconstrained visions thus appear to reflect different temperaments that eventually coalesce into different ideologies (Bacon's idols of the cave). Our temperaments have a lot to do with the information we deem worthy of our attention, and they may therefore go a long way to explaining the content of the knowledge we ponder and bring to the table. The prospect of a happy peace between the constrained and unconstrained visionaries thus faces formidable ideological barriers built on a foundation of differences in the temperaments, which provide the physiological underpinnings of our personalities. Temperament has heritable components such as *mood* (happy/sad), *sociability* (introverted/extraverted), *reactivity* (calm/excitable), *activity level* (high/low), and *affect* (warm/cold) ranging from the 0.40s to the 0.60s (Bouchard et al., 2003).

Many unconstrained scholars still reject the idea of genes affecting human traits, particularly traits such as values and attitudes, strongly believing that we get our ideological and political views and values where we get our dinner—at the kitchen table. In my opinion, those who hold this belief missed the bus because there is copious evidence flowing down the information highway that genes influence all personality and cognitive traits (for comprehensive reviews, see Bouchard & McGue, 2003; Cary, 2003; Moffitt, 2005; Walsh & Bolen, 2012). Political scientists Alford, Funk, and Hibbing (2008:323) note that "gene–culture interaction is the key to understanding the source of political attitudes and behaviors, just as it is the key to understanding most physical and behavioral aspects of the human condition." A large number of studies find heritability coefficients for liberalism–conservatism—which map closely to the unconstrained–constrained visions—in the mid-0.50s (e.g., Bell, Schermer, & Vernon, 2009), and neuroscientists are finding that different political orientations are correlated with variant brain structures (Jost & Amadio, 2012; Kanai, Feilden, Firth, & Rees, 2011).

Geneticists do not expect to find genes "for" (no one should ever use the expression "genes for" when referring to any quantitative trait; if they do, you can be sure they know nothing about genetics) an Aristotelian or Platonic worldview or a Sowellian vision by rummaging around among our chromosomes. Likewise, neuroscientists do not expect to discover red and blue color-coded neuronal pathways taking the left or right highways to the prefrontal cortex. Rather, our visions are synthesized genetically via our temperaments that serve as physiological–emotional substrates guiding and shaping our environmental experiences via the processes of gene–environment correlation and gene × environment interaction in ways that increase the likelihood of developing traits and attitudes that color our world in hues most congenial to our individual natures (Carmen, 2007; Olson, Vernon, & Harris, 2001; Smith et al., 2011).

If genes account for between 40 and 60% of the variance in the subtraits that make up temperament and for approximately 50% of our political ideologies, then the environment accounts for the remaining variance. Thus, although our visions are resistant to change, they are certainly not impossible to change. The Platonic/Aristotelian, constrained/unconstrained dimensions are continua along which people may shift back and forth according to the issue at hand, and they are certainly not rigid dichotomies. Only a few dogmatic fundamentalists are glued tightly to the tails of the distribution. The point, however, is that temperament trumps reason in so many ways that matter. If it did not, we would not see such eminently *reasonable* thinkers as Plato and Aristotle, and all the constrained and unconstrained scholars of today that follow in their footsteps, differing so widely on important issues that are suffused with emotion.

I am optimistic that criminologists can circumvent ideological barriers if they allow themselves in the spirit of true scholars to survey the full array (not just one's favorite elephant part) of scientific knowledge available. The sheer weight of the whole elephant will eventually wear down ideological and temperamental opposition. I have elsewhere documented a number of prominent social scientists from diverse fields who have been "dragged by the data" to positions they formerly found ideologically distasteful. They had minds open enough (or perhaps temperaments that are relatively easily soothed) to allow alien ideas a place to germinate. There is no reason that the dialectic process of thesis, antithesis, and synthesis cannot work in criminology. As well as being a barrier to advancement, different ideologies are necessary to provide this creative dialectic, but if one side quits and takes its ball home, then the whole game is over. Change and advancement need a driving force, and that is provided by healthy opposition. When we have Hegel's "interpenetration of opposites," we create an upward spiral of positive change rather than a circle going nowhere.

Conclusion

The wars we witness over science are the same ones that have raged ever since the first two philosophers sat down to contemplate issues of importance. Ideology is one of the major barriers we have to obtaining knowledge, but ideology—one's general picture of how the world is or should be—provides humans with a way of making sense of diverse matters. Ideology may thus be functional for individuals by giving them a place to hang their hats, but it is detrimental to science because it retards progress by leading to attacks on scientists who pursue "distasteful" topics that do not fit one's ideology. As in so many areas, the ideological divide in criminology consists of the Aristotelian constrained visionaries and the Platonic dreamers of the unconstrained vision. In the modern American context, we may call them conservatives and liberals, respectively. These two groups plainly favor different criminological theories, with self-identified conservatives favoring individualistic theories and self-identified liberals favoring mostly structural or learning theories. Moderates tend to favor structural and individualistic theories approximately equally. If we can overcome the hurdle of temperamental differences, perhaps theories that combine the individualistic with the social may hold the key to advancing criminology. My ideological bias is unabashedly for biosocial theories, theories that by definition include all aspects of what make us human—evolutionary history, biological inheritance, developmental experiences, and sociocultural context.

11

Ideology and Causation

Ideology and the Causes of Crime

Given the role of ideological visions in criminologists' theory choices, it is not surprising that ideology is also significantly related to the causes of criminal behavior they consider important. Cooper, Walsh, and Ellis (2010) presented means (scores ranged from 0 = "not important at all" to 10 = "highly important") for each of the 24 alleged causes of crime, broken down by ideological category. Predictably, conservatives and moderates favored individual-level explanations ("Stop whining and pull up your socks, man!") most strongly, and liberals and radicals favored external social explanations ("Stop blaming the victim, racist!") most strongly. The top three factors for conservatives were (in order): "Lack of empathy and concern for others," "Impulsiveness and risk-taking tendencies," and "Unstable family life." The top three favored by moderates were: "Lack of empathy and concern for others," "Poor discipline practices," and "Unstable family life." Liberals favored: "Unfair economic system," "Lack of educational opportunities," and "Peer influences" most strongly, and radicals favored: "Unfair economic system," "Bias in law enforcement," and "Lack of educational opportunities." The only alleged cause considered "important" (a mean score of 5 or higher) across all four ideological categories was "Lack of empathy and concern for others," although conservatives and moderates scored it significantly higher than liberals and radicals. Four "causes" considered important for which there was no significant difference in mean scores across ideological categories were: "Peer influences," "Unstable family life," "Alcohol abuse," and "Hard drugs."

Our discipline is in dire need of some form of stabilizing and unifying influence because we seem to be talking past each other (Bacon's idols of the marketplace) on significant issues. Even where there is agreement about what "causes" are important, the "causes of the causes" are very much in dispute. Think of how Ronald Akers, Travis Hirschi, Richard Chambliss, James Q. Wilson, and Terrie Moffitt, each feeling their own part of the elephant, would account for the agreed upon "causes" listed previously. One would talk about social reinforcement, one about poor supervision, one about moral poverty, another about financial poverty, and one would blame the whole shebang on capitalism. Only Terrie Moffitt in this distinguished list feels all parts of the criminological elephant from neurons to neighborhoods in her work.

Neutralizing Ideology by Feeling the Whole Elephant

The only way criminology can neutralize the corrosive effects of ideology is to induce scholars to feel the whole metaphorical elephant without privileging any single part, as Terrie Moffitt and a few others have done (Beaver & Walsh, 2011). It is not so much an open mind that is needed to do this as it is a dampening of visceral reactions long enough to allow temperamentally incongruent ideas a chance to step inside. Once they are allowed to do that, we might find that they are very friendly and helpful.

As we move from the philosophical past to the scientific present, we should remember that humans are biological, psychological, and cultural animals with phylogenic and ontogenic histories that we need to understand. This point was made many years ago by Nobel Laureate ethologist Nikolas Tinbergen (1963) with his famous four questions. Tinbergen maintained that in order to understand any nontrivial behavior of any animal, it is necessary to inquire about the adaptive function of the behavior, its phylogenic history, its development history, and its mechanisms of proximate causation. Even here, we must acknowledge our debt to philosophy in terms of Aristotle's four fundamental causes. Aristotle believed that "we do not have knowledge of a thing until we have grasped its why, that is to say, its cause" (in Falcon, 2011:2). We will take altruism as an example to examine Tinbergen's levels, because altruism is in many ways the polar opposite of criminality. Altruism is an active concern for the welfare of others motivating the altruist to ease the pain of others and to offer them resources, whereas criminality is an active concern only for one's self, motivating the criminal to take the resources of others.

The *function* question (Aristotle's final cause) asks what the adaptive features of altruism are; that is, what are the evolutionary fitness consequences of helping others at a cost to the self? Helping others ultimately helps the self because it leads to reciprocal helping and enhances the altruist's reputation as a reliable cooperator. Mutual help and support aids all members of a social group to do things such as avoid predators and cooperate in hunting and gathering, and it is involved in many other features of social life. Because these things have obvious fitness consequences, there will be strong selection pressures for altruistic behavior (Gintis, 2003).

The *phylogeny* question (Aristotle's formal cause) asks how a functional trait or behavior came to be over the course of the evolutionary history of the species. Empathy underlies the urge to come to the aid of others, and empathy is a deep emotional quality of vital importance to any species with altricial young. Although the heritability of empathy is roughly the same for both genders, as we have seen, females are invariably found to be more empathetic than males, regardless of the methods used to assess it (Campbell, 2006b). Parental care and mother–child bonding serve as templates for later social bonding and for helping behavior that aids in forging those bonds. Recall that parental attachment is the foundational element of the social bond in Hirschi's (1969) social control theory, and which the "typical" criminal is said to lack.

The *development* question (Aristotle's efficient cause) asks why a functional trait or behavior varies in frequency and strength from one person to another. Strong genetic influences on empathy and altruism account for a great deal of the variance, but all traits and behaviors are either nourished or starved by developmental experiences. Altruism is a highly prosocial trait that serves as a buffer against antisocial behavior, and it is thus not surprising that caring parents strive to cultivate the genetic seed for it in their children (Warneken & Tomasello, 2009). To the extent that persons are motivated by empathy ("feeling the pain" of others) to behave altruistically, by doing so they remove their own distress. The removal of something aversive is reinforcement, and the behavior that led to it is likely to be repeated. This is an indication of the "multiplier effect" (Dickens & Flynn, 2001) by which genetic propensities are cultivated and magnified in interaction with environmental circumstances.

The *causation* question (Aristotle's material cause) asks what are the proximate mechanisms underlying altruism. Altruism is motivated by an empathetic understanding of why someone needs help, and empathy is underlain by brain chemistry (oxytocin). Performing the altruistic act facilitates the release of chemicals that target the reward areas of the brain (dopamine); thus, the helper is reinforced internally as well as externally by the enhancement of his or her reputation in the eyes of others as kind and dependable. This chemical reward we receive from helping others is yet another piece of evidence that helping behavior was important to our distant ancestors because nature has built in mechanisms that reward us internally only when we do things that promote her grand goal of survival and reproductive success (Moll et al., 2006).

Tinbergen's four questions allow us to examine any behavioral issue from the most distal to the most proximate level. No one carries out a research agenda animated by all of them, but all levels must be mutually consistent; that is, there should be no contradictions as we move from one level to another. No biologist hypothesizes a relationship between a hormone or neurotransmitter and behavior that contradicts the known chemistry of those substances, just as no chemist would advance a hypothesis that contradicts the elegant laws of physics. Likewise, no hypothesis about behavior at a higher level of analysis should contradict what is understood at a more fundamental level. Once we agree that this is a reasonable and desirable thing, we have the dim beginning of a coherent and consistent human science that blends smoothly into biology in the same way that biology blends smoothly into chemistry and chemistry into physics.

Visions and Theories

Durkheim and Merton

Emile Durkheim and Robert Merton are well-known sociologists with opposite visions. The constrained Durkheim had a naturalistic view of human nature and saw that humans seek to maximize pleasure and minimize pain (Schmaus, 2003). Durkheim was a realist in the anti-nominalist sense, viewing human nature as something that is "substantially the same among all men in its essential qualities" (1951:247), although he realized that "one sort of heredity will always exist, that of natural talent" (1951:251). Because all persons do not possess the same means to accomplish the things necessary to satisfy their common appetites: "a moral discipline will therefore still be required to make those less favored by nature accept the lesser advantages which they owe to the chance of birth" (1951:151). This moral discipline is provided by society, which is "the only moral power superior to the individual [for] it alone has the power necessary to stipulate law and to set the point beyond which passions must not go" (1951:149).

Durkheim clearly saw criminal behavior to be the default option of individuals unimpeded by moral norms. Society and its institutions control the natural selfish and acquisitive nature of human beings and will do so as long as social solidarity is strong and society is not visited by the plague of anomie. According to Durkheim, anomic conditions serve as "releasers" of criminal behavior, not motivators, and this release will occur at lower thresholds for some individuals than for others. He recognizes this when he remarks: "Thus, since there cannot be a society in which the individuals do not diverge to some extent from the collective type, it is also inevitable that among these deviations some assume a criminal character" (1982:101).

Robert Merton was almost an ideal type unconstrained visionary who only mentioned "human nature" (always it seems in scare quotes) to assert that something or another was not "rooted" in it (e.g., Merton, 1948). Merton's anomie theory is limited to the role of culture and social structure and ignores individual differences. The "root" cause of crime is not to be found within individuals whose insatiable appetites must be kept under control by strong normative controls but, rather, in structural–cultural contradictions. He agreed with Durkheim that the inability to attain resources legitimately generates strain, which may lead to efforts to obtain them illegitimately. Rather than viewing society as a positive force *restraining* individuals from adopting illegitimate options, Merton's unconstrained vision led him to view society (at least capitalist society) as a negative force that *motivated* such behavior. This is not surprising because as Seymour Lipset (1994) pointed out, Merton saw himself as a revolutionary socialist.

Acquisitiveness is inherent in human nature for Durkheim; for Merton, it was caused by a society that exalted monetary success over anything else. Anomie was also viewed differently by these two men. For Durkheim, anomie was an occasional condition rising and declining according to levels of social stability, whereas Merton viewed it as a permanent condition of capitalist society generated by the cultural/structural disjunction between goals and means (Merton, 1968). Although both men viewed crime as a consequence of anomie, for Durkheim, anomie acts to *release* natural inclinations previously restrained, whereas for Merton, these inclinations are socially constructed traits that are *caused* by anomie (Passas, 1995).

Akers and Hirschi

Social learning theories exemplified by differential association theory and Ronald Akers's extension of it are firmly in the unconstrained camp because they tend to disdain the idea of an innate human nature. Social learning theories have an underlying implicit assumption that human beings are naturally good until corrupted by society, which implies that criminology's task is to explain why inherently good social animals commit antisocial acts. Social learning theorists emphasize that social structure and culture frames and shapes human relationship patterns, and they explore the lessons delinquents and criminals come to learn from them. In other words, social learning theorists believe that the default option for humans unsullied by malevolent neighborhoods, families, peers, and so on is to be good social animals, and so they ask "What causes crime?" How the sum of inherently good individuals equals a bad society is never addressed.

Conversely, social control theorists believe that the default option for humans not taught to behave well is to behave poorly, so they ask "Why don't most of us commit crimes?" After all, crime is a way to acquire valued resources with minimal effort. The classical view of human nature is the view that constrained visionaries such as Durkheim and Travis Hirschi take as a given. We are preeminently concerned with our own well-being; thus, getting something for nothing at someone else's expense comes naturally to us unless we are properly socialized. Socialization, cultivation, training, civilizing, or whatever else we choose to call it wakens the social emotions in us so that we come to value and respect the rights and property of others and we develop an orientation toward wanting to do good. Gwynn Nettler (1984:313) stated it most colorfully on behalf of the social control position: "If we grow up 'naturally,' without cultivation, like weeds, we grow up like weeds—rank." In other words, we learn to be good, not bad.

Most criminologists realize that unsocialized children become "spoiled brats." It is thus difficult to see how the default option (the "natural" outcome of unsocialized children) can be anything other than Nettler's rank weeds. For the control tradition—whether it be Durkheim's society, the Chicago school's natural ecological areas, or Hirschi's family—the ambient control agents are the "good guys" producing flowers where weeds would otherwise be. When these institutions fail in their task, society becomes anomic, natural areas become disorganized, families become dysfunctional, and widespread moral breakdown and crime result.

Efforts to answer the natural behavioral propensities of humans at birth empirically have revolved around longitudinal studies of behavior from infancy onward. Data show that the frequency of hitting, biting, and kicking peaks at approximately age 2 years and declines by approximately 66% by age 12 years among socialized children (Tibbetts & Hemmens, 2010). A study tracing the trajectory of physical aggressive behavior among children showed that the trend was for aggressive behavior to diminish among low and moderately aggressive children, but it increased during adolescence among those defined as "highly aggressive" during toddlerhood and subsequently decreased to levels observed at age 6 years (Tremblay, 2008). Tremblay (2008:2619) summarizes the literature on this issue by stating: "By monitoring the development of physical aggression from infancy onwards, recent longitudinal studies show that human infants spontaneously use physical aggression and that humans learn not to physically aggress rather than learn to aggress." There are no studies running counter to this—that is, studies showing a profound distaste for aggressive acts among saintly toddlers that dissipates with age as they are exposed to a malevolent society. This does not mean that we are born bad. We are necessarily born selfish, as are all animals, and it is this self-centeredness that must be reined in lest it turn bad. Harmful environments most assuredly strengthen antisocial impulses, often to toxic levels, but they do not create them.

Applying Tinbergen
Social Learning Theory

To briefly explore the usefulness of exploring criminal behavior across Tinbergen's four domains, I use social learning and control theories, the two most popular theories among contemporary criminologists (Cooper et al., 2010). Cao (2004:97) points out that social learning theories have a blank slate concept of human nature and assume "a passive and unintentional actor who lacks individuality ... because of its limited conception of human nature learning theories generally also ignore the differential receptivity of individuals to criminal messages." By couching the processes of learning antisocial behavior in terms of operant psychology, Akers improved on differential association theory, but he did not venture into the question of individual differences in the ease or difficulty of learning prosocial or antisocial behavior. Some people naturally find hell-raising more exiting (and thus more reinforcing) than others, some are more susceptible to short-term rewards because they are impulsive, some are better able to appreciate the long-term rewards of behaving well, and some are more ready to engage in aggressive behavior than others because of their temperaments: "Constitutions affect the impact of environment. What we learn and how well we learn it depends on constitution.... The fire that melts the butter hardens the egg" (Nettler, 1984:295).

In response to criticisms that his theory neglects individual differences, Akers replied that it does not:

> *An individual in a low crime group or category who is nevertheless more exposed to criminal associations, models, definitions, and reinforcement than someone in a high crime group or category will have a higher probability of committing criminal or deviant acts.*
>
> *(1999:482)*

This is an explanation in terms of different *environments*, not different *individuals*. It reinforces Cao's (2004) point that Akers's theory suffers from the sociological appetite for positing equipotential individuals who enter different environments at one end and emerge from the other as saints or sinners based solely on environmental exposure.

One of the causal variables with no significant difference across ideological categories in the Cooper et al. (2010) study was peer influence. Criminologists have long struggled to explain the ubiquitous age–crime curve relying on peer influence: "Age-specific [crime] rates differ because individuals are differentially exposed to the learning variables at different ages" (Akers, 1998:338). No one doubts that the number of delinquent friends an individual has is a powerful predictor of one's own antisocial behavior, but this "explanation" only describes what it purports to explain; it does not explain why the influence of peers suddenly becomes so powerful, or why association with peers so often leads to antisocial behavior. With his usual penetrating insight, Nettler (1984:104) wrote: "To explain the 'age effect' one has to abandon sociological and sociopsychological theories of crime causation and revert to physiology, to ways organisms differentially function with age."

The tremendous neurohormonal changes that take place during adolescence indicate that there are *physical* reasons for the immature and often antisocial behavior of adolescents. So much of what goes on in the teen brain leads many scientists to the belief that we have been designed by natural selection to behave precisely as we do during adolescence (Powell, 2006; Walsh, 2009c). The immaturity of the teen brain facilitates the tendency to assign faulty attributions to the intentions of others. In other words, a brain on "go slow superimposed on a physiology on fast forward" explains why many teenagers "find it difficult to accurately gauge the meanings and intentions of others and to experience more stimuli as aversive during adolescence than they did as children and will do so when they are adults" (Walsh, 2002:143). As Richard Restak (2001:76) stated: "The immaturity of the adolescent's behavior is perfectly mirrored by the immaturity of the adolescent's brain." There are so many changes going on in the adolescent's brain and body that affect behavior that natural scientists are mystified by social scientists' neglect of them in their theorizing about adolescent antisocial behavior.

Self-Control Theory

Self-control theory is also deficient in its treatment of individual differences. Because of widely varying temperaments, some children learn self-control easily and others only with great difficulty. The theory attributes self-control levels solely to parenting, and it ignores children's effects on parents. Lilly, Cullen, and Ball (2007:110) point out, however, that "research suggests that parents may affect levels of self-control less by their parenting styles and more by genetic transmission." John Wright and colleagues (2009:83) go further and state that "*all* scientific data indicate that self-control is housed in the frontal and prefrontal cortex, that self-control is strongly influenced by genetic factors expressed in the brain, and that self-control involves a complex, dynamic balancing of limbic and cortical functioning."

Naomi Friedman and colleagues (2008) found that individual differences in executive functions (self-control being one such function) are almost entirely genetic in origin. This does not mean that executive functioning *per se* is almost entirely genetic, or that it is impervious to targeted training. Executive functioning can be quite strongly related to training and thus affect the population *mean*, but individual differences (i.e., population *variance*) can still be almost entirely genetic. In other words, mean levels of self-control in a population can move upward under the influence of parental training, but it will still drag a constant level of variation (the basis of computing heritability) along with it. Parental effects establish a certain level of self-control in their children, but they account for little population *variance* in self-control. As Wright and Beaver (2005:1190) point out: "For self-control to be a valid theory of crime it must incorporate a more sophisticated understanding of the origins of self-control."

Another problem with self-control theory is that it claims too much for its central construct. Caspi and colleagues (1994:187) contend that crime proneness is defined at a minimum by both low self-control (which they call low constraint) and negative emotionality, which is the tendency to experience many situations as aversive and to react to them with irritation and anger more readily than with positive affective states. Negative emotionality is strongly related to self-reported and officially recorded criminality, and it is inversely associated with constraint. Individuals high on negative emotionality but also high on self-control are able to hold their anger and irritability in abeyance, but if a person high on negative emotionality is also low on self-control, the risk for violent behavior is great.

Impulsiveness, a central component of low self-control, is moderately to strongly heritable (Caspi et al., 1994; Lykken, 1995), and it is strongly related to low levels of the serotonin metabolite CSF 5-HIAA (cerebrospinal fluid 5-hydroxyindoleacetic acid) in human and nonhuman animals (Bernhardt, 1997). The median estimate of the heritability of serotonin level is between 0.55 and 0.66 (Hur & Bouchard, 1997). As we have seen, serotonin is a modulator of behavior, and poor serotonin turnover is a brain with defective brakes, resulting in a runaway brain that frequently fails to think before acting. Low serotonin, therefore: "may be a heritable diathesis for a personality style involving high levels of negative affect and low levels of constraint, which generates in turn a vulnerability to criminal behavior" (Caspi et al., 1994:188).

Robert Agnew (2005) has taken Tinbergen seriously to develop a theory based on these two "super traits" (he calls them self-control and irritability) that neatly integrates concepts and research from genetics, evolutionary psychology, and neuroscience, and shows how the various components influence each other developmentally across the lifespan. He identifies five *life domains*—personality, family, school, peers, and work— that interact and feedback on one another across the lifespan (rGE and GxE). Agnew states that personality traits set individuals on a particular developmental trajectory that influences how others in the family, school, peer group, and work domains react to them (evocative rGE). People with low self-control and irritability are likely to evoke negative responses from family members, school teachers, peers, and workmates that exacerbate those tendencies. Agnew goes on to state that "biological factors have a direct effect on irritability/low self-control and an indirect effect on the other life domains through irritability/low self-control" (2005:213). He also notes that neuroscience claims that the immaturity of adolescent behavior mirrors the immaturity of the adolescent brain, and that teens experience massive hormonal surges that facilitate competitiveness and aggression. Neurohormonal changes during adolescence *temporarily* increase irritability/low self-control among adolescents who limit their offending to that period, whereas for those who continue to offend, irritability and low self-control are *stable* characteristics.

The Tautology Argument

The tautology barb has been tossed back and forth most notably in criminology by proponents of social learning and self-control theories. Ronald Akers (1991)calls self-control theory tautologous, and Hirschi and Gottfredson (2000) repay the compliment. The enmity between advocates of these two theories is hardly surprising because they hold radically different philosophical views about the nature of the human animal. The tautology charge is so frequently made that it is necessary to understand what it means and how we can deal with it. To call a theory tautological is to accuse it of containing a series of self-reinforcing statements that are true by definition. Such theories are said not to be nonfalsifiable and thus to be useless. Criminology is in deep trouble if its two most popular theories are useless.

Those who hold these two theories dear should not be overly concerned about the tautology gibe because this indictment has been made against one of science's grandest theories—the theory of evolution by natural selection—almost from its beginning. In a logical tautology such as "all mothers are females," the predicate adds nothing to the subject save redundancy because the statement is true by definition. The charge of tautology in natural selection is made by stating that it is summed up as "survival of the fittest." But which ones are the fittest? The fittest are the ones that survive. Because the consequent is contained in the antecedent, the assertion cannot be falsified. Although this criticism is logically true on its face, it loses its power when followed by the assertion that the relational claim that the fittest survive is false.

"Survival of the fittest" is a catchy phrase, but it is not a description of the theory of natural selection. Fitness is correlated with, but not identical to, survival; it is a measure of reproductive success, not a trait or set of traits that inevitably leads to survival. The superiority of one trait variant over another is *expressed* by its fitness, not *defined* by it in the sense that mothers are defined by their femaleness. The power of the theory does not rest on the survival *of* the fittest organisms but, rather, on the specification of environmental conditions that select *for* adaptive traits. Heritable variation leads to differential reproductive success (fitness); this is a predictive statement that can be verified or falsified, and therefore it is not an analytic proposition that is true simply by definition (Endler, 1986; Wilson & Wilson, 2007).

The theory of natural selection has enormous explanatory power and has been so successful that it is one of the mysteries of the philosophy of science that the tautology argument keeps popping up. After all, if natural selection was an empty tautology, it would not have had the enormous success that it has had. As Stephen Jay Gould so well stated: "We are always ready to watch a theory fall under the impact of new data, but we do not expect a great and influential theory to collapse from a logical error in its formulation" (1976:1). Physical and biological scientists do not have the aversion to tautologies that social scientists do:

> *We think that it is no more a problem for the theory of natural selection ... that it has at its heart a "tautology"—more accurately a (nonempirical truth) of mathematics—than it is for physics that it relies on such mathematical truths as 2 + 2 = 4.*
> (Matthen & Ariew, 2005:356)

According to some philosophers of science (Kauffman, 2000), well-known formulas such as $E = mc^2$ and $F = ma$ are tautologies of the bluest blood. They are called tautologies because the first and second terms in each equation are equivalent, as the equals signs attest. Of course, this *equivalence* is not the same as saying that one side of each of these equations is *defined* by the other, since all the concepts contained in them (energy, mass, light, force, and acceleration) are independently defined, as are natural selection and fitness. Then we have the neuroscientists' version of survival of the fittest: "The neurons that fire together wire together, those that don't, won't" (Penn, 2001:339). This statement is true by definition; rather like saying that it will either rain tomorrow or it will not. Both are empirically verifiable, although the latter (a formal or rhetorical tautology) is of little import unless your area is suffering a surfeit or deficit of the stuff. On the other hand, the first truism is of scientific importance because it tells us in a pithy manner how the brain wires itself in voltage-dependent ways (a series of electrochemical processes independently defined) in response to environmental experiences (Shi, Cheng, Jan, & Jan, 2004); the reasoning is circular, but we pick up an awful lot of information as we go around.

Social Learning and Social Control Theories Are Not Tautological

Returning to criminology, what can we determine about tautology in social learning and self-control theories? What I have said in defense of natural selection can be transported whole to both theories. The psychological basis for social learning theory avers that behavior is controlled by its consequences, which is a kind of ontogenic "natural selection" of the behavioral repertoires of individuals. If a behavior is reinforced, it will likely be repeated; if it is punished, it likely will not. The tautology claim is easy to spot here: Bill consistently does X because he has been reinforced for doing so. How do we know he has been reinforced? Because he consistently does X. The language is definitely circular and asserts the truth about Bill's behavior, but it is not true by definition. The notion that a person's behavior reflects his or her history of reinforcement is necessary (but hardly sufficient) for understanding behavior, and very important for parents and therapists wishing to shape the future behavior of others. If a person does X at time 1 and receives Y as a consequence, and we note that he or she has an increased propensity to engage in X at many subsequent occasions, we have a deductive model by which we can make predictions about the effects of Y on the frequency of X. Of course, this has not explained why the person is reinforced by Y for doing X. Others may find that doing X is not at all reinforcing, and that behavior may be extinguished. But the fact that we need additional information to explain behavior does not negate the fact that operant conditioning is the most powerful shaper of behavior that we know of (Toates, 2009).

With regard to tautology in self-control theory, it has been said that "the propensity toward crime and low self-control appear to be one and the same" (Akers & Sellers, 2004:125). This is a criticism difficult to sustain because self-control is measured in many ways that are not synonymous with "propensity to commit crime." The dimensions of low self-control include impulsiveness, orientation to the present, risk-taking, and lack of conscientiousness and empathy. All of the traits are related to criminal behavior (what would be the good of talking about them if they were not?), but they are hardly synonymous with it, as their respective correlations with criminal behavior are a long way from 1.0. All of them are independently defined and measured, just like mass, force, acceleration, fitness, and so on. If we could measure the constituent parts with the same precision that physicists can measure their variables, then we might be able to develop succinct equations indicating the relationship between criminal behavior and its putative causal factors that indicate their equivalence in the same manner as $F = ma$. Of course, we never will. Human beings are much too complex to be captured by such elegant simplicity.

In summary, a statement is a tautology if it is true *only* because of its logical form (i.e., by definition). Many analytical statements, so often tarred as tautologies, are true by virtue of the meaning of their independently defined constituent terms. Such "closed systems" should never be sneered at as "mere tautologies" because they are greatly valued in advanced sciences. We should keep in mind the words of Harold Kincaid (2002:299), America's premier philosopher of the social sciences: "Every causal claim can be turned into a tautology by the simple device of changing 'A caused B' into 'the causes of B caused B.'"

Conclusion

Contemporary criminologists disagree about the relative utility of the current crop of criminological theories, so it is no surprise that they also disagree about the various causes nominated by those theories. Even when there are causes that all ideological categories consider "important," there are arguments about the "causes of the causes." None of the arguments lack utility, but they all need to be considered dispassionately. It is my contention that if we follow Tingerben's advice and examine behavior at the functional, phylogenic, developmental, and causal mechanism levels, we should be able to get a better grasp on the phenomena of our discipline. That is, we should feel the whole elephant while also confronting the idols of the marketplace that so bedevil criminology.

We examined the role of visions in criminological thought by first examining two theorists—Durkheim and Merton—who shared a theoretical tradition but who had opposite visions. Anomie, crime, greed, society, and human nature are concepts viewed quite differently by these two men. We also discussed the two most popular theories among contemporary criminologists—social learning and control theories—that also have quite different, even opposite, ideas about the fundamental nature of our subject matter. Can we imagine, for example, chemistry having completely opposite conceptions of the elements? We are in real trouble here and in dire need of applying Tinbergen's famous four questions. I attempted to do this in the briefest of fashions, but it has been done in thousands of articles and numerous books by biosocial criminologists. Unfortunately, many of these articles and books are either unknown or ignored by most of those in the criminological community who prefer to hug the familiar sociological coastline rather than to sail beyond the horizon where "there be monsters."

We also discussed the tautology indictment, an accusation most often made against social learning theorists by control theorists, and against control theorists by social learning theorists. It was shown that the hard sciences do not have the same aversion to empirical tautologies and view them as desirable. It was also shown that both social learning and self-control theories have nothing to fear from the tautology barb because it has been applied to some of the grandest ideas in science. The tautology argument is used apparently only by those who are confused about what it means. By the standards of physical and natural science, as well as by the standards of philosophers of science, social learning and self-control theories are not circular redundancies going round and round and never forward any more than is the theory of natural selection.

12 ⊞

The Philosophy and Science of Human Nature

Arguments over Human Nature

Criminology is a discipline concerned with issues relating to people who have violated the rules of civilized society by committing acts society has called criminal. The issues we are most concerned with are at bottom moral issues relating to why some people commit crimes or why most of us do not, and what should be done with those who do after arrest and conviction. We tend to ask these questions without bothering to ask about the fundamental nature of our subject matter—that is, about the nature of the human material with which we work. The only criminology work premised on an articulated human nature that I have seen is Wilson and Herrnstein's *Crime and Human Nature* (1985). Wilson and Herrnstein argue that any serious social inquiry must issue from an understanding of human nature, and they write that they could have explored it by studying things such as sexuality or politics but chose to do it in the context of crime because crime "more dramatically than other forms of behavior, exposes the connection between individual dispositions and the social order" (1985:20).

To ask what human nature is probably constitutes the most fundamental question we can ask about ourselves outside of the metaphysical. All theories of human conduct contain an underlying vision of human nature, although they differ radically, and some scholars claim that there is no such thing: "Man has no nature, he only has a history" (Ruffie, 1986:297). The claim that there is no human nature is the path of least resistance because it relieves those who make it of the burden of pondering the issue any further. Those of us who claim that humans have a nature are asserting a realist claim (as opposed to a nominalist claim), because the assertion is that the abstraction called humanness is real and that every member of the species *Homo sapiens* shares that abstraction. It is also essentialist because it asserts that every member of the species has some qualities essential to being included in that species rather than in some other. No denial of weak versions of nominalism or social constructionism is contained in this assertion. It does not deny nominalism because each instantiation of humanness is assuredly a unique representation of it. Neither does it deny social constructionism because how we cultivate our nature depends greatly on sociocultural ideas of morality and correct behavior.

Three "Human Natures"?

We may tiptoe around the argument and please almost everyone by asserting that in a real sense, humans have three "natures." The first is our evolved Darwinian nature that supplies all the sturdy foundations and scaffolding. The second is a Durkheimian social nature molded in different ways by ecology and history building a wide variety of facades around that scaffolding. Third is a Sartresque existentialist nature in which we are condemned by our free will to construct our own natures, and thus there is a variety in the interior décor favored by the individual. The natures posited by Durkheim and Sartre speak of cultural and individual variation, whereas Darwinian nature speaks of central tendency—the monomorphic constant underlying all. This is the human nature we have to come to grips with if we are to better comprehend the others superimposed on it. Talk of "culture" and "free will" to explain human practices and behavior goes only so far and cannot be understood if decoupled from a common human evolutionary history. As Henry Plotkin (2011:454) stated: "The biological and social sciences can be, and must be, married within a single theoretical structure [but this] can only be realized within an expanded theory of evolution." To try to understand human behavior without an understanding of our evolutionary history is analogous to speaking of mixing compounds as if ionic and covalent bonding are irrelevant, which is OK in the kitchen but not in the chemistry laboratory.

Unconstrained visionaries are the most hostile to the idea of an innate human nature because such a nature militates against dreams of human and social perfection. These are often the same people who urge us to respect one another on the basis of our common humanity, but surely it is incoherent to exhort us to do anything on the basis of something that supposedly does not exist. Be that as it may, unconstrained visionaries on the far left might quote Marx in his sixth 1844 *Theses on Feuerbach* as their basis for denying a human nature: "Feuerbach resolves the essence of religion into the essence of man. But the essence of man is no abstraction inherent in each single individual. In its reality it is the ensemble of the social relations" (1978b:145). Although it is self-evident that "man" only becomes fully human in the "ensemble of social relations," to assert that human nature is nothing but such an ensemble extinguishes human dignity and relegates us to little more than mindless cells in the social sponge.

It was by no means necessarily Marx's position that humans are "nothing but" an ensemble of social relationships because in other works he wrote eloquently about the "essence of man." As noted previously, for Marx, the essential feature of any species is the activity that distinguishes it from every other species. For humans, that feature is the ability to *create* their environment consciously rather than merely submitting to it as given as nonhuman animals do. This free and creative activity, wrote Marx, is the distinguishing human *species being*: "man's spiritual essence, his human essence" (in Sayers, 2005:611). Later in *Capital,* the "mature" Marx wrote: "To know what is useful for a dog, one must study dog nature…. Applying this to man, [we] must first deal with *human nature* in *general,* and then with human nature as *modified* in each historic epoch" (Marx, 1967:609; italics added). Marx was boldly stating that there is a universal human nature and strongly implying that any theory of human behavior must necessarily start with a theory of Darwinian general nature, as well as a Durkheimian nature modified by a particular culture with a particular mode of production.

Liberals less to the left than Marxists might invoke John Locke's *tabula rasa* to assert their nominalist claim that there is no human nature. This view is congenial to them because defects in human beings can be blamed on defective social scripts inscribed by society (about which they ditch their nominalism and become realists), and because it grants them license to believe that they can mold these empty organisms in any way desired by rewriting those scripts. They may also believe that an innate human nature implies "genetic determinism." It does not, and I suggest that far more damage to humanity has been done by a blank-slate view of humans because the environmental determinism implied by it is a more sinister form of determinism since the determinant is external to the actor.

It has been argued by a number of political philosophers (e.g., Strauss, 2006) that Thomas Hobbes's totalitarian Leviathan was deduced from the nominalist position that society was just a collection of particular individuals with no common humanity that might rebel against anything the sovereign might command. The blank-slate idea is assuredly a totalitarian's dream because if humans have no innate nature that chaffs against whatever grates against it, they can indeed be knocked into any shape dictated by state ideology. Stalin, Mao, Pol Pot, and their like murdered in excess of 100 million people in their belief that they could take empty organisms and turn them into the "new Soviet, Chinese, or Cambodian man" (van den Berghe, 1990:179). The sins of these and other Marxist "reformers" issue partly from a profound misunderstanding of human nature. Commenting on Mao's "reforms," Frans de Waal (2001:278) writes that they:

ignored the human tendency to work first for the family, and only secondarily for the greater good of society. Hard work comes a lot easier when it feeds hungry mouths at home than hungry mouths elsewhere. Cooperatives established under communism can be said to have been in stark violation of human nature.

Of course, this is why it is so imperative to understand human nature. A view of human nature that sees each person as a unique individual born with a suite of biological traits with which to interact with the world is both more scientifically defensible and respectful of human dignity than blank-slate views that delight political megalomaniacs demanding that everyone conform to their visions of the world.

It is not at all clear how Locke's *tabula rasa* could lead logically to the dismissal of the concept of a human nature. After all, Locke was the champion of natural rights, and the notion of natural rights strongly implies inborn dispositions shared by all humans favoring those particular rights. Locke was an individualist without being a nominalist, because one does not necessarily imply the other, and the phrase "human nature" was prominent in his vocabulary, with Locke believing that morality was "a fact so firmly rooted in the soil of human nature" (in Trigg, 1999:71). He was at one with numerous philosophers and scientists before and after his time in thinking that we naturally seek pleasure and avoid pain, and that our ethics are ultimately built on self-interest (although he seemed ambivalent on this point, at times viewing morality as a gift of God). He was aware of the great diversity of cultural practices and how these led to different ways of expressing human nature. It was these Durkheimian cultural varieties that were to be inscribed on Locke's blank sheet, but it was a Darwinian scroll that they were to be written on—the cultural specifics of human nature are absent at birth, but the biological generalities are present. Unfortunately for the extreme view of *tabula rasa*, all of neuroscience and evolutionary biology tells us that a blank-slate brain lacking in algorithms built in by eons of evolution that "frame" the vagaries of environmental challenges for organisms is an impossibility for any animal species (Mitchell, 2007; Pinker, 2002; Quartz & Sejnowski, 1997).

What Is Human Nature?

Let us acknowledge that human nature is a concept less than sharply defined. Darwinism makes it clear that we should expect fuzzy boundaries around any taxonomical grouping of living things. Nevertheless, to describe the nature of anything, we list its special features and nominate those that are unique (or quantitatively enhanced) that differentiate it from everything else that is not it. If Marx was correct that the defining feature of humans is our ability to consciously create our environments, we must identify the component design features that uniquely allow us to do so. The most important of these features include culture, language, large brain size relative to body size, intelligence, self-consciousness, foresight, agency, spirituality, social emotions, a theory of mind, and moral sensibility. The sum of these and other less important features may be rightly called human nature, even if none separately, or all jointly, are necessary and sufficient to define it. The relevant information for the design and expression of these features is contained in the species genome, and the universality of them is strongly supported by a number of studies. Studies across at least 50 cultures with vastly different social, cultural, economic, religious, and political differences, and consisting of many thousands of subjects, confirm that the same personality constructs are present in all cultures, and that they correlate with the same behavioral outcomes in all of them (Costa, Terracciano, & McCrae, 2001; McCrae & Terracciano, 2005; Schmitt, Realo, Voracek, & Allik, 2008).

Like everything that exists in the world, humans have a nature. To be sure, it is a malleable nature, but malleability is part of the definition of human nature. We change and adapt to environmental challenges, and we have done so over eons of evolutionary time. Nature has assuredly preferred plasticity over fixity for humans, but the view that we have no nature places humanity above nature, and it implies that an ontological set of principles completely distinct from that which is applied to other animals is required to understand human behavior. Humans are unquestionably unique, but we are not uniquely unique. Every animal species is unique in ways that define it apart from other species, and every human being is unique from every other member given the almost infinite number of possible permutations of genes and developmental experiences that shape each person. None of this talk of uniqueness contradicts the fact that humans have a shared nature underlying their individual uniqueness.

No one doubts that human nature is developed or constrained contingently by culture and history. It is patently obvious that hunter/gatherers, agrarians, and industrial workers living in vastly different times and cultures express their natures differently, but we should not let the variance blind us to the central tendency. These differing expressions are variations on a common theme running through time and place, but there are definite limits to how far we can stretch our natures. Melford Spiro, a self-confessed former cultural determinist, realized this after studying vastly different cultures throughout the world. His struggles with the data led him to reach the conclusion that "I could not make sense of my findings so long as I continued to operate within the postulates of strong cultural determinism and relativism.... I could see no way of accounting for [my findings] short of postulating a pancultural human nature" (1999:8).

If anyone believes that humans are infinitely malleable and that human nature places no constraints of the kinds of cultures humans can construct, he or she might just believe that the hypothetical Bongo-Bongo culture, presented by David Buss (2001:973) to illustrate what human nature most assuredly is *not*, might actually be a possibility:

> *They live in peace and harmony and don't get into social conflicts; sex roles are reversed, with women being masculine and aggressive, men being feminine; husbands don't care if their wives have sex with other men, and women don't care if their husbands give the bulk of the meat from the hunt to their lovers; they lack envy, jealousy, and avarice; men find older women who are grandmothers to be more sexually attractive than young women; they lack status hierarchies and are perfectly egalitarian; and they channel acts of altruism as much toward other people's children as their own.*

To deny human nature is an arrogant parochialism that disconnects us from the sweep of history, from other cultures past and present, and makes the ideas of the ages inaccessible and irrelevant. It also commits us to the notion that humans from different cultures and centuries lived in distinct and isolated universes with nothing except their morphology in common with other humans from other times and places. Yet the writings of the past strongly suggest the notion of a universal human nature. Grosvenor (2002:434) tells us that "it is the existence of perennial traits that enables us to understand, for example, the motivations of characters in the plays of Shakespeare or Sophocles, even though they were written in times radically different from our own." If there is no universal human nature beneath cultural variation, the stories from ancient and distant cultures would mystify us, but they do not. We all understand Antigone's struggles to secure a decent burial for her brother. We appreciate the profound lessons of Plato's allegories; Raskolnikov's struggle with depression, self-identity, and guilt; and the loyalty, sense of betrayal, and desire for revenge in *Forty-Seven Rōnin*. The ideas bequeathed to us by these writers are still as potent and relevant today as they were in their own time. If they were not, why is Sun-Tzu's *Art of War*, written in sixth-century BCE China, required reading in modern military academies, and even in business schools, throughout the world?

Although recognizing major differences in cultural values and practices across time and space, the eminent philosopher David Hume also recognized the central tendency inherent in the variation when he wrote:

> *It is universally acknowledged that there is a great uniformity among the actions of men, in all nations and ages, and human nature remains still the same in its principles and operations ... would you know the sentiments, inclinations and course of life of the Greeks and Romans? Study well the temper and actions of the French and English.*

(in Trigg, 1999:83)

If human beings in all cultures at all times did not have the same hopes, aspirations, character traits, emotions, feelings, goals, needs, and moral strengths and weaknesses, it would indeed be difficult, or even impossible, to grasp the wisdom and lessons bequeathed to us by the past. If we do not believe in a shared human nature, I ask the same question I asked of relativists: How can we denounce the inhuman if we do not know what the human is? As anthropologist Donald Brown wrote more than 20 years ago: "Whatever the motive may be for resisting the idea that there is a human nature whose features shape culture and society, its intellectual foundations have all but collapsed" (1991:144).

Natural Selection and Human Nature

The reason why all humans share a common nature is that we share a common evolutionary history. Because of this history, we share a common genome, which is the chemical archive of millions of years of evolutionary wisdom accumulated by the ruthless process of natural selection. Natural selection is a process that *reacts* to genetic variance by preserving favorable variants and discarding unfavorable ones; it does not *induce* variation. Any functional genes currently part of our genome are there because they provided some sort of advantage to our ancestors in the form of survival and reproductive success. Evolution by natural selection is a trial-and-error process that changes a breeding population's gene pool over time by the selective retention and elimination of genes as they become adaptive or maladaptive in their environments. The nature of any living thing, from potatoes to people, is the sum of its design features: "Human nature may be defined as our collection of adaptations" (Kennair, 2002:27). These adaptive features arose and promoted their increased frequency via an extended period of selection because they increased reproductive success, the ultimate goal of all living things.

Despite the exponential gains made in biology during the past half-century, there are social scientists who do not accept the evolutionary origins of the human behavioral repertoire and dismiss the idea as "genetic determinism" (e.g., Rose & Rose, 2000). We may all agree that there is no other scientifically viable explanation for morphological design other than evolution by natural selection but disagree with the assertion that, likewise, there is no other scientific explanation for the origin of basic psychological and behavioral design.

Kenrick and Simpson (1997:1) state that "to study any animal species while refusing to consider the evolved adaptive significance of their behavior would be considered pure folly ... unless the species in question is *Homo sapiens*." John Alcock (2001:223) also comments on the strange notion that human behavior has escaped evolution:

To say that human behavior and our other attributes cannot be analyzed in evolutionary terms requires the acceptance of a genuinely bizarre position, namely, that we alone among animal species have somehow managed to achieve independence from our evolutionary history.

Plomin (2003:533) likewise asserts that "the behavioral genomic level of analysis may be the most appropriate level of understanding for evolution because the functioning of the whole organism drives evolution. That is, behavior is often the cutting edge of natural selection." It is behavior, or rather the consequences of behavior, that creates new variants, and then—and only then—can natural selection begin the process of selective retention or elimination of the genes underlying them. This is not the language of genetic determinism. I am referring to traits and general propensities to behave in one way rather than in another, not specific behaviors; the genome does not waste precious DNA coding for behavioral specifics.

Those who deny a human nature have constructed a straw man version of it that is unrecognizable to biologists. After constructing and engaging their figure, they proclaim victory and walk away unscathed, leaving their real opponent wondering what the flurry was all about. Their straw man human nature amounts to a timeless and immutable Aristotelian *per se* essence, but that particular straw was harvested and burned in the nineteenth century in Darwin's *Origin of Species*. We are designed to incorporate environmental information into our neural architecture in somatic time and into our genomes in evolutionary time, and thus we change ontogenically and phylogenically. Because species undergo the process of evolution, we can rule out any conjunction and/or disjunction of feature we could nominate as *timelessly* necessary and sufficient for membership in our species. All modern humans came out of Africans with dark skin and wooly hair, and all were once tiny Australopithecines with crania not much larger than those of modern chimps with whom they shared a common lineage. Further back in the mists of time, we were creatures who reproduced asexually in the primordial muck, and so on back to the Big Bang where it all began. This philosophical rewind to the fact that we ultimately are all, in Carl Sagan's famous line, "made of star stuff" (1980:233), tells us in some sense that nothing can be essentialist in the way that human nature's detractors want to construct it, so they may deconstruct it with ease. This does not rule out the use of the current features to distinguish human from nonhuman, or even to say that such features are essential to defining humans from all life-forms that are not human. After all, we have been the way we are for a very long time. As Lisa Gannett (2010:367) asserts, we can rule out the strong essentialist "*really* real" concept of human nature of the philosopher of Platonic sentiments for the "merely real" concept of the Darwinian biologist.

Gene–Culture Coevolution and Human Nature

Evolutionary accounts do not ignore culture as often claimed; they simply remind us that "psychology underlies culture and society, and biological evolution underlies psychology" (Barkow, 1992:635). Ultimate-level explanations complement, not compete, with proximate-level explanations because nature (genes) and nurture (cultural learning) constitute a fully integrated reciprocal feedback system. Genes and culture are both information transmission devices, with the former laying the foundation (the capacity) for the latter, and the latter then influencing the former (What genetic variants are useful in this culture at this time and when should they be expressed?). Tinbergen's four questions are particularly useful when exploring gene–culture evolution. If a novel trait emerges that happens to be useful and desirable in a given culture, those displaying the trait will be advantaged in terms of securing resources and mates, and thus the alleles underlying the trait will be preserved and proliferate in the population gene pool. It is in this sense that there can be no human culture without human biology and no human biology without human culture. There is ample evidence for this relating to numerous human traits, especially for important ones such as intelligence and altruism (Gintis, 2003; Richerson & Boyd, 2010; Walsh & Bolen, 2012).

Culture drives selection not only for psychological and behavioral traits but also for changes in morphology, which leads to further increases in our psychological and behavioral repertoires. Sophisticated gene technology has revealed that the rate of genomic change has been approximately 100 times greater during the past 40,000 years than it was during the 5-million-year-long Pleistocene. This almost exponential change is due largely to the greater challenges posed by living in ever larger social groups: "[T]he rapid cultural evolution during the Late Pleistocene created vastly more opportunities for further genetic changes, not fewer, as new avenues emerged for communication, social interaction, and creativity" (Hawks, Wang, Cochran, Harpending, & Moyzis, 2007:20757). Our most human characteristics evolved during the Pleistocene epoch, but we do not operate with brains forged exclusively during that epoch. During the approximately 1.5 million years that separated *Australopithecus afarensis* and *Homo erectus*, hominid cranial capacity doubled from a mean of 450 cc to a mean of 900 cc, and it increased by another 70% to approximately 1350 cc from *Homo erectus* to modern *Homo sapiens*, indicating a rapid increase in intelligence (Bromage, 1987). This very rapid increase (on an evolutionary timescale) indicates that the selective pressures for the brain areas needed to negotiate social relationships must have been extremely strong.

A number of studies of hominid crania dating as far back as 1.9 million years show more robust increases in cranial capacity in areas with greater population density, and in colder and most northerly areas of the world in which food procurement was most problematic (Ash & Gallup, 2007; Kanazawa, 2008). Bailey and Geary (2009:77) found that latitude was strongly related to cranial capacity ($r = 0.61$), but population density was more strongly related ($r = 0.79$), and they concluded that the burden of evolutionary selection has moved from "climactic and ecological to social." Living in large social groups and facing ecological challenges to food procurement thus drive changes in brain morphology to accommodate the increasing brain mass needed to carry the structures associated with both intelligence and the social emotions. In many ways, the human brain is an artifact of culture because culturally created environments have influenced both the anatomy and the function of the human brain above and beyond the influences posed by the challenges of the physical environment (Mithen & Parsons, 2008). Even today, new genetic variations affecting the brain's structure and function have been discovered as it continues to evolve in response to new ecological and social conditions (Evans et al., 2005; Mekel-Bobrov et al., 2005).

Human Nature: Good, Bad, or Just Selfish?

Do humans learn to be good or bad, or are we just selfish? This broad issue subsumes several others, the most important for criminology being the origins of criminal behavior. Once again, Sowell's visions constitute the basic fault line, with the unconstrained and constrained visionaries viewing the issue in entirely different ways. Unconstrained visionaries look for the special causes of the evils of this world, and they deny that humans have an innate nature. This being the case, the causes of evil must be sought in human institutions, and human institutions can be changed. The optimism of unconstrained visionaries leads them to believe in solutions to social problems and to see no intractable reason why the crime problem cannot be solved given sufficient moral and financial commitment to the task.

Perhaps the best known unconstrained philosopher is Jean-Jacques Rousseau. Rousseau considered civilization to be a cancer on the human body, viewed private property as the source of wars and crime, and idealized the prestate days of the "noble savage." According to Durant and Durant (1967:29), Rousseau thought that "'man is naturally good'; he becomes bad chiefly through social institutions that restrain or corrupt his tendencies to natural behavior." Rousseau did not mean that humans are born unblemished and that left alone their natural goodness would shine through. He insisted that self-restraint and respect for others can only come through moral training, so here he is a constrained visionary. The innate goodness he saw in prestate humans consisted of their oneness with nature, a condition to which he knew we could not return.

French philosopher the Marquis de Condorcet was more of an unconstrained visionary than Rousseau. Condorcet traced all evil to forces outside the person:

> *Is there any vicious habit, any practice contrary to good faith, any crime, whose origin and first cause cannot be traced back to the legislation, the institutions, the prejudices of the country wherein this habit, this practice, this crime can be observed.*
>
> *(Condorcet, 1794)*

His faith in reason, human perfectibility, and in solutions is evident when he writes: "The moral goodness of man, the necessary consequence of his constitution, is capable of indefinite perfection like all his other faculties, and that nature has linked together in an unbreakable chain truth, happiness and virtue" (Condorcet was arrested and murdered by his fellow dreamers full of the "moral goodness of man" during the French Reign of Terror.)

Constrained visionaries believe that there are few solutions available to us in the social world; there are only prudent trade-offs because evil lies in the failure of social institutions to rein in natural human impulses. It is instructive that most moral philosophers have asked what makes a virtuous person rather than what makes a bad one, which reveals what they thought was the default condition. The constrained view sees civilization and society as good (of course, there are terrible societies and murderous civilizations), and is fearful of romanticized visions of perfection because such visions invariably lead to nightmares.

Although Plato held romantic ideas of Utopianism and human perfectibility and may be considered an unconstrained visionary, his allegory of the Ring of Gyges is particularly apt as an illustration of the constrained view of human nature. Gyges was a respectable young shepherd in the service of the king of Lydia who came upon a gold ring in a cave that allowed him to become invisible whenever he turned it on his finger. When Gyges realized the possibilities this opened for him, he went to the court, seduced the queen, murdered the king, and took over the kingdom. Plato's point is that with the ring's gift of invisibility, no one is so virtuous that they could resist all temptation to act unjustly in the name of self-interest. Putting the words into the mouth of Glaucon, Plato (1960:44) asserts that:

> *no man can be imagined to be of such an iron nature that he would stand fast in justice. No man would keep his hands off what is not his own when he could safely take what he liked out of the market, or go into houses and lie with anyone at his pleasure, to kill or release from prison whom he would, and in all respects be like a God among men.*

For Plato, it seems that conscience was the inner voice that makes us behave well only when others are looking.

The position of the constrained vision is not that humans are born bad but, rather, that they are born, like Gyges, selfish. This was the position of Durkheim, Marx, and Weber, who could be seen as the "holy trinity" of sociology. They all agreed with Talcott Parsons that each new generation of infants was a recurrent "barbarian invasion," and that without socialization they would grow up uncivilized (Brown, 1965:193). Durkheim wrote of the insatiability of human appetites, which can lead to crime unless a "moral discipline" provided by society prevents it. There is much evidence throughout Marx's writings that he viewed humans as primarily motivated by self-interest (Jost & Jost, 2007). For instance, Marx and Engels wrote that right-thinking communists "do not put the moral demand: love one another, do not be egoists, etc.; on the contrary, they are well aware that egoism, just as much as selfishness, *is* in definite circumstances a necessary form of self-assertion for individuals" (in Replogle, 1990:695). Finally, Walter Wallace (1990:209) notes that "Weber quite unmistakably regards personal self-interest as innate and universal among humans.... For Weber: personal self-interest is already fixed by genetic inheritance in all human individuals and needs no further fixing there by external imposition."

None of these theorists believed that selfishness is bad; rather, they considered it a necessary part of human nature, just as it is a necessary part of the nature of all animals if they are to survive their early years. Infants cannot know or be concerned with the effect the necessary demands they make will have on others—they *must* be selfish. David Hume believed that if humans were not motivated by self-interest, there would be no noble emotions such as compassion and justice (Gill, 2000). As we shall see in Chapter 13, this is the position of evolutionary theorists, who view natural selfishness as necessary for all animals and the basis of human altruism and cooperation. Even Rousseau agreed with this. He believed that *amour de soi* (self-love) is the essence of human beings, necessary for self-preservation and the basis of all positive emotions (Hoffmann, 1963). It is this innate and necessary self-centeredness that has to be contained by the realization that our wants and needs are inextricably bound up with the wants and needs of others, which is basically what Freud (1965:80) had in mind with his socialization dictum: "Where id was, there shall ego be."

Conclusion

It is surely true that like everything from ants to zebras, humans have a nature produced by the process of natural selection. We may be free to forge our own natures as the existentialist philosophers insist, and we may have natures intimately and inescapably connected to our cultures as the sociologists and anthropologists insist, but societies and individuals do not construct these natures out of nothing. There is a preexisting nature that puts constraints on our constructions; to insist otherwise is to perversely insist that we among all animals have managed to escape our evolutionary history. The denial of human nature, writes sociologist Terry Leahy (2012:13), is to ignore "the elephant in the room." Such a denial also destroys our bridges with the past and turns Horace's famous apothegm on its head to say "everything human other than that found in my own time and culture is alien to me." Given the cross-cultural studies on the universality of similar personality traits and emotions, the fact that we understand the plots and characters in literature written in vastly different times in vastly different cultures, and the work being done in the neurosciences, it is increasingly difficult to deny the existence of a universal human nature. The idea of a human nature and the discoveries made about it are indispensable to the progress of criminology, as they are to all human sciences, lest we fall into a deadening postmodern relativism in which all claims of truth are equally valid.

Human nature can be viewed as the sum of all human evolutionary adaptations, among which (and shared with all sexually reproducing animals) is self-interest. This is important to criminologists because it supports the various control theories on the importance (and "good guy" role) of society and its institutions in socializing each generation in prosocial ways. If social institutions fail in their allotted task of cultivating human nature, the default result will be criminal behavior and other forms of deviance. Almost all the great moral philosophers recognized this in their concerns to discover what makes a person good. Like all animals, we are necessarily born selfish. Whereas this is good if selfishness, as understood by evolutionary theorists and by the philosophers discussed here, is mobilized for prosocial ends, it is bad only in the absence of cultivation.

13 ⠿

Feminist Criminology and Contending Metaphysics

Feminism

Broadly defined, feminism is a set of theories and strategies for social change that takes gender as their central focus in attempting to understand social institutions, processes, and relationships. Feminism is both a social movement and a worldview that holds that women suffer oppression and discrimination in a society run for men by men who have passed laws and created customs to perpetuate their privileged position. Feminists employ a set of theories and strategies for social change in directions that improve the lot of women in ways consistent with these demands (Flavin, 2001). The general theoretical stance of feminism is highly critical of the social, political, and economic status quo. The core concepts and concerns of feminism (gender, patriarchy, oppression, etc.) have been taken by feminist criminologists and applied to their work (Irwin & Chesney-Lind, 2008).

The feminism label has been applied to such a large and diverse set of perspectives ("liberal," "socialist," "radical," "Marxist," "sameness," "difference," "gender," "equity," "evolutionary," "womanism," etc.) that it is impossible to capture something called "feminism" with a single stroke. We need to pare the concept down to some essentials so that we can talk sensibly about it. Because we have already set the tone earlier in the book by opposing science with social constructionism, we will accept Anne Campbell's (2006a:63) three broadly defined groups of feminists. She identifies *"social construc-tionists* (who reject scientific method as commonly understood) and *liberals* (who accept scientific method but seek to redress the past anthropocentrism of the topics studied and conclusions reached)." She further divides liberal feminists into *environmental liberals*, who view gender differences as solely resulting from gender socialization and gender roles, and *evolutionary liberals*, who see gender differences residing in the brain and ultimately resting on Darwinian sexual selection.

Feminist Metaphysics and Gender

Social Constructionist Feminists

Because there is no one monolithic feminism, there is no single feminist system of metaphysics. "Feminist" ontology and epistemology run the entire gamut of positions we have previously examined. As Campbell (20006a) intimated, many feminists who call sociology and psychology home tend to distrust sciences and to favor nominalism over realism and universalism, idealism over materialism, and rationalistic qualitative studies of situation-specific factors over empirical quantitative studies of general phenomena. Feminists who embrace science (Campbell's evolutionary liberals) favor the opposite ontologies and epistemologies. Let us discuss the different ways these groups view gender.

The concept of gender is a major cornerstone of feminist criminology and feminism in general. The use of the term "gender" was traditionally confined to the masculine and feminine grammatical categories of language, but with the rise of the feminist movement in the 1960s, it came to be used to refer to categories of human males and females (Nicholson, 1994). Gender is often used as a synonym for sex (useful to avoid connotations of copulation), but for social scientists the terms "sex" and "gender" refer to different but overlapping concepts. *Sex* refers to one's biological status as a male or female based on chromosomal, hormonal, and gonadal distinctions. *Gender* refers to historical social or cultural categories about how femininity and masculinity are molded and expressed in a particular culture, subculture, or situation.

For biologists, the relationship between sex and gender is analogous to that between genotype and phenotype. Just as the phenotype (anything measurable about the individual, such as height, blood pressure, IQ, personality, and blood sugar levels) is the result of the raw material provided by the genes interacting with the physical, social, and cultural environment; sex provides the raw material out of which gender is fashioned. The same genome can produce a wide variety of phenotypes, depending on its developmental experiences, and the same karyotype (XX or XY) can lead to a variety of gendered traits and behaviors depending on to what it is exposed. Thus, gender is a fluid and dynamic construction built upon the superstructure of sex. Many constructionist feminists, however, deny that gender is based on anything material, viewing it entirely built from ideational "social stuff" such as gender socialization and gender roles. Barbara Ehrenreich and Janet McIntosh (1997:12) call this "gender from nothing" position the "new secular creationism" and claim that it "threatens the credibility of feminism."

For social constructionists, gender is something that seeps into a blank-slate mind via socialization and the performance of gendered social roles as we learn how to "do gender" at home, school, and work. At a very young age, children self-socialize in a process by which incoming information is labeled and boxed as male or female, which then becomes the basis for enhanced attention and concern about gender-appropriate behavior. Although this is an accurate account of the process of coming to see the self as a gendered male or female, it ignores the fact that the information to which children pay attention is biased by their sex-specific biology, and it implies a rather arbitrary process that could easily be otherwise. However, longitudinal studies show that young children prefer to interact with their own sex and prefer sex-congruent toys *before* they are able to correctly sort pictures of girls and boys into appropriate piles (Campbell, Shirley, & Candy, 2004; Trautner, 1992). Campbell (2006a:79) stated: "Children seem to need neither the ability to discriminate the sexes nor an understanding of gender stereotypic behavior to show sex differences." Children strongly resist efforts to get them to play with opposite-sex toys or to play in sex-integrated groups, and they "quickly return to same-sex partners when adult supervision is reduced" (McIntyre & Edwards, 2009:87). The evidence seems to indicate that what some dismiss as "gender stereotypes" are in fact reasonably accurate assessments of gender differences: Differences lead to stereotypes; stereotypes do not lead to differences.

Social roles are also said to subconsciously mold gender identities, which implies that as strict sex roles diminish, so should gender differences. Eagly and colleagues (2004:289) aver that the "demise of many sex differences with increased gender equality is a prediction of social role theory." Social role theorists therefore expect gender differences to be strongest in traditional patriarchal cultures in which sex roles are most distinct. Empirical findings are contrary to their expectation. Costa, Terracciano, and McCrae's (2001) study of personality across 26 cultures ($N = 23,031$) showed that gender differences were most pronounced in modern *egalitarian* cultures in which traditional sex roles are minimized. Another study (McCrae & Tarracciano, 2005), using different measures and 50 cultures ($N = 11,985$), found exactly the same result, as did Schmitt et al.'s (2008) study of 55 cultures ($N = 17,637$). Finally, Merten's (2005) study of emotional reactions among 42,638 participants in a variety of cultures once again showed that gender differences *increase* as gender equality increases.

Although these findings may shock social constructionists, they mesh perfectly with the behavior genetic principle that as the environment becomes more equal for a trait, the more innate factors dominate. There are only two sources of trait variance—environmental and genetic—so the more one source is equalized, the more the influence of the other stands out. In the less constraining environments of modern egalitarian societies, individuals are freer to act in ways consistent with their innate proclivities. Increased personality difference in egalitarian societies is simply a function of the natural tendency of the sexes to develop different levels of the same traits and personalities. Schmitt, Realo, Voracek, and Allik (2008) maintain that traditional cultures with large resource and gender inequalities may represent the greatest departure from the egalitarian hunter–gatherer cultures that characterized our species for more than 99.9% of its history.

Evolutionary Feminists

Opposing the ideational notions of constructionist feminists are the materialist notions of those feminists Campbell (2006a) calls evolutionary liberals. For these feminists, sex differences, and therefore gender differences, in personality and behavior begin with the different reproductive roles and strategies nature has imposed on the sexes. Males produce sperm (which are simply little bags of chromosomes with tails) by the millions every day. Females are born with all the precious nutrient-rich eggs (which are 85,000 times larger than a single sperm) they will ever have (~500) (Bateman & Bennett, 2006). Because of the rarity of egg cells, a female's unconscious imperative is to choose wisely which male she will allow to fertilize them (Campbell, 2009). This is the basis for Darwin's theory of sexual selection, which remains the basis in biology for explaining sex differences across the animal kingdom.

Sexual selection, like natural selection, causes changes in the relative frequency of alleles in populations in response to environmental challenges, but in response to sex-specific mating challenges rather than general sex-neutral ecological challenges (Qvarnstrom, Brommer, & Gustafsson, 2006). Males and females inhabit the same ecological niches in which natural selection operates in sex-neutral ways, but they inhabit different mating environments that ultimately produce different sex-based natures. Sexual selection theory is far too complicated to be explained in a short section, but it boils down to the fact that sexual selection has forged trait and behavioral differences in males and females that are adaptive in pursuing their reproductive success (Davies & Shackleford, 2008; Walsh, 2013).

There are two ways in which members of any species can maximize reproductive success: Parenting effort and mating effort. Parenting effort is the proportion of reproductive effort invested in rearing offspring, and mating effort is that proportion allotted to acquiring sexual partners. Because humans are born more dependent than any other animal, parenting effort is particularly important to our species. The most useful traits underlying parenting effort are altruism, empathy, and nurturance (Rowe, 1996). Female parental investment necessarily requires an enormous expenditure of time and energy, but the only *obligatory* investment of males is the time and energy spent copulating. Reproductive success for males increases in proportion to the number of females to whom they have sexual access, and thus males have evolved a propensity to seek multiple partners. Mating effort emphasizes quantity over quality (maximizing the number of offspring rather than nurturing a few), although maximizing offspring numbers is obviously not a conscious motive of any male seeking sex.

Reproductive success among our ancestral females rested primarily on their ability to secure mates to assist them in raising offspring in exchange for exclusive sexual access, and thus human females evolved a much more discriminating attitude about sexual behavior (Geary, 2000). According to evolutionary biologists, the inherent conflict between the reckless and indiscriminate male mating strategy and the careful and discriminating female mating strategy drove the evolution of traits such as aggressiveness and the lowering of trait levels (relative to female levels) such as empathy and constraint that help males to overcome both male competitors and female reluctance. The important point is that although these traits were designed by natural selection to facilitate mating effort, they are also useful in gaining nonsexual resources via illegitimate means (Quinsey, 2002; Walsh, 2006).

Conversely, traits that facilitate parenting effort underlie prosocial activity: "Crime can be identified with the behaviors that tend to promote mating effort and noncrime with those that tend to promote parenting effort" (Rowe, 1996:270). Because female reproductive success hinges more on parenting effort than mating effort, females have evolved higher levels of the traits that facilitate it (e.g., empathy and altruism) and lower levels of traits unfavorable to it (e.g., aggressiveness) than males. Of course, both males and females engage in both mating and parenting strategies, and both genders follow a mixed mating strategy. It is only claimed that mating behavior is more typical of males and parenting effort is more typical of females.

Sex-differentiated evolution leading to different levels of a variety of traits linked to pro- and antisocial behavior requires brain mechanisms controlling these traits. Neuroscientists explain gender differences as resting on a foundation of differential neurological organization shaped by a complicated blend of prenatal genetic and hormonal processes that reflect sex-specific evolutionary pressures. Most measured gender differences are small and fairly inconsequential, but the differences that are most salient to core gender identity—that is, at the center of one's identity as male or female— are large and have neurohormonal underpinnings (Hines, 2004, 2011; Lippa, 2002). Male and female brains are thus both similar and different, but the interesting questions lie not in similarity but in the differences and what these differences mean for gendered personalities and behaviors.

Doreen Kimura informs us that sexual selection pressures ensure that males and females arrive in this world with "differently wired brains," and these brain differences "make it almost impossible to evaluate the effects of experience independent of physio-logical predisposition" (1992:119). Similarly, neuroscientists de Vries and Sodersten (2009:589) state: "Thousands of studies have documented sex differences in the brain in practically any parameter imaginable." These differences begin with the genes encoded on the sex chromosomes specifying an XX female or an XY male: "These genes are differentially represented in the cells of males and females, and have been selected for sex-specific roles. The brain is a sexually dimorphic organ and is also shaped by sex-specific selection pressures" (Arnold, 2004:1). This sex differentiation begins with the male-specific Y chromosome that carries the SRY ("sex determining region of the Y chromosome") gene (Arnold, Xu, Grisham, Chen, & Kim, 2009). In all mammals, maleness is induced from an intrinsically female form by processes initiated by this gene at approximately the sixth week of gestation. The major function of the SRY gene is to induce the downstream autosomal genes to begin the development of the testes.

When the testes are developed, they produce androgens that activate androgen receptors in the brain to masculinize it or, perhaps more correctly, to defeminize it. This brain sexing takes place during the second half of gestation, and as a result: "the structure and functioning of these regions become altered, as are the behaviors they control ... high concentrations of prenatal androgens result in male-typical behavior ... female-typical behavior develops in the absence of androgens" (Yang, Baskin, & DiSandro, 2010:154). Once prenatal androgens have sensitized receptors in the male brain to their effects, there is a second surge from approximately the second week of life to approximately the sixth month of life that further "imprints" the male brain, and then there is a third surge at puberty that activates the brain circuits organized prenatally to engage in male-typical behavior (Sisk & Zehr, 2005). Because of the additional steps required to switch the male brain from its "default" female form, significantly more males than females suffer from many types of neurological problems, such as attention deficit hyperactivity disorder (ADHD), delayed language, and autism; many things can go awry when perfectly good systems are meddled with.

Two Major Issues of Feminist Criminology

Feminist criminologists rightly complain that female crime has been virtually ignored by mainstream criminology. Despite the fact that women are responsible for only a small proportion of crime, feminists want to draw on women's "ways of knowing" to explain it (Daly & Chesney-Lind, 1988:490). Feminist criminologists thus want to put women on the criminological agenda and to interpret female crime from a feminist perspective. Two major issues on the agenda of feminist criminology are: (1) Do traditional male-centered theories of crime apply to women? and: (2) What explains the universal fact that women are far less likely than men to involve themselves in criminal activity (Price & Sokoloff, 1995)? The first of these issues is known as the generalizability problem.

The generalizability problem is "the quest to find theories that account equally for male and female offending" (Irwin & Chesney-Lind, 2008:839). The implication of this is that mainstream theories do not equally account for the criminal behavior of both genders. The argument is basically that the concepts on which traditional theories are based are "inscribed so deeply by masculinist experience that this approach will prove too restrictive, or at least [if applied to women] misleading" (Daly & Chesney-Lind, 1988:519).

Eileen Leonard (1995) has examined some of the most popular theories of crime causation with an eye to determining if they can be applied to female criminality and concludes that they cannot. For instance, she maintains that Merton's anomie theory cannot be applied to women because women are socialized to be successful in relationships, to get married, and to raise families, not to pursue financial success. The failure to succeed in either male or female cultural goals produces strain, and although it may be true that males commit crime as innovative means of attaining their *success* goals, it is illogical to view female crimes as innovative means to their *relationship* goals. Likewise, Leonard contends that if the status concerns focused on by subcultural theories were equally salient for males and females in lower-class areas, male and female crime rates would be similar. Because they are not, she dismisses these theories as inadequate for explaining female crime. Leonard is thus implicitly rejecting any explanation for gender differences in criminal behavior other than learned norms and values.

The Generalizability Problem Is Not a Problem

Unless we conceive of men and women as two entirely different species, any adequate criminology theory should be able to account for both male and female offending: "Males and females are not raised apart and exposed to an entirely different set of developmental conditions" (Bennett, Farrington, & Huesmann, 2005:280). Female offenders are found in the same places as male offenders—that is, among single-parent families located in poor, socially disorganized neighborhoods, which was recognized by Sheldon Glueck and Eleanor Glueck (1934) almost 80 years ago. Theories that limit themselves to demographic factors thus generalize to females. For sociologically trained criminologists, this is a conundrum because the main variable that matters is the environment, and people—whether we are talking about races, genders, or any other division of humanity—are essentially all alike. Biosocial criminologists certainly do not make this assumption, and they are thus not surprised that different people are differentially affected by the same environmental conditions. Males and females are affected to different degrees by the same demographic risk factors for crime, but risk factors are risk factors for both males and females (Steffensmeier & Haynie, 2000).

Individual-level correlates of male offending, such as low self-control, low IQ, conduct disorder, ADHD, and low empathy, are also correlated with female offending (Moffitt, Caspi, Rutter, & Silva, 2001), which again Glueck and Glueck pointed out in 1934. A British cohort study of 16,000 children born in 1970 concluded that "despite the much higher prevalence of antisocial behavior among boys, associations between early risk factors and antisocial outcomes were very similar for girls and boys" (Murray, Irving, Farrington, Colman, & Bloxsom, 2010:1205). For many reasons, females are less likely to be affected by risk factors at the same level than are males. Gwynne Nettler attributes female resistance to risk factors to greater female durability: "Environments—good or bad, and whichever facet of them is considered—affect males, the less viable of the sexes, more strongly than they do females, the more durable segment of the species" (1982:138).

That males and females respond in similar ways (albeit more or less strongly) to the same environmental factors is evidenced by the large correspondence of male and female crime rates. Campbell, Muncer, and Bibel (2001:484) report Pearson correlations between male and female violent and property crime *rates* over time in the United States of 0.95 and 0.99, respectively, and almost identical correlations from British data (0.98 and 0.99, respectively) and from a number of other countries in the same range. These correlations tell us that no matter how wide the gender gap in criminal behavior is across and within nations, when male rates rise, so do female rates, and when male rates fall, so do female rates. Large gender differences in offending thus exist over a wide range of cultures and conditions, even though these conditions affect the crime rates of both sexes/genders similarly in terms of raising or lowering them.

Because male and female crime rates march in lockstep despite the large difference in these rates, the risk factors proposed by mainstream criminology cannot account for gender *differences* in the incidence and prevalence of offending. If we are constrained to operate under a strict environmentalist paradigm, then these risk factors should be experienced by males and females similarly, and thus the incidence and prevalence of offending should be roughly equal for each gender. The fact that they decidedly are not implies that there is something about gender *per se* that intervenes between environmental stimulus and behavioral response that is responsible for the different level of offending between males and females. These differences influence the level of environmental instigation required for a person to cross the threshold from law-abiding behavior to criminal behavior (Steffensmeier & Haynie, 2000). All evidence points to the fact that when females cross that line, they do so at higher thresholds; thus, we may argue that the generalizability problem is not a problem, and that there is only one problem worthy of serious pursuit in feminist criminology: Why is this so? This is the gender ratio problem.

The Gender Ratio Problem

Unlike the nit-picking involved in the generalization problem, the gender ratio problem is real and urgent. We saw in Chapter 8 that Bernard, Snipes, and Gerould (2010:299) believe that the "gender ratio problem may be considered the single most important fact that criminology theories must be able to explain." The huge gender differences in criminal behavior are not in dispute by feminists or anyone else: "Women have had lower rates of crime in *all nations*, in *all communities* within nations, for *all age groups*, for *all periods in recorded history*, and for practically *all crimes*" (Leonard, 1995:55; italics in original). Leonard emphatically writes that the gender ratio is true across *all* age groups, cultures, and historical periods. The task of explaining the wide criminal gap Leonard describes is the gender ratio problem. Because most feminist criminologists, like their male counterparts, are primarily trained in sociological criminology, efforts to explain the gender ratio have been limited to differences in socialization patterns and social role expectations.

Early Feminist Theoretical Efforts: Women's Liberation and Crime

The gender-as-socially-constructed idea was expressed in Freda Adler's (1975) masculinization hypothesis. Adler's social role perspective led her to conclude that with the decrease in sex-segregated roles, we should eventually see a convergence of male and female crime rates. The adoption of male roles would result in female attitudes and behavior becoming masculinized, and thus women eventually would commit crimes at rates matching those of males:

> *In the same way that women are demanding equal opportunity in fields of legitimate endeavor, a similar number of determined women are forcing their way into the world of major crimes ... increasing numbers are women are using guns, knives, and wits to establish themselves as full human beings, as capable of violent aggression as any man.*
>
> *(1975:15)*

Rita Simon (1975) offered a different view, claiming that increased participation in the workforce affords women greater opportunities to commit job-related crime. Simon denied Adler's notion that to engage in crime women would have to become more masculine. She even argued that female violence will decrease rather than increase due to occupational involvement outside of the home. This is because women's "motivation to kill," she said, arises from the exploitation, frustration, and dependency that supposedly come from the traditional housewife role, and these feelings would be reduced by outside employment.

The *economic marginalization hypothesis* is another theory linking women's liberation to female crime. It argues that Adler and Simon did not pay sufficient attention to patriarchy and the extent to which it allows males the power to control females' labor and sexuality (Hunnicutt & Broidy, 2004). According to this hypothesis, both increasing crime and growing poverty rates among women are indirectly related to the women's liberation movement because, as women struggled to free themselves from the power of men, they inadvertently freed men from their traditional roles as providers. The sexual revolution, coupled with the decline in the traditional modes of male respect for women, has led to enormous increases in out-of-wedlock births and divorce. These in turn have led to single-female-headed households and the feminization of poverty, which motivates women to engage in economically related crimes such as prostitution, drug sales, and shoplifting (Reckdenwald & Parker, 2008).

Mears, Ploeger, and Warr (1998) maintain that the genders differ in criminal behavior because they differ in exposure to delinquent peers, and because males are more likely to be affected by delinquent peers than females because females have a greater sense of morality, greater empathy, and different cognitive skills that inhibit their behavior. This merely states that "boys will be boys" and "girls will be girls." We would like to know *why* males are more likely to be exposed (or to expose themselves) to delinquent peers and *why* they are more affected by them once they are exposed. We should also like to know *why* females have greater empathy, a greater sense of inhibitory morality, and different cognitive skills.

We are told by Mears et al. (1998) that females are less likely to be exposed to delinquent peers because they are more strictly supervised, and they are more morally inhibited because they are socialized more strongly to conformity. The way children are socialized and supervised impacts decisions to misbehave for both genders, but controlling for supervision level results in the same large gender gap in offending; that is, comparably supervised boys have higher rates of delinquency than girls (Gottfredson & Hirschi, 1990). Further adding to the misery of this position is a meta-analysis of 172 studies that found a slight tendency for boys to be *more* strictly supervised than girls (Lytton & Romney, 1991). Another surprising finding from Lytton and Romney's meta-analysis was how few parent-initiated (as opposed to child-initiated) behaviors and socialization patterns were gender differentiated.

Adding Materialism to Idealism

Our brief discussion of the idea that gender differences in criminal offending are the result of purely ideational processes leads me to conclude with Dianna Fishbein (1992:100) that "cross cultural studies do not support the prominent role of structural and cultural influences of gender-specific crime rates as the type and extent of male versus female crime remains consistent across cultures." Parents in all cultures socialize males and females differently because they *are* different—the biological dog wags the cultural tail. Sanderson (2001:198) insists that socialization patterns "simply represent social confirmation of a basic biological reality that is easily recognized by people in all societies."

Because the gender gap is found across time and cultures, it is a constant, and we know that we cannot explain a constant by a variable. The invariance of the gender gap must be explained by something that itself is invariant, which socializing practices are not. The invariant is sex-specific developmental physiology undergirded by sex-specific evolutionary pressures. We cannot continue to infer the power of gender-differentiated norms from the gender-differentiated behavior that these norms supposedly explain. Richard Udry (1994:563) calls such reasoning circular and states that "the reason for this tautology is that we, as social scientists, can't think of any other way to explain sex differences." As Alice Rossi (1984) maintained in her presidential address to the American Sociological Association, if feminists continued to rely on disembodied phenomena to explain sex/gender differences, and if they continued to ignore the fact that humans have genes, brain, hormones, and an evolutionary history, they would become irrelevant in the scientific world.

This is not the place to survey the voluminous literature in biosocial criminology on sex differences in criminal behavior. I gave a "bare bones" explanation in terms of gender differences in empathy and fear, both of which have strong evolutionary underlays in terms of evolutionarily relevant sex role differences, in Chapter 8. In my *Feminist Criminology through a Biosocial Lens* (2011a), I surveyed all individual traits associated with pro- and antisocial behavior for which there is a robust literature linking them to genetics and neurobiology. Males are consistently and strongly found to be higher on all traits linked to antisocial behavior, such as impulsiveness, low self-control, ADHD, conduct disorder, alcoholism, and psychopathy, and females consistently and robustly show higher levels of all traits linked to prosocial behavior, such as altruism, empathy, guilt proneness, conscientiousness, and agreeableness. All these syndromes have material correlates in the genome and the brain (i.e., they are heritable and are linked to sex differences in specific areas of the brain), and the ultimate reason why we consistently see sex differences in the genome and brain is explained by the logic of evolution. Sarah Bennett and colleagues (2005:273) provide a thumbnail sketch of why we should not be surprised to find male–female differences in antisocial behavior but, rather, would be dumbfounded if we did not find such differences:

> *Males and females vary on a number of perceptual and cognitive information-processing domains.... The human brain is either masculinized or feminized structurally and chemically before birth. Genetics and the biological environment in utero provide the foundation of gender differences in early brain morphology, physiology, chemistry, and nervous system development. It would be surprising if*

these differences did not contribute to gender differences in cognitive abilities, temperament, and ultimately, normal or antisocial behavior.

Conclusion

Feminism is an emancipatory movement, not a scientific theory. Feminist criminology can be considered as but a small part of that movement. Some strands of feminism reject science as a path to knowledge altogether, viewing it as "classist, racist, and especially masculinist" (Jagger, 1986:158). According to a survey of academic psychologists, most self-identified feminists reject traditional science, viewing it as an outdated method of acquiring knowledge and unsuitable to feminist enterprise (Unger, 1996). This strand of feminism wants nothing to do with a method of obtaining knowledge that points to the biological underpinnings of gender because the traits and behaviors imputed to women and considered biologically have been used to oppress them. Ian Hacking (1999:96) notes that feminists often view the tools of science as tools that "have been used against them ... women are subjective, men are objective. They argue that those very values, and the word objectivity, are a gigantic confidence trick." Biological findings can be used by misogynists to denigrate and oppress women only if we allow them to do so, and only if we fail to counter the ignorance that underpins their arguments. The pursuit of social justice is a *moral* imperative regardless of what science does or does not have to say about any observed differences between the sexes.

Science must be our unfettered guide to understanding human behavior because it is about what empirically *is*, not what morally *ought* to be. We would do well to remember, however, that empirical observations are guided perceptions and as such are fallible. But guided perceptions are all that we have, and they have proved monumentally successful in making progress in all sorts of domains. It would be surprising if science did not produce justified knowledge in the area of sex differences. The findings of science should not be construed as antithetical to the emancipatory goals of feminism. Justice does not rest on what science discovers about sameness or on differences between the sexes but, rather, on law and reasoned moral discourse. Whatever legitimate complaints women have about their historical treatment, it is hardly legitimate to say that because these tools have been used in this way, the tools themselves are illegitimate. Misogynists will jump on any bus—science, religion, politics, and so forth—that will take them where they want to go. But because they jump on the bus, it does not mean that the bus should be consigned to the scrap heap.

14

Origins of the Intuition of Justice

Pre-Naturalist Ideas of Justice

What is justice? Where does the human sentiment for it come from? What is its relationship to various processes such as cooperation, conflict, altruism, empathy, sympathy, and punishment? My dictionary's definition of justice goes around in circles, defining it as "the maintenance or administration of what is just." It previously defines *just* as "conforming to a standard of correctness; righteous; merited; deserved" and gives as synonyms the terms *fair* and *upright*. Because the predicate is contained in the subject, this definition does not do us much good. But we cannot expect too much from dictionaries because the question of the origin of moral sensibilities such as justice has occupied philosophers for centuries. Supreme Court Justice Potter once said that he could not define obscenity but knew it when he saw it. We too have difficulty defining justice but know it when we see it. Given that justice is intimately woven into our discipline, we should expect to see a lot of pondering over its origins and meaning, but we do not.

Although both Plato and Aristotle waxed eloquently about justice, they never set forth a coherent theory of it and saw it merely as a function of reason and virtue. In more modern times, John Rawls's *A Theory of Justice* (1971) is perhaps the most influential non-naturalistic theory of justice. Rawls's theory is in the tradition of social contract theorists such as Hobbes and Rousseau, who posited a time in prehistory when rational men found it prudent to enter a social contract in which they would surrender much of their autonomy to powerful leaders in exchange for peace and justice. Rawls joined them in positing an "original position" corresponding to their "state of nature" in which humans were neither Hobbes's brutal beasts nor Rousseau's noble savages but simply "mutually disinterested" in one another (1971:12). It is necessary to Rawls's argument that humans in the original position be free, rational, and equal, and be under no prior obligations or constraints because they were charged with developing a social system under a "veil of ignorance" regarding the talents and characteristics they would bring to it or their place in it. Under such conditions of rational ignorance, Rawls avers, all individuals would accept the principle of equality as a *prima facie* obligation, and that for Rawls is justice.

Rawls's theory posits a wholly unrealistic hypothetical set of conditions and explores what would happen *if* they obtained; it is thus more a thought experiment than a theory because a theory proper is supposed to be premised on facts. It is a normative model presenting Rawls's vision of distributive justice that separates justice from dessert: "The principles of justice that regulate the basic structure and specify the duties and obligations of individuals do not mention moral dessert, and there is no tendency for distributive shares to correspond to it" (1971:311). Equality was Rawls's *summum bonum*, but he was not a radical egalitarian because he believed that inequality is acceptable if it is to the advantage of the worst-off individuals in society (the "difference principle" mentioned in Chapter 7). That is, justice permits social and economic inequalities because greater rewards naturally attach to certain occupations that require extensive preparation. However, everyone should have an equal opportunity to compete for these occupations, and the only way that can be reasonably assured is for the government (i.e., the taxpayer) to provide free education for all beyond high school.

The Rawlsian model is counterfactual, and although counterfactual ideas may produce interesting novels, they are not much good in science. Far from being "mutually disinterested," hominids evolved in the context of several millions of years of living in small, hierarchically structured social groups with strong attachments to the in-groups and animosity toward out-groups. Humans were almost certainly more equal by necessity in the "original position" but never free (in terms of having access to alternative modes of thought and existence), and they have always been more emotional than rational (Krebs, 2008; Wilson, 1998). Rawls's work is a piece of brilliant deductive logic promoting his vision of morality, but it has no place for emotion or for pre-contractual social solidarity. It offers no thoughts on justice's origins or how or why justice is integral to human nature. It is not a theory of what justice *is* but rather a polemic about what Rawls believes it *should* be, nor is it a theory of how and why the human intuition of justice came to be.

A Sense of Justice as an Evolved Adaptation

Aristotle's definition of justice can be paraphrased as "treating equals equally and unequals unequally according to relevant differences" (Walsh & Stohr, 2010:133). Most moral philosophers accept this meritocratic definition, which is contrary to the Rawlsian idea of justice. It is, of course, a definition and not an explanation of its origins and purpose any more than Rawls's is an explanation. The definition sums up Aristotle's ideas of distributive and corrective (retributive) justice, and boils down to a judgment that there is or is not a correspondence between what persons receive and what they are entitled to or deserve.

Aristotle's definition accords well with equity theory, which has dominated the study of justice in the social sciences for decades. Equity theory is based on the assumption that humans seek to maximize their benefits and minimize their costs, a goal that can be best accomplished in a social setting by developing social norms for equitably distributing resources (Wagstaff, 1998). The theory asserts that outcomes are just in social relationships when those who have made the largest contributions receive the greatest rewards and those who have damaged social relationships the most receive the most severe reprisals, but once again it does not address justice's origins.

Equity theory, based squarely on the social learning of morality, emphasizes rational judgments of morality and fairness, ignoring naturalism and emotion completely. Yet, as de Jong (2011:118) asserts: "Morality is mostly a matter of intuition, sentiments, and emotional intuitions ... and is the product of a coevolution of individual mental mechanisms and social and cultural institutions." In this view, moral reasoning is a *post hoc* rationale for moral intuitions ("I *feel* this is wrong [or right], and here are my *reasons* why"). Prinz (2007) also views reasoned judgments as cognitive elaborations that are secondary to emotional appraisals. Scholars such as these follow in the tradition inaugurated by Charles Darwin, who linked his moral sensibilities to the deepest regions of human nature. This insight is expressed in Immanuel Kant's testimony that the only two things he could be absolutely sure of were "the starry heavens above and the moral law within" (in Thomas, 1962:255). If justice and other moral sentiments are part of human nature with an evolutionary history, they had adaptive consequences.

We recognize justice because we recognize injustice, and we recognize injustice by *felt* outrage at experiencing injustice, not by reference to some legal rule we have pondered upon. The first identifiably moral statement made by children, and often quite forcibly, is surely "That's not fair!" How do children arrive at that conclusion, and why is it so immediately compelling? Reacting to perceived injustice the way children do reflects a deep emotional concern provoked by physiological arousal mechanisms motivating them to do something about it. This affective state arrives long before children are able to articulate any moral reasoning for their felt injustice, and something so readily and strongly activated argues for its status as an adaptation shaped by natural selection. Finkel, Harré, and Rodriguez Lopez (2001:7) call these "not fair" complaints "common-sense justice" because they "are uttered long before children come into contact with any formal introduction to general moral principles."

Justice and Selfishness

The just desserts concept of justice has been criticized on the grounds that it is motivated by selfishness and based on conservative notions of meritocratic capitalism, whereas "true" justice implies cooperation (Cela-Conde, Burgess, Nadal, & Olivera, 2010). It is difficult to view cooperative behavior as motivated by selfishness rather than by a sense of fairness, unless the sense of fairness is itself motivated by selfishness, as evolutionary biologists aver (Wilson & Wilson, 2007). Selfishness as commonly understood is not conducive to *adaptive* selfishness as understood by evolutionary scientists. As normally understood by the nonbiologist, selfishness is taken to mean greed, cheating, a lack of concern for others, egotism, Machiavellian manipulation, and insensitivity. Acting thusly may be self-serving in the short term, but it is certainly self-destructive in the long term, and self-destruction is surely not indicative of a sensible concern for one's self-interest.

Rawls's theory of justice assumed human nature to be selfish, which is why his scheme demanded a veil of ignorance in the original position as to the traits, abilities, and circumstances people would have in the society they were to be part of. He knew that each person would be concerned with advancing his or her own position in life, and he assumed that all would be "mutually disinterested" in the interests of others. It is only because people are rational and preeminently concerned with themselves that they would agree to the difference principle so that society's distributive shares will not be unduly influenced by factors (individual and family characteristics, traits, and connections) that are arbitrary from a moral standpoint. Rawls clearly sees selfishness in a manner similar to the evolutionary biologist.

Selfishness in the evolutionary sense is normatively neutral because evolutionists recognize that all organisms have evolved to be principally concerned with their own survival and reproduction, and will do what they have to do in order to realize those concerns (Tang, 2011). For the evolutionist, altruism and selfishness are not opposites; on the contrary, altruism is driven by concerns for the self, although its self-serving nature is rarely consciously perceived. We benefit ourselves (intrinsically or extrinsically, immediately or later) by cooperating, behaving altruistically, and acting justly. Because others benefit from nonexploitive selfishness as well, selfishness is a positive thing, even highly desirable in a social species (Krebs, 2008).

This is not an insight specific to modern evolutionists. As we discussed previously, philosophers from Kant to Rousseau and all three founding fathers of sociology (Durkheim, Marx, and Weber) viewed selfishness as a good thing when properly cultivated. We may add John Duns Scotus to this pantheon of great thinkers. Scotus, perhaps the greatest mind of the Middle Ages, saw all activity sparked by love but insisted that this love was necessarily self-centered because nature exhorts us to seek above all things our continued survival (Vos, 2007). Although individual organisms are adapted to act in their best interests, not to behave for the good of the group, their fitness goals are best realized by adhering to the rules of cooperation and altruism—by "being nice"—and that is "for the good of the group." Thus, even though altruism is ultimately self-serving, this does not diminish the value of fairness and altruism to its beneficiaries.

Justice and Emotions

Evolutionary explanations are ultimate-level explanations that ask "why" questions rather than "how" questions. For instance, a neuroscientist might explain the benefits of altruism to the self by indicating that reward centers in the altruist's brain light up when he or she performs some act of kindness (Lee, 2008). An evolutionary biologist will want to know why extending benefits to others was so important to individual fitness in evolutionary environments that natural selection has built in mechanisms to reward us when we do. These ultimate and proximate explanations complement one another; they do not compete with one another, and neither do naturalistic and cultural explanations.

Social learning and moral reasoning certainly play a role in specifying what the acts are that anger and outrage us when injustice is perceived. What is right or wrong, just or unjust, is often culturally specific (*mala prohibita* acts), and those who are angered by such acts will feel emotionally reassured that justice is done when offending parties are chastised. Other acts (*mala in se* acts) are universally proscribed (at least when directed against members of the in-group) because they militated against our common ancestors' survival and reproductive success. Cultural variation in the acts that engage the sense of injustice does not gainsay the universality of the sentiment. The arousal of evolved sentiments in situations different from those originally responsible for their selection is not unusual. Evolved tendencies are extended and reshaped by our cultures by providing us with moral norms that engage them, even if those norms have no obvious fitness benefits. For instance, the human nurturance of non-kin or of animals, or having a singular sexual attraction toward one's own sex are behaviors that have no fitness benefits for the self. They are examples of the diffusion of evolved propensities to engage in activities that are similar and that do have obvious fitness benefits—that is, nurturing of one's own offspring and being attracted to reproductive partners.

Justice and Evolution

Evolutionary theorists have the basic premise that any human feature, process, emotion, or behavior that is universal (and found to varying degrees among nonhuman animals also) is a biological adaptation. With Dennis Krebs (2008:232), I argue that the "overarching function of a sense of justice is to induce members of groups to uphold fitness-enhancing forms of cooperation." In other words, the sense of justice is an adaptive solution to problems faced by our distant ancestors living in groups. This felt sense of justice is a secondary emotion formed from a mix of primary affective states that evolved to serve purposes other than fairness and equity but have been coopted to serve that purpose. Many of the emotions that comprise the sense of justice are usually thought of as serving quite different, and even opposite, purposes, such as anger versus pleasure and the desire for revenge versus sympathy. These emotions have palpable physiological referents, as does the intuition of injustice (anger, sadness, and depression) and justice when injustice is assuaged (relief, satisfaction, and happiness). *Justice* is the term we use to describe the higher-order abstraction that has evolved from the interplay of these emotions and cognitions.

A sense of justice is observed in its rudimentary forms among many mammalian species, especially among primates (de Waal, 1996; Wilson, 1998). Scholars who limit their study of morality to rationality argue that morality requires belief, and belief requires language. They would therefore conclude that animals such as chimps do not have language and thus cannot know what it is to act morally. Language makes emotions accessible to reasoning, but it does not make them happen, as any animal lover knows.

As it does for humans, justice, "doing the right thing," reflects a sense of social regularity among these animals involving a set of cognitive and emotional algorithms, defined as:

> *a set of expectations about the way in which oneself (or others) should be treated, and how resources should be divided, a deviation from which expectations to one's (or the other's) disadvantage evokes a negative reaction, most commonly protest in subordinate individuals and punishment in dominant individuals.*
>
> *(de Waal, 1991:336)*

In short, justice is an abstract concept that nonetheless has palpable physiological components that are activated when the prescriptive and proscriptive rules that regulate social peace and harmony are disrupted. But what are the evolutionary sources of the ensemble of emotional and cognitive algorithms that demand justice? Like any other feature of physical and mental development, these algorithmic processes arise from epigenetic rules. These rules explicitly recognize that genes alone do not determine social and mental development. There are many plausible routes from genes to behavior, which depend on culture, situational factors, and the complex interaction of gene products. As moral development theorists such as Piaget (1968) and Kohlberg (1984) have pointed out, moral behavior is learned in stages, and we are somehow innately "prepared" to embrace it more fully as we mature. This "prepared learning" is what biologists call canalization, or biased pathways in our development.

Experience-Expected and Experience-Dependent Development

The terms "epigenetic rules," "prepared learning," and "canalization" recognize that when we use the term "innate," we do not mean that the feature so considered is present at birth in its final form, fixed, or unalterable. These terms mean that we have specialized computational systems that allow us to acquire vital characteristics as we interact with our species-expected environments. That is, we arrive in this world with neurological computational systems that allow us to take advantage of experiences that occur naturally in our species-typical environments. Neuroscientists call these developmental processes *experience-expected* and *experience-dependent* (Schon & Silven, 2007).

Experience-expected mechanisms are hardwired and shared by all members of a species and reflect its phylogenic history (Gunnar & Quevedo, 2007). They have evolved as neural readiness during certain critical developmental periods to incorporate environmental information that is vital to an organism and ubiquitous in its environment. Certain developmental processes, such as sight, speech, depth perception, affectionate bonds, mobility, and sexual maturation, are vital, and natural selection has provided for mechanisms designed to take advantage of experiences occurring naturally within the normal range of environments. Pre-experiential rudimentary brain organization (built-in assumptions) frames or orients our experiences so that we will respond consistently and stereotypically to vital stimuli (Black & Greenough, 1997; Geary, 2005).

Experience-dependent mechanisms, on the other hand, reflect the brain's ontogenic plasticity. The development of the brain of each individual will depend on experience acquired in the organism's developmental environment and involves "collaboration of genetic and environmental influences across the lifespan" (Depue & Collins, 1999:507). In other words, the brain wires itself in ways directly reflecting its experience, and the earlier and more frequent the experience, the more entrenched those neuronal pathways will be. Brain plasticity is greatest in infancy and early childhood, but a certain degree is maintained across the lifespan so that every time we experience something, we shape and reshape the nervous system in ways that could never have been preprogrammed (Walsh & Bolen, 2012).

The acquisition of language is a useful example for what is meant by experience-expected/experience-dependent developmental processes. The computational machinery for acquiring language, while innate, requires input from the environment to trigger it. Because hearing others speak is an experience-expected feature of human phylogenic and ontogenic environments, these mechanisms are triggered automatically and we learn to speak ("develop" is a better word because we acquire language almost effortlessly as if by osmosis). We know of rare children who were not exposed to language at critical developmental junctures who are never able, or barely able, to speak despite their language acquisition devices being intact. On the other hand, what language(s) we speak is entirely an experience-dependent feature determined by our cultures of rearing.

Reciprocal Altruism

Reciprocal altruism is the extending of a benefit to another with the unspoken expectation of obtaining a like benefit from the recipient at some later date. As Max Weber maintained, human social life involves competition for status and power—the perennial coinage of male reproductive success. It is this competition over scarce resources "that constitutes the core of a great many of moral problems involving justice" (Charlesworthy, 1991:351). Without great struggles to be settled, there would not have been any selection pressure for the evolution of moral systems, once again emphasizing the interdependence of conflict and cooperation in social life.

The conflict between the norm of cooperation and the natural desire to put one's own interests ahead of others is illustrated in the familiar prisoner's dilemma of game theory (Axelrod, 1984). The paradox in this game is that although the payoff for cheating when the other actor does not is high, if both cheat, they are both worse off than if they had cooperated with one another. The lesson of the prisoner's dilemma game is that mutual cooperation produces the best payoff for individuals in a *group*, but it also shows how difficult cooperation is to achieve in circumstances of limited communication. In a single game of prisoner's dilemma, defecting always yields the best payoff for the one who defects, so the question is how cooperation can exist in social species where there is (and there always is) competition for resources and mating opportunities. Evolutionary theory posits that cooperation will only be favored by natural selection if cooperators interact with other cooperators who are able to recognize and remember conspecifics in previous instances of cooperation and noncooperation (Broom, 2006).

A population of cooperators provides an obvious target-rich niche for cheats who signal cooperation but then default, thus gaining resources at zero cost to themselves. "Cheating" is a general term used by evolutionists to describe any antisocial behaviors that lead to feelings of injustice in victims. Cheats prosper in a population of unconditional cooperators ("suckers") and would soon drive them to extinction. Having destroyed the system they feed on, the problem then becomes that cheats have only other cheats with whom to interact. A population of cheats is also very unlikely to thrive because in situations of frequent interaction, it breeds an ambiance of alienation and suspicion in which few are willing to cooperate with conspecifics. This should lead to rapid selection for cooperation among a population of cheats (Machalek, 1996).

Pure suckers and pure cheats are thus unlikely to exist in large numbers in any social species, as computer simulations and mathematical models of evolutionary scenarios have consistently found (Boyd & Richerson, 1992). Almost all social animals, including humans, are grudgers who employ a strategy evolutionary game theorists call *tit-for-tat*. Grudgers are conditional cooperators who can be cheated because they abide by the norms of mutual trust and cooperation and expect the same from others. Unlike suckers, once cheated, grudgers will react differently to cheaters in the future by not offering them cooperation in obtaining resources. The evolution of reciprocal altruism requires the frequent reversal of donors and recipients with the intelligence to recognize one another, as well as to recognize cheats (Crawford, 1998). Thus, cheaters interact with populations of "grudgers" in a *repeated* game of prisoner's dilemma (as opposed to a single game in which the best strategy is always to cheat) in which players adjust their strategies in tit-for-tat ways according to their experience with other players in the past (Machalek, 1996). Chronic cheaters (we call them *criminals*) are only able to maintain their strategy by frequent changes of location, meeting and cheating a series of grudgers who are susceptible to one-time deception. Cheaters move from place to place, job to job, and relationship to relationship, moving on again when their reputation catches up to them (Ellis & Walsh, 1997: Wiebe, 2011).

Human beings, as a species of grudgers, engage in many behaviors characterized as altruistic, but as the previous discussion illustrates, altruistic behavior is typically contingent on reciprocal behavior on the part of recipients unless directed at close genetic kin. Because it is discriminative and tends to cease when recipients do not reciprocate, altruism must have been ultimately designed to serve the purposes of the altruist.

This does not mean that we possess genes urging us to behave altruistically in order to gain resources and to maximize our reproductive success, or that we make rational cost–benefit calculations when deciding to help others. We cooperate and behave altruistically because our distant ancestors who behaved altruistically enjoyed greater reproductive success than those who did not, thus passing on the genes for the structures and neurotransmitters that underlie altruism. It is so built into us that most of us engage it almost automatically when we perceive someone is in need. Our immediate rewards for helping others are feelings of contentment and self-satisfaction—we feel plain good about ourselves when helping others. Our more distant reward is the unspoken promise of reciprocal behavior in the future, but even if the recipient of our beneficence is a stranger we are unlikely to meet again, we still receive the surge of neurochemicals that make us feel good (Brunero, 2002). Brain imaging studies consistently show that our pleasure centers "light up" when either giving or receiving something valued, but also that brain areas associated with the pleasures of social attachments only fire when giving (Moll et al., 2006). Modern science has vindicated Jesus's proclamation that "It is more blessed to give than to receive."

Fairness and Equality Redux

The concept of fairness is integral to justice. In Chapter 11, we saw that "unfair economic system" was the most popular putative cause of crime for liberal and radical criminologists, and in Chapter 7 we addressed the concept of equality. But what does it mean to be fair or unfair? Fairness appeals to our moral sentiments because it is a process by which we expect to "make things right." We feel sorry for individuals burdened with disabilities they did nothing to create, and we would like to make it right for them. But having sympathy for such individuals does not tell us how their position in life coheres with the moral issue of fairness. As I previously noted, fairness is an issue saturated with contradictory notions; we all praise it but differ as to when its promise is fulfilled. Constrained visionaries view fairness as an equal opportunity *process*—a nondiscriminatory chance to play the game—which can be guaranteed by law. This is the natural liberty concept that permits inequalities based on talent and effort. Unconstrained visionaries tend to view fairness as equality of *outcome*—which no power on earth can guarantee, as even Rawls agreed.

In the constrained view, unequal outcomes are considered fair if the process is fair, and the process is fair if everyone is subjected to the same rules and judged by the same standards. With the rules of the game and the standards of judgment held constant, the only things that vary are the qualities that individuals bring to it. Life is like a poker tournament; we all get dealt our hands and must play the best way we can within the rules of the game. We can hone our skills and pray to lady luck; we win some and we lose some, but we cannot all win jackpots. Fairness has nothing to do with it. We can only talk of fairness or unfairness if some entity has the power to distribute resources, but no one is in charge of handing out parents, genes, or environments; we just find ourselves existing and, as the existentialists insist, must do our best with what we have been dealt.

Noble Prize-winning economist and philosopher Friedrich Hayek had the following to say about fairness (note my emphasis on *if*):

> *The manner in which the benefits and burdens are apportioned by the market mechanism would in many instances have to be regarded as very unjust if it were the result of a deliberate allocation to particular people. But this is not the case. Those shares are the outcome of a process the effect of which on particular people was neither intended nor foreseen by anyone.*
>
> *(1976:64)*

The insinuation of the moral issue of fairness into social issues helps us to understand why we often see unconstrained visionaries viciously attacking constrained visionaries, but rarely see the opposite. As Thomas Sowell (1987:227) states: "Implications of bad faith, venality, or other moral and or intellectual deficiencies have been much more common in the unconstrained vision's criticism than *vice versa*." It is the fusion of so many issues with their notions of morality that leads unconstrained visionaries to consider those who disagree with them as immoral supporters of inequality rather than simply wrongheaded. They seem to believe that if apparently intelligent and well-educated individuals oppose programs they believe could improve the lives of the less fortunate, those individuals must be evil. On the other hand, constrained visionaries rarely accuse their opponents of deliberately opposing the common good, even if they view these individuals as inadvertently doing just that. Constrained visionaries view their opponents as well-meaning but naive and unrealistic, and rarely do they resort to *ad hominem* attacks in response to an argument.

Unconstrained visionaries tend to value Kant's deontological ethics whereby only "good" intentions are moral. Constrained visionaries tend to favor consequentialist ethics that judge political actions (but not necessarily individual ones) as good or bad by their consequences, not by their intentions, noting that the path to hell is paved with good intentions. Consequentialist ethics accord with Kant's disdained empirical morality (e.g., the honest shopkeeper who is honest because he does not want to drive his customers to the competition), which is not morality *per se* because the shopkeeper's honesty policy is followed only for practical reasons that benefit himself. For Kant, only acts performed solely from duty and good will are truly moral, *regardless of the consequences*. Thus, if we are to be good deontologists, policies such as Prohibition and the current drug war are moral because they were derived from good moral intentions (to prevent the use of mind-altering substances that often lead to violence and other undesirable consequences), despite their negative consequences. For the same reasons, unconstrained visionaries consider capitalism to be immoral (at least amoral) despite the bounty it provides us, because it is a system built on self-interest and meritocracy, which was not moral for Kant, and neither is it for those with complaints about an unfair economic system.

Conclusion

Justice is a concept close to the heart of criminology, but discussions of its nature and origins are extremely difficult to find in our discipline. Such discussions tend to be found only in biological and philosophical journals—in the first instance because biologists are interested in the ultimate origin of things pertaining to living creatures, and in the second instance because philosophers like to peer beyond what is immediately apparent. Yet most philosophers are so enamored with reason that they tend to ignore emotion as a key player in human affairs. This is obvious in Rawls's quite brilliant but counterfactual thought experiment leading him to his "difference principle." Emotions appear to be far more important than reason in the fairness calculus, which should not be surprising given that the emotional brain evolved eons before the rational brain. Emotions move us to demand that we be treated fairly; reason helps us to articulate why.

Fairness is viewed differently by constrained and unconstrained visionaries, which often leads to the latter accusing the former of intellectual venality. The unconstrained visionary tends to view fairness as something close to Rawls's difference principle—a principle that explicitly denies dessert principles on moral grounds, given that no one "deserves" the genes or family they inherit, and therefore no one deserves the advantages and disadvantages these genes and families grant. We saw in Chapter 7 that experiments in a variety of countries show that an overwhelming number of people throughout the world intuitively opt for allotting rewards according to dessert principles (Chan, 2005). According to dessert principles, fairness is getting what one deserves according to one's contribution in a society in which the free market (the sum of millions of individual choices) determines worth. Any system attempting to artificially enforce equality of outcome as opposed to equality of opportunity can only do so at the expense of the human intuition of justice and by, to quote Durkheim again: "external constraints to the detriment of the achievement of justice" (in Anne Rawls, 2003:333).

15

Punishment
Its Justifications and Its Role in the Evolution of Justice

Philosophical Justifications for Punishment

Punishment is the application of painful stimuli in response to some norm violation committed by the person being punished. Because punishment typically involves the state doing deliberate harm to individuals in the name of the people, philosophers consider it a practice in need of strong moral justification. The traditional justifications of punishment—deterrence, incapacitation, rehabilitation–reintegration, and retribution—ebb and flow in popularity according to the ideology of the times. Moral philosophers refer to the first four justifications as "consequentialist," meaning that punishment is justified by the consequences assumed to come from it; that is, punishment is a means to an end. Retribution is the only nonconsequentialist position because it justifies punishment based on its intrinsic moral worth, regardless of any benefits that may flow from its application (Wood, 2010a).

Plato's theory of punishment is particularly interesting because it combines "ultra-conservatism with radical innovation" (Ladikos, 2000:167). Plato is considered a reformist in the mold of Cesare Beccaria (1764/1963) in his concern for criminals, urging Athenians to foreswear retribution in favor of reform. He considered crime a disease of the soul that could be cured, but like most of us, he could never get beyond the concept of blameworthiness (Mackenzie, 1981). Despite his reformist reputation (although "reform" is, of course, relative to what came before) in his penal code, he advocated for the death penalty for seven offenses, including murder, temple robbing, subversion, and theft of public property (Hunter, 2009). His Utopianism outlined in the *Republic* makes it clear that he favored the state over individual rights, and that harsh punishment was necessary to deter others from harming the polis. Plato was thus a deterrence theorist favoring punishment because of its supposed consequences or utilitarian value. For the consequentialist, the basis for judging any policy, practice, or conduct morally acceptable is their desirable consequences. Aristotle also believed in deterrence, but thought the death penalty only appropriate for willful murder and treason (Anckar, 2004).

Deterrence has long been considered the primary function of punishment. Specific deterrence, the effect of the imposed punishment on the future behavior of the person punished, does not seem to work very well when we consider parolee recidivism rates of approximately 67% by the third year after release from prison (Stohr & Walsh, 2012). On the other hand, few of us would dispute the general deterrent effect of punishment on those who have witnessed it but not personally experienced it. Punishing criminal offenders serves as an example to the rest of us of what may happen if we violate the law. Radzinowicz and King (1979:296) stated it well:

> *People are not sent to prison primarily for their own good, or even in the hope that they will be cured of crime. Confinement is used as a measure of retribution, a symbol of condemnation, a vindication of the law. It is used as a warning and deterrent to others. It is used, above all, to protect other people ... from the offender's depredations.*

Some philosophers reject general deterrence as a moral justification (but not as a practical one) because it suggests that it is defensible to punish innocent people for the greater social good (Wood, 2010b).

The justification for incapacitation is aptly summarized by James Q. Wilson's (1975:391) remark that "wicked people exist. Nothing avails except to set them apart from innocent people." It is also exemplified by Enrico Ferri's concept of social defense, which avers that the purpose of punishment is not to deter or to rehabilitate but, rather, to defend society from criminal predation. The only reasonable rationale for punishing offenders is to incapacitate them for as long as possible so that they no longer pose a threat to the peace and security of society. Incapacitation obviously "works" while criminals are incarcerated. Elliot Currie (1999) uses robbery rates to illustrate this, stating that in 1995, there were 135,000 inmates in prison whose most serious crime was robbery, and that each robber on average commits 5 robberies per year. Had these robbers been left on the streets, they would have been responsible for an additional $135,000 \times 5$ or 675,000 robberies in addition to the 580,000 actual robberies reported to the police in 1995.

Rehabilitation and reintegration are also consequentialist justifications, but they are more forward-looking by their focus on the future behavior of criminals than backward-looking at what they have done. Plato was a believer in rehabilitation for some offenses because he considered criminal behavior to be a moral sickness caused by the domination of the appetitive soul rather than by the reasoned soul, and believed that education would furnish offenders with moral skills and thus they would become just (Ladikos, 2000). The twentieth-century medical model also viewed criminal behavior as a moral sickness requiring treatment, although later rehabilitative models viewed criminals in terms of their "faulty thinking" rather than sickness, and in need of "programming" rather than "treatment." The rehabilitative goal is to change offenders' attitudes so that they come to accept that their behavior was wrong, not to deter them by the threat of further punishment. The goal of reintegration is to use the time criminals are under correctional supervision to prepare them to reenter free society as well-equipped to do so as possible.

Reintegration is not much different from rehabilitation, but it is more pragmatic, focusing on concrete programs such as job training rather than attitude change.

The rehabilitation model is criticized by conservatives as "molly coddling" and lacking in truth in sentencing, and it is criticized by liberals and libertarians for both forcing offenders into treatment against their will and contributing to sentencing disparity (it does so because it requires indeterminate sentencing because some people are "cured" faster than others). Yet we continue to try to rehabilitate criminals with the realization that whatever helps the offender helps the community. We are mindful of former United States Supreme Court Chief Justice Warren Burger's famous lines: "To put people behind walls and bars and do little or nothing to change them is to win a battle but lose a war. It is wrong. It is expensive. It is stupid" (in Stohr & Walsh, 2012:246). I think most of us would agree with this, but if we choose to justify punishment from any of the consequentialist positions, we are using the person being punished as an instrument for the greater good. This is immoral, according to nonconsequentialists.

Kant's Deontological (Nonconsequentialist) Retributionism

Nonconsequentialism is a deontological position that avers that any policy, practice, or conduct is to be morally judged by the motives behind it, not by the consequences that flow from it. If punishment is to be justified, it must be on its own intrinsic merits, which leads to a retributionist justification. California is among the states that have explicitly embraced retribution in their criminal code (California Penal Code Sec. 1170a): "The Legislature finds and declares that the purpose of imprisonment for a crime is punishment" (cited in Barker, 2006:12). Because many modern criminologists probably abhor retribution as little more than state-sanctioned revenge (Rosebury, 2009), and because the retributive spirit appears to be strong in the criminal justice system today, we need to spend a little more time with it.

Immanuel Kant is the foremost philosophical proponent of retributive justice. To understand Kant's retributionism, we have to understand his philosophy of duty and his strong beliefs about human reason, agency, and autonomy. He believed that human beings are differentiated from other animals in that they are commanded by reason, and that it is from reason that we derive all duties and obligations. All humans have a duty to act out of reverence for moral law set by Kant's concept of the categorical imperative. A categorical imperative is a principle stating that a moral act is objectively necessary (should or ought to be done) "in itself" regardless of any further end; it says "Do this," not "Do this *if.*" Any action consistent with such an imperative is good (moral) regardless of its consequences. Kant viewed categorical imperatives as *a priori* universal laws that guide us toward duty: "Act as if the maxim of your action were to become through your will a universal law of nature" (1964: 89). In his *Groundwork of the Metaphysics of Morals*, Kant wanted to find "the ground of a possible categorical imperative" that should be an "end in itself, and absolute value." He finds this ground in "man," who "exists as an end in himself, not merely as a means for arbitrary use for this or that will" (1964:95). "Man," in all his actions, must always be regarded as an end in himself regardless of whether his actions are directed at himself or at others. Based on this discussion of "man" as an end in himself, Kant reformulates the categorical imperative: "Act in such a way that you always treat humanity, whether in your own person or in the person of any other, never simply as a means, but always at the same time as an end" (1964:96).

This respect for humans as ends in themselves and not as means to some other end naturally flows toward a retributionist position on punishment. Punishing criminals for instrumental reasons or subjecting them to rehabilitative treatment is wrong because it treats them as means to an end, not as ends in themselves. Criminals are commanded by reason just as everyone else and thus live in accordance with maxims—universal moral standards ("Act as if the maxim of your action were to become through your will a universal law of nature"). Accordingly, if a criminal robs, rapes, or murders, he or she is both violating the autonomy of others and endorsing these acts as universal laws, saying in effect that others should also act in this way. By punishing criminals, the state is thus treating them in accordance with their own maxims; that is, how they think others should be treated. In other words, the state is allowing criminals to decide how they will be treated and is thereby respecting their judgment and autonomy. Thus, Kant says of the criminal: "His own evil deed draws the punishment upon himself" (in Rachels, 1986:123). For Kant, retribution is a "just desserts" model that demands that punishment match the degree of harm criminals have inflicted on their victims. This is the most honestly stated justification for punishment because it both taps into our primitive punitive urges and posits no secondary purpose for it. According to an editorial in the *New York Daily Tribune* in 1853, Karl Marx noted that "there is only one theory of punishment which recognizes human dignity in the abstract, and that is the theory of Kant." Similarly, Logan and Gaes (1993:252) claim that only retributive punishment "is an affirmation of the autonomy, responsibility, and dignity of the individual."

Contrary to Kant, philosopher Michael Zimmerman (2011) considers retribution to be immoral because he is a hard determinist who believes that people should be punished for what they are responsible for, and that depends on what they can control. Like Kant, Zimmerman wants each person to be his or her own lawmaker by deciding what is and is not morally wrong, but he draws opposite conclusions. Whereas Kant says that a man's decision to commit a crime "draws punishment upon himself," Zimmerman says that if criminals do not believe that what they have done is morally wrong, they do not deserve retribution. Zimmerman rejects Kant's view of humans as free agents in his assumptions that many of our personal actions are "beyond our control" (completely determined by outside forces). Note, however, that Zimmerman is only calling retribution immoral; he recognizes that the state must respond to harms done and has no quarrel with incapacitation and rehabilitation. Of course, these are word games; sitting in prison is experienced as punishment by the inmate regardless of the particular justification we apply to it.

Detecting Cheats in Cooperative Groups

I now return to the issues presented in Chapter 14 to examine the role of punishment in *Homo sapiens'* evolving sense of justice. Criminologists want to morally justify the state purposely inflicting harm on criminals in the name of the people, but as scientists they want to go beyond that to examine naturalistic explanations for why the urge to punish is present in us and is so strong.

In order to be successful in cooperative social groups, humans evolved mechanisms for detecting cheats and for dissuading them from further cheating (Nowak, 2006). As with most other behavioral adaptations, these mechanisms involve emotions. We feel contentment and joy when we acquire resources, sadness and frustration when we do not, envy when others have more, and anger when others try to take resources from us. Because reproductive success is the raison d'être of all sexually reproducing organisms, the emotions accompanying the loss of resources that facilitate this goal became the basis for detecting cheats and the desire to retaliate against those who may have expropriated their resources (Barkow, 2006).

Retaliation, revenge, punishment, or whatever we choose to call it, was vital to the fitness concerns of our distant ancestors. It has been repeatedly shown in computer simulation games (e.g., the prisoner's dilemma) that in a mixed population of cooperators and cheats, cheats always do better than cooperators in the absence of punishment (Klein, 2012; Nowak, 2006). This is borne out in empirical research when "doing better" is defined in its most evolutionary sense—access to sex partners. A review of 51 studies relating number of sex partners to criminal behavior found 50 of them to be positive and 1 nonsignificant, and a review of 31 other studies found that age of first sexual contact was significantly negatively related to criminal behavior in all 31 studies (Ellis & Walsh, 2000). Molecular genetic studies of dopamine-related genes also find significant relationships between sexual behavior and criminal behavior, with the most antisocial individuals having an average of approximately twice the number of sex partners than prosocial subjects (Beaver, Wright, & Walsh, 2008; Guo, Tong, & Cai, 2008).

The continued presence of chronic cheats among us indicates that we have imperfect ability to detect them. Evolutionary biologists posit that a coevolutionary "arms race" similar to the coevolution of predator and prey has molded the sensibilities of cooperators and cheats alike. Cooperators have undergone evolutionary tuning of their senses for detecting cheats, and cheats have evolved mechanisms that serve to hide their true intentions, such as the dulling of the neurohormonal mechanisms that regulate the social emotions (Gorelik, Shackelford, & Salmon, 2011). The fact that the genetic studies cited previously find that common genes underlie both antisocial behavior and high levels of sexual activity also strongly indicates that noncooperative behavior has had positive fitness consequences. Natural selection is morally neutral; it pounces on anything—morally repugnant or not—that leads to reproductive success.

As important as emotions are in detecting cheats, natural selection does not pass judgment on emotions, or even on the behaviors they motivate if the behaviors do not result in enhanced fitness. As with operant conditioning in somatic time, it is the *consequences* of the behavior motivated by the emotion upon which natural selection operates (Cziko, 1996). Reciprocal altruism generates positive emotions that reinforce further altruism, which sustains the *modus vivendi* of any social species, but what of the negative emotions that accompany being cheated? As de Waal (1996:160) points out: "A taste of revenge is the other side of the coin of reciprocity." Victims feel angry and hurt at being treated unfairly, and they feel confusion and frustration at losing the expectation of predictability ("I scratched your back, but you didn't scratch mine!"). The sum of these evolved emotions amounts to "moral outrage." Without moral outrage, there would be no motivation to react against those who violate the norms of reciprocity, cheats would have thrived without the threat of punishment in our ancestral environments, and we would have evolved as a quite different species of animal (Nowak, 2006).

Second- and Third-Party Punishment

It is no use feeling angry and hurt when victimized if those feelings do not generate behavior designed to prevent its reoccurrence. Negative feelings accompanying victimization are assuaged by punishing violators because punishment signals the restoration of fairness and predictability (the perception that cheaters may be less likely to cheat in the future and that potential cheaters may be deterred). The positive feelings accompanying the punishment of those who have wronged us, coupled with the reduction of negative feelings, provide powerful reinforcement, as suggested by the popular saying, "vengeance is sweet." A number of brain imaging studies have shown increased blood flow to reward centers in the brain when subjects witness the punishment of those who have wronged them (de Quervain et al., 2004; Klein, 2012). As noted previously, evolution only provides endogenous chemical rewards in response to actions that increase fitness; thus, the urge to punish must be an adaptive feature of human nature.

Punishment aimed at discouraging cheats is observed in every social species. Clutton-Brock and Parker's (1995) review gives many examples of punishing behavior, referred to as *moralistic* or *retaliatory aggression*, among nonhuman animals. Among chimpanzees, our closest genetic relatives, alpha males take on the role of what has been termed *control behavior*, which includes the punishment of troop members who bully and exploit others (de Waal, 1996). This is called second-party punishment. Why should some members of a group punish noncooperators for the benefit of other members? It is a costly and risky role, but it confers a number of fitness-enhancing benefits on alpha males. An alpha male typically shows a preference for the weaker party in most disputes, which both serves to develop grassroots support among the weaker rank and file and to level the hierarchy, and thereby increase the gap between him and the relatively more powerful members of the group who might seek to replace him (de Waal, 1996).

The maintenance of the alpha male's dominance through coalition building and favoritism toward weaker members not only yields him additional resources and the favors of females but also coincidentally confers benefits on the entire group. A fair leader, one who can stop disputes from tumbling out of control with impartiality and a minimum of force, is hard to come by. By the judicious use of dominance and authority, the alpha male introduces equity and justice to the group, albeit as an inadvertent consequence of pursuing his own fitness ends (de Waal, 1996). Numerous computer simulation studies of human altruistic punishment (so called because the punisher receives no material gain) have conclusively shown that the punisher receives many benefits, including an increased likelihood of receiving future benefits, with enhanced status in the group being the most valuable because high status attracts females (Ule, Schram, Rieddl, & Cason, 2009). dos Santos, Rankin, and Wedekind (2011:376) conclude that "reputation is the key to the evolution of punishment, and that simple reputation games can explain the high preservation of punishment in humans."

In human societies, it is rarely possible (and even illegal) to punish those who have harmed us ourselves (first-party punishment). Neither is punishment meted out by second-party punishers such as troop alpha males who benefit themselves by punishing wrongdoers on behalf of others. Punishment in modern societies is meted out by third-party punishers who are individuals not directly harmed and who will not directly benefit from their punitive actions. Numerous experiments have shown that third parties will punish cheats at a cost to themselves. A study of 1762 subjects from five continents found that in all populations, people are willing to punish defectors who have harmed unknown others (Henrich et al., 2006). This study also found that "societies with high degrees of punishment will also exhibit more altruistic behavior" (2006:1770). This suggests that altruism and punishment coevolved in the sense that "third-party punishment of norm violations ('I punish you because you harmed him') seems especially crucial for the evolutionary stability of cooperation and is the cornerstone of modern models of criminal justice" (Buckholz & Marois, 2012:655).

From Vengeance to Justice

We have thus far examined punishment as a form of revenge designed to deter cheaters from expropriating valued resources. The desire to "get even" is a primitive one that, if left untamed, can tear a social group apart by generating a cycle of tit-for-tat blood feuds, which have been the norm throughout human history (Boehm, 2011). Even given that there are well-founded evolutionary reasons for retributionist feelings aimed at wrong-doers, we must reflect on the moral propriety of acting on them. That is, just because these feelings are natural, it does not mean that we *ought* to act on them unalloyed by rational considerations. To believe that what is natural is necessarily a moral guideline for truth is to fall afoul of the naturalistic fallacy. To give in to our feelings leads to the kind of situation observed among the Yanomamo Indians. Chagnon (1988) estimates that approximately 30% of adult male deaths among the Yanomamo are related to revenge feuds, which generate and expand the very injustice that "righteous" revenge was supposed to assuage. The urge for vengeance, while an *adaptation*, is not *adaptive* in large social groups. As Susan Jacoby (1983:13) states:

The struggle to contain revenge has been conducted at the highest level of moral and civic awareness at each stage in the development of civilization. The self-conscious nature of the effort is expectable in view of the persistent state of tension between uncontrolled vengeance as destroyer and controlled vengeance as an unavoidable component of justice.

Although moral outrage responses are guided by evolved brain mechanisms universally, the way we respond to wrongdoers is shaped by culture. Culture may engage or neutralize the emotions that temper punishment with mercy, or it may allow vengeful passions to run wild. Cesare Beccaria's lasting influence in our discipline rests in part on his recognition that the brutal acts of retribution (and other injustices) that were common in his time, and often based on the arbitrary vengeance requirements of powerful aristocrats, resulted in general distrust and social alienation. For Beccaria, the purpose of punishment should be deterrence, not vengeance, and this could be accomplished by punishments that just exceeded the benefits obtained from a specific crime. Beccaria's work was so influential that many of his recommended criminal justice reforms were implemented in a number of European countries within his lifetime (Durant & Durant, 1967:321).

Such radical change over such a short period of time across many different cultures suggests that Beccaria's rational reform ideas tapped into and broadened other evolved emotions (particularly sympathy and empathy) among the political and intellectual elite of Enlightenment Europe. We tend to feel empathy for those whom we view as being "like us," and empathy often leads to sympathy, which may translate the vicarious experiencing of the pains of others into an active concern for their welfare. Vignette studies have shown, as evolutionary theory would predict, that people tend to recommend more lenient punishment for criminals whom they perceive to be similar to themselves (reviewed in Miller & Vidmar, 1981). With cognition and emotion gelled into the Enlightenment ideal of the basic unity of humanity, justice became both more refined and more diffuse (Walsh & Hemmens, 2011).

Writing in the century following Beccaria, Emile Durkheim (1964) viewed crime and punishment as central to social life. Just as evolutionary psychologists view cheating as vital to the evolution of cooperation, Durkheim viewed deviance as being necessary for social solidarity. Durkheim's view is analogous to what was said previously about the coevolution of altruism and punishment in the sense that the former needs the latter. Punishing criminals maintains solidarity, in part, because the rituals of punishment reaffirm the justness of the social norms, particularly those concerning reciprocal altruism. Durkheim recognized that the urge to punish is inherent in human nature, and that it serves an expiatory role, but he also recognized that we can temper the urge with sympathy. He observed that over the course of social evolution, humankind had largely moved from retributive to restitutive justice. For Durkheim, retributive justice is driven by the natural passion for punitive revenge that "ceases only when exhausted ... only after it has destroyed" (1964:86). Restitutive justice, on the other hand, is driven by simple deterrence and is more humanistic and tolerant, although it is still "at least in part, a work of vengeance" because it is still "an expiation" (1964:88–89). Both forms of justice satisfy the human urge for social regularity by punishing miscreants, but repressive justice oversteps its adaptive usefulness and becomes socially destructive. Restitutive justice offers a balance between helping to calm moral outrage, on the one hand, and exciting the emotions of empathy and sympathy, on the other hand.

Reconciliation and Reintegration: Forgiveness Tit-for-Tat

Although a simple strategy of tit-for-tat reciprocity has been shown to be highly effective for generating cooperative behavior in small groups, and tit-for-tat modified by punishment for defectors in larger groups, natural selection is operating simultaneously on too many alternate strategies to opt for fixity (Wilson & Wilson, 2007). If two strict tit-for-tat strategists play one another and one cheats (purposely or otherwise), it tends to launch a long series of mutual punitive response resulting in a loss for both. Work in game theory indicates that a measure of forgiveness may work better to maintain social cooperation rather than always paying back defectors in kind (Rand, Ohtsuki, & Nowak, 2009). If people play strict tit-for-tat (always punishing noncooperation in kind) in their relationships, they risk losing a valuable relationship if the cheating incident was uncharacteristic of the person or accidental (Wagstaff, 1998). As Machalek and Cohen (1991:221) state: "Forgiving strategies can transform a pattern of mutual cheating by not remaining permanently punitive but instead by cooperating, even when the other strategy cheats." A large number of game theory studies have found that strict tit-for-tat can amount to punishment that is just too costly for the punisher, that all parties tend to suffer to some extent, and that the generous (forgiving) tit-for-tat strategy invariably prevails (Rand et al., 2009).

The generous tit-for-tat strategy forgives a one-shot betrayal by responding with cooperation rather than retaliation in the next round of the game, and in most circumstances it will return the players to mutual cooperation. Of course, we are dealing with game theory here, with its idealized laboratory conditions and assumption of rational actors; the real world is expected to be far more complicated. However, the predictions based on game theoretical models have been remarkably consistent with real-world findings on numerous occasions (Levitt & List, 2007). Cosmides and Tooby (1992) offer the example of the Ache tribe of Paraguay (and certain other hunter/gatherer tribes), which responds differently to hunters who cheat than to gatherers who cheat. Meat is a scarce and valued resource, and it is shared equally by all when available, which is often a matter of luck and hunting skills. Plant food is a low-variance item, the availability of which depends only on the effort spent on gathering it. Arguments erupt when plant gatherers are perceived as not pulling their weight. Punishing lazy gatherers has no adverse effect on the availability of plant food; it is still there for the gathering. Given the highly variable nature of meat acquisition, however, tribal members are more forgiving of hunters whom they perceive as cheating. It is recognized that a charge of cheating can be the result of a false perception (hunting is often a matter of sheer luck as much as effort). If as a result of the false charge the hunter is punished by ostracism, the whole tribe will lose a valuable cooperator in the tricky business of hunting for meat, and the meat supply will become less stable and predictable.

Continuing to invite cooperation in the face of defection is not a "sucker" strategy because it is not one that tolerates continued cheating. It is similar to sentencing an offender to probation rather than prison, thus leaving the door open to future mutually advantageous cooperation between offender and community. The "forgiving tit-for-tat" strategy is captured most familiarly in Braithwaite's (1989) concept of reintegrative shaming. It is Braithwaite's position that we should retaliate against tit-for-tat defectors, but that retaliation should be conciliatory rather than permanently punitive. Punishment (and the shame accompanying it) should be reintegrative and motivate offenders to evaluate themselves and their behavior, not disintegrative. Both the offender and the community benefit by methods used to express our disapproval of offenders that conform to the reintegrative ideal. If we always respond to defecting with strong punitive reactions, the community loses a potentially valuable cooperator, and the offender becomes—to his or her great disadvantage—alienated from it.

Reconciliatory behavior is common among primate species, which indicates that forgiving tit-for-tat had some positive fitness consequences. This is not to assert that forgiveness is "natural" (i.e., forged by natural selection) in the same sense that moral outrage and the desire to punish apparently are natural. It is more a rational evaluation of the costs and benefits involved than emotional. However, in restorative justice programs, victims who confront their victimizers in controlled settings and offer forgiveness to them report feeling positive (a sense that justice had been done) about the experience (reviewed in Latimer, Dowden, & Muise, 2005). Forgiveness is contingent on the wrong done being not too egregious, on payment of restitution, on written and verbal apologies, and on the assurance of some consequences for the offender. Thus, even forgiveness has rather strong elements of tit-for-tat.

Restorative justice principles that tap the offender's capacity for empathy with the victim are most fully implemented by juvenile justice agencies. Juvenile agencies implicitly recognize that delinquent behavior is normal behavior; indeed, the young male who does not engage in some sort of delinquent behavior is statistically abnormal (Moffitt, 1993). Adolescence and young adulthood is a period of intense intermale competition ultimately (if not always consciously) aimed at securing more mating opportunities than the next male (McKibbin & Shackleford, 2011; Wiebe, 2011). To adopt a strategy of strict tit-for-tat rather than forgiveness tit-for-tat with juvenile offenders, whose physical desires and abilities have temporarily outrun their neurological maturity, would be severely counterproductive. Forgiveness tit-for-tat in game theory thus provides a degree of evolutionary and mathematical justification for restorative justice, which is the only corrections model aimed at reintegrating offenders back into the community with the help of the community. This is a consequentialist position at odds with Kantian deontology, but it is both more practical and (I believe contra Kant) more moral than punishment for its own sake, even if we are treating criminals as means to an end.

Conclusion

The concept of punishment has occupied philosophers for centuries. They all agree that it is necessary, but they differ in their justifications. We discussed it in terms of consequentialism and nonconsequentialism, with emphasis in Kant's deontological non-consequentialism whereby the state punishes criminals simply because they deserve it. To punish criminals as a means to an end is to treat them as less than autonomous human beings. We may agree that this position is both the most honestly stated one and one that respects criminals as responsible human beings. However, most of us do things for utilitarian purposes; that is, we expect what we do will have some desired consequences, and thus simple retribution does not cut it for most of us.

Our analysis of cheating and punishment suggests that cheating has been essential to the evolution of cooperation because it gave rise to the coevolutionary arms race that strengthened the social emotions that demand justice and punishment. By helping to extinguish the negative emotions (anger and frustration) associated with victimization of self or others, and generating satisfaction upon witnessing the imposition of sanctions against the miscreant, punishment reinforces our sense of the justness of moral norms (Gorelik et al., 2011; Machalek, 1996; Nowak, 2006). Thus, as Durkheim asserted, punishment is vital to the maintenance of a just society. However, it was also argued that strict tit-for-tat strategies can be harmful, and that forgiveness tit-for-tat is useful for the purposes of reconciliation and reintegration into the community.

References

Adams, J. (1971). *In defense of the Constitution of the United States* (Vol. 1). New York: De Capo Press. (Original work published 1778).

Adler, F. (1975). *Sisters in crime: The rise of the new female criminal.* New York: McGraw-Hill.

Adler, F., Mueller, G., & Laufer, W. (2001). *Criminology and the criminal justice system.* Boston: McGraw-Hill.

Agnew, R. (1992). Foundation for a general strain theory of crime and delinquency. *Criminology, 30,* 47–87.

Agnew, R. (2005). *Why do criminals offend? A general theory of crime and delinquency.* Los Angeles: Roxbury.

Agnew, R. (2011). *Toward a unified criminology: Integrating assumptions about crime, people and society.* New York: New York University Press.

Akers, R. (1991). Self-control as a general theory of crime. *Journal of Quantitative Criminology, 7,* 201–211.

Akers, R. (1994). *Criminological theories: Introduction and evaluation.* Los Angeles: Roxbury.

Akers, R. (1997). *Criminological theories: Introduction, evaluation, and application.* Los Angeles: Roxbury.

Akers, R. (1998). *Social learning and social structure: A general theory of crime and deviance.* Boston: Northeastern University Press.

Akers, R. (1999). Social learning and social structure: Reply to Sampson, Morash, and Krohn. *Theoretical Criminology, 3,* 477–493.

Akers, R., & Sellers, C. (2004). *Criminological theory: Past and present.* Los Angeles: Roxbury.

Alcock, J. (2001). *The triumph of sociobiology.* New York: Oxford University Press.

Alford, J., Funk, C., & Hibbing, J. (2008). Beyond liberals and conservatives to political genotypes and phenotypes. *Perspectives on Politics, 6,* 321–328.

Almgren, G. (2005). The ecological context of interpersonal violence. *Journal of Interpersonal Violence, 20,* 218–224.

Alves, N., Fukusima, T., & Aznar-Casanova, S. (2008). Models of brain asymmetry in the processing of emotions. *Psychology & Neuroscience, 1,* 63–66.

Amin, A. (2010). The remainders of race. *Theory, Culture & Society, 27,* 1–23.

Amodio, D., Master, S., Lee, C., & Taylor, S. (2007). Neurocognitive components of the behavioral inhibition and activation systems: Implications for theories of self-regulation. *Psychophysiology, 44,* 1–9.

Anckar, C. (2004). *Determinants of the death penalty: A comparative study of the world.* New York: Routledge.

Anderson, E. (1994). The code of the streets. *The Atlantic Monthly, 5,* 81–94.

Anderson, E. (1999). *Code of the street: Decency, violence, and the moral life of the inner city.* New York: Norton.

Armstrong, D. (1989). *Universals: An opinionated introduction.* Boulder, CO: Westview.

Arnett, J. (1995). Broad and narrow socialization: The family in the context of cultural theory. *Journal of Marriage and the Family, 57,* 617–628.

Arnold, A. (2004). Sex chromosomes and brain gender. *Nature Reviews: Neuroscience, 5,* 1–8.

Arnold, A., Xu, J., Grisham, W., Chen, X., & Kim, Y. (2009). Minireview: Sex chromosomes and brain differentiation. *Endocrinology, 145,* 1057–1062.

Arrigo, B., & Bernard, T. (2002). Postmodern criminology in relation to radical and conflict criminology. In S. Cote (Ed.), *Criminological theories: Bridging the past to the future* (pp. 250–257). Thousand Oaks, CA: Sage.

Ash, J., & Gallup, G. (2007). Paleoclimatic variation and brain expansion during human evolution. *Human Nature, 18,* 109–124.

Axelrod, R. (1984). *The evolution of cooperation.* New York: Basic Books.

Ayala, F. (2010). The difference of being human: Morality. *Proceedings of the National Academy of Sciences, 107,* 9015–9022.

Badcock, C. (2000). *Evolutionary psychology: A critical introduction.* Cambridge, UK: Polity.

Bailey, D., & Geary, D. (2009). Hominid brain evolution: Testing climactic, ecological, and social competition models. *Human Nature, 20,* 67–79.

Barak, G. (1998). *Integrating criminologies.* Boston: Allyn & Bacon.

Barker, V. (2006). The politics of punishing: Building a state governance theory of American imprisonment variation. *Punishment & Society, 8,* 5–32.

Barkow, J. (1989). *Darwin, sex and status: Biological approaches to mind and culture.* Toronto: University of Toronto Press.

Barkow, J. (1992). Beneath new culture is an old psychology: Gossip and social stratification. In J. Barkow, L. Cosmides, & J. Tooby (Eds.), *The adapted mind: Evolutionary psychology and the generation of culture* (pp. 627–637). New York: Oxford University Press.

Barkow, J. (Ed.). (2006). *Missing the revolution: Darwinism for social scientists.* Oxford: Oxford University Press.

Bartels, A., & Zeki, S. (2004). The neural correlates of maternal and romantic love. *NeuroImage, 21,* 1155–1166.

Bartollas, C. (2005). *Juvenile delinquency* (7th ed.). Boston: Allyn & Bacon.

Bateman, P., & Bennett, N. (2006). The biology of human sexuality: Evolution, ecology, and physiology. *Verbum et Ecclesia, 27,* 245–264.

Beaver, K. (2009). Molecular genetics and crime. In A. Walsh, & K. Beaver (Eds.), *Biosocial criminology: New directions in theory and research* (pp. 50–72). New York: Routledge.

Beaver, K., & Walsh, A. (2011). *The Ashgate research companion to biosocial theories of crime.* Farnham, UK: Ashgate.

Beaver, K., Wright, J., & Walsh, A. (2008). A gene-based evolutionary explanation for the association between criminal involvement and number of sex partners. *Social Biology, 54,* 47–55.

Beccaria, C. (1963). *On crimes and punishment.* H. Paulucci (Trans.). Indianapolis, IN: Bobbs-Merrill. (Original work published 1764).

Bell, E., Schermer, J., & Vernon, P. (2009). The origins of political attitudes and behaviors: An analysis using twins. *Canadian Journal of Political Science, 42,* 855–879.

Bell, M., & Deater-Deckard, K. (2007). Biological systems and the development of self-regulation: Integrating behavior, genetics, and psychophysiology. *Journal of Developmental & Behavioral Pediatrics, 28,* 409–420.

Bennett, S., Farrington, D., & Huesmann, L. (2005). Explaining gender differences in crime and violence: The importance of social cognitive skills. *Aggression and Violent Behavior, 10*, 263–288.

Bentham, J. (1948). A fragment on government and an introduction to the principles of morals and legislation. In W. Harrison (Ed.). Oxford: Blackwell. (Original work published 1789).

Berger, P., & Luckmann, T. (1966). *The social construction of reality: A treatise in the sociology of knowledge.* Garden City, NY: Anchor Books.

Bernard, T., Snipes, J., & Gerould, A. (2010). *Vold's theoretical criminology.* New York: Oxford University Press.

Bernhardt, P. (1997). Influences of serotonin and testosterone in aggression and dominance: Convergence with social psychology. *Current Directions in Psychological Science, 6*, 44–48.

Bhaskar, R. (1978). *A realist theory of science.* Brighton, UK: Harvester Press.

Bishop, R. (2006). Determinism and indeterminism. In D. M. Borchert (Ed.), *Encyclopedia of philosophy* (2nd ed.). Farmington Hills, MI: Macmillan.

Black, J., & Greenough, W. (1997). How to build a brain: Multiple memory systems have evolved and only some of them are constructivist. *Behavioral and Brain Sciences, 20*, 558–559.

Blair, R. (2004). The role of the orbital frontal cortex in the modulation of antisocial behavior. *Brain and Cognition, 55*, 198–208.

Blair, R. (2007). The amygdala and ventromedial prefrontal cortex in morality and psychopathy. *Trends in Cognitive Sciences, 11*, 387–392.

Boehm, C. (2011). Retaliatory violence in human prehistory. *British Journal of Criminology, 51*, 518–534.

Boghossian, P. (2006). *Fear of knowledge: Against relativism and constructivism.* New York: Oxford University Press.

Bohan, J. (1993). Regarding gender: Essentialism, constructionism, and feminist psychology. *Psychology of Women Quarterly, 17*, 5–21.

Boots, D. (2011). Neurobiological perspectives of brain vulnerability in pathways to violence over the life course. In K. Beaver, & A. Walsh (Eds.), *The Ashgate research companion to biosocial theories of crime* (pp. 181–211). Farnham, UK: Ashgate.

Bouchard, T., & McGue, M. (2003). Gene tic and environmental influences on human psychological differences. *Journal of Neurobiology, 54*, 4–45.

Bouchard, T., Segal, N., Tellegen, A., McGue, M., Keyes, M., & Krueger, R. (2003). Evidence for the construct validity and heritability of the Wilson–Patterson conservatism scale: A reared-apart twins study of social attitudes. *Personality and Individual Differences, 34*, 959–969.

Boudon, R. (2003). Beyond rational choice theory. *Annual Review of Sociology, 29*, 1–21.

Boyd, R., & Richerson, P. (1992). Punishment allows for the evolution of cooperation (or anything else) in sizable groups. *Ethology and Sociobiology, 13*, 171–195.

Box, S. (1987). *Recession, crime and punishment.* Totowa, NJ: Barnes & Noble.

Braithwaite, J. (1981). The myth of social class and criminality reconsidered. *American Sociological Review, 46*, 36–57.

Braithwaite, J. (1989). *Crime, shame, and reintegration.* Cambridge, UK: Cambridge University Press.

Brembs, B. (2011). Towards a scientific concept of free will as a biological trait: Spontaneous actions and decision-making in invertebrates. *Proceedings of the Royal Society: Biological Sciences, 278*, 930–939.

Brennan, P., Raine, A., Schulsinger, F., Kirkegaard-Sorenen, L., Knop, J., Hutchings, B., et al. (1997). Psychophysiological protective factors for male subjects at high risk for criminal behavior. *American Journal of Psychiatry, 154*, 853–855.

Bromage, T. (1987). The biological and chronological maturation of early hominids. *Journal of Human Evolution, 16,* 257–272.

Broom, D. (2006). The evolution of morality. *Applied Animal Behavior Science, 100,* 20–28.

Brown, D. (1991). *Human universals.* New York: McGraw-Hill.

Brown, R. (1965). *Social psychology.* New York: Free Press.

Brunero, J. (2002). Evolution, altruism and internal reward explanations. *Philosophical Forum, 33,* 413–424.

Buck, R. (1999). The biological affects: A typology. *Psychological Review, 106,* 301–336.

Buckholtz, J., & Marois, R. (2012). The roots of modern justice: Cognitive and neural foundations of social norms and their enforcement. *Nature Neuroscience, 13,* 655–661.

Buss, D. (2001). Human nature and culture. *Journal of Personality, 68,* 955–978.

Buss, D., & Malamuth, N. (1996). Introduction. In D. Buss, & N. Malamuth (Eds.), *Sex, power, and conflict: Evolutionary and feminist perspectives* (pp. 3–5). New York: Oxford University Press.

Byrnes, J., Miller, D., & Schafer, W. (1999). Gender differences in risk taking: A meta-analysis. *Psychological Bulletin, 125,* 367–383.

Camilleri, K. (2005). Heisenberg and the transformation of Kantian philosophy. *International Studies in the Philosophy of Science, 19,* 271–287.

Campbell, A. (1999). Staying alive: Evolution, culture, and women's intrasexual aggression. *Behavioral and Brian Sciences, 22,* 203–214.

Campbell, A. (2006a). Feminism and evolutionary psychology. In J. Barkow (Ed.), *Missing the revolution: Darwinism for social scientists* (pp. 63–99). Oxford: Oxford University Press.

Campbell, A. (2006b). Sex differences in direct aggression: What are the psychological mediators? *Aggression and Violent Behavior, 6,* 481–497.

Campbell, A. (2009). Gender and crime: An evolutionary perspective. In A. Walsh, & K. Beaver (Eds.), *Criminology and biology: New directions in theory and research* (pp. 117–136). New York: Routledge.

Campbell, A., Muncer, S., & Bibel, D. (2001). Women and crime: An evolutionary approach. *Aggression and Violent Behavior, 6,* 481–497.

Campbell, A., Shirley, L., & Candy, J. (2004). A longitudinal study of gender-related cognition and behaviour. *Developmental Science, 7,* 1–9.

Cao, L. (2004). *Major criminological theories: Concepts and measurement.* Belmont, CA: Wadsworth.

Carey, G. (2003). *Human genetics for the social sciences.* Thousand Oaks, CA: Sage.

Carmen, I. (2007). Genetic configurations of political phenomena: New theories and methods. *Annals of the American Academy of Political and Social Science, 614,* 489–496.

Caspi, A., McClay, J., Moffitt, T. E., Mill, J., Martin, J., Craig, I. W., et al. (2002). Role of genotype in the cycle of violence in maltreated children. *Science, 297,* 851–854.

Caspi, A., Moffitt, T., Silva, P., Stouthamer-Loeber, M., Krueger, R., & Schmutte, P. (1994). Are some people crime-prone? Replications of the personality–crime relationship across countries, genders, races, and methods. *Criminology, 32,* 163–194.

Cauffman, E., Steinberg, L., & Piquero, A. (2005). Psychological, neuropsychological, and psychophysiological correlates of serious antisocial behavior in adolescence. *Criminology, 43,* 133–176.

Cela-Conde, C., Burgess, L., Nadal, M., & Olivera, A. (2010). Altruisme et impartialite: Selection non-naturelle? *Comptes Rendus Biologies, 333,* 174–180.

Cernkovich, S., Giordano, P., & Pugh, M. (1985). Chronic offenders: The missing cases in self-report delinquency research. *Journal of Criminal Law and Criminology, 76,* 705–732.

Chagnon, N. (1988). Life histories, blood revenge, and warfare in a tribal population. *Science, 239,* 985–992.

Chambliss, W. (1976). *Criminal law in action.* Santa Barbara, CA: Hamilton.

Chan, H. (2005). Rawls' theory of justice: A naturalistic evaluation. *Journal of Medicine and Philosophy, 30,* 449–465.

Chandy, L., & Gertz, G. (2011). *Poverty in numbers: The changing state of global poverty from 2005 to 2015.* Washington, DC: Brookings Institute.

Charlesworthy, W. (1991). The development of the sense of justice. *American Behavioral Scientist, 34,* 350–370.

Charlton, B. (2009). Clever sillies: Why high IQ people tend to be deficient in common sense. *Medical Hypotheses, 73,* 867–870.

Chen, Z., & Kaplan, H. (2003). School failure in early adolescence and status attainment in middle adulthood: A longitudinal study. *Sociology of Education, 76,* 110–127.

Chiao, J., & Ambady, N. (2007). Cultural neuroscience: Parsing universality and diversity across levels of analysis. In D. Cohen (Ed.), *Handbook of cultural psychology* (pp. 237–254). New York: Guilford.

Clark, R., & Cornish, D. (1985). Modeling offenders' decisions: A framework for research and policy. In M. Tonry, & N. Morris (Eds.), *Crime and justice annual review of research* (pp. 147–185). Chicago: University of Chicago Press.

Clark, T. (2007). *Encountering naturalism: A worldview and its uses.* Somerville, MA: Center for Naturalism.

Clarke, J. (1998). *The lineaments of wrath: Race, violent crime, and American culture.* New Brunswick, NJ: Transaction Publishers.

Cleveland, H., Wiebe, R., van den Oord, E., & Rowe, D. (2000). Behavior problems among children from different family structures: The influence of genetic self-selection. *Child Development, 71,* 733–751.

Clutton-Brock, T., & Parker, G. (1995). Punishment in animal societies. *Nature, 373,* 209–216.

Coffey, P. (2008). *Cathedrals of science: The personalities and rivalries that made modern chemistry.* Oxford: Oxford University Press.

Cohen, A. (1955). *Delinquent boys.* New York: Free Press.

Cohen, A. B. (2010). Just how many different forms of culture are there? *American Psychologist, 65,* 59–61.

Collier, A. (1994). *Critical realism: An introduction to the philosophy of Roy Bhaskar.* London: Verso.

Condorcet, M.-J. (1794). *Historical view of the progress of the human mind.* Available at http://www. faculty.fairfield.edu/faculty/hodgson/Courses/progress/CondorcetChapt10.html. Accessed 22.11.11.

Congressional Budget Office. (2011). *Trends in the distribution of household income between 1979 and 2007.* CBO Publication No. 4031. Washington, DC: Author.

Cooper, A., Perkins, A., & Corr, P. (2007). A confirmatory factor analytic study of anxiety, fear, and behavioral inhibition system measures. *Journal of Individual Differences, 4,* 179–187.

Cooper, J., Walsh, A., & Ellis, L. (2010). Is criminology ripe for a paradigm shift? Evidence from a survey of American criminologists. *Journal of Criminal Justice Education, 21,* 332–347.

Corning, P. (2002). The re-emergence of "emergence": A venerable concept in search of a theory. *Complexity, 7,* 18–30.

Cornish, D., & Clarke, R. (1986). *The reasoning criminal.* New York: Springer-Verlag.

Corr, P. (2004). Reinforcement sensitivity theory and personality. *Neuroscience and Biobehavioral Reviews, 28,* 317–332.

Corredoira, M. (2009). Quantum mechanics and free will: Counter-arguments. *NeuroQuantology, 7*, 449–456.

Coser, L. (1965). *Men of ideas: A sociologist's view.* New York: Free Press.

Coser, L. (1971). *Masters of sociological thought.* New York: Harcourt Brace Jovanovich.

Cosmides, L., & Tooby, J. (1992). Cognitive adaptations for social change. In J. Barkow, L. Cosmides, & J. Tooby (Eds.), *The adapted mind: Evolutionary psychology and the generation of culture* (pp. 163–228). New York: Oxford University Press.

Costa, P., Terracciano, A., & McCrae, R. (2001). Gender differences in personality traits across cultures: Robust and surprising findings. *Journal of Personality and Social Psychology, 81*, 322–331.

Craig, M., Catani, M., Deeley, Q., Latham, R., Daly, E., Kanaan, R., Picchioni, M., McGuire, P., Fahy, T., & Murphy, D. (2009). Altered connections on the road to psychopathy. *Molecular Psychiatry, 14*, 946–953.

Crawford, C. (1998). The theory of evolution in the study of human behavior: An introduction and overview. In C. Crawford, & D. Krebs (Eds.), *Handbook of evolutionary psychology: Ideas, issues, and applications* (pp. 3–42). Mahwah, NJ: Erlbaum.

Cronin, H. (2003). Getting human nature right. In J. Brockman (Ed.), *The new humanist: Science at the edge* (pp. 53–65). New York: Barnes & Noble.

Cullen, F. (2003). Foreword to J. Crank, *Imagining justice.* Cincinnati, OH: Anderson.

Cullen, F. (2005). Challenging individualistic theories of crime. In S. Guarino-Ghezzi, & J. Trevino (Eds.), *Understanding crime: A multidisciplinary approach* (pp. 55–60). Newark, NJ: LexisNexis Matthew Bender/Anderson.

Cullen, F. (2009). Foreword to A. Walsh & K. Beaver, *Biosocial criminology: New directions in theory and research.* New York: Routledge.

Currie, E. (1999). Reflections on crime and criminology at the millennium. *Western Criminology Review, 2*, 1–14.

Cziko, G. (1996). *Three lessons of biology for psychology: The adapted mind, within organism selection, and perceptual control.* Evanston, Illinois: Paper presented at the annual meeting of the Human Behavior and Evolution Society, Northwestern University. June 1996.

D'Alessio, S., & Stolzenberg, L. (2003). Race and the probability of arrest. *Social Forces, 81*, 1381–1397.

Daly, K., & Chesney-Lind, M. (1988). Feminism and criminology. *Justice Quarterly, 5*, 497–538.

Darwin, C. (1981). *The descent of man, and selection in relation to sex.* Princeton, NJ: Princeton University Press.

Datetskaya, A. (2010). The Soviet communist party and the spirit of capitalism. *Sociological Theory, 28*, 377–401.

Davidson, R., Putman, K., & Larson, C. (2000). Dysfunction in the neural circuitry of emotion regulation—A possible prelude to violence. *Science, 289*, 591–594.

Davies, A., & Shackleford, T. (2008). Two human natures: How men and women evolved different psychologies. In C. Crawford, & D. Krebs (Eds.), *Foundations of evolutionary psychology* (pp. 261–281). Danvers, MA: CRC Press.

Davis, B. (2000). The scientist's world. *Microbiology and Molecular Biology Reviews, 64*, 1–12.

Dawkins, R. (1998). Postmodernism disrobed. *Nature, 394*, 141–143.

Day, J., & Carelli, R. (2007). The nucleus accumbens and Pavlovian reward learning. *The Neuroscientist, 13*, 148–159.

DeFina, R., & Arvanites, T. (2002). The weak effect of imprisonment on crime: 1971–1998. *Social Science Quarterly, 83*, 635–653.

Degler, C. (1991). *In search of human nature: The decline and revival of Darwinism in American social thought*. New York: Oxford University Press.

De Haan, W., & Vos, J. (2003). A crying shame: The over-rationalized conception of man in the rational choice perspective. *Theoretical Criminology, 7*, 29–54.

de Jong, H. (2011). Evolutionary psychology and morality: Review essay. *Ethical Theory and Moral Practice, 14*, 117–12b.

DeLisi, M., Beaver, K., Vaughn, M., & Wright, J. (2009). All in the family: Gene × environment interaction between DRD2 and criminal father is associated with five antisocial phenotypes. *Criminal Justice and Behavior, 36*, 1187–1197.

DeLisi, M., Kosloski, A., Drury, A., Vaughn, M., Beaver, K., Trulson, C., et al. (2011). Never desisters? An empirical illustration of the life-course persistent offender. In M. DeLisi, & K. Beaver (Eds.), *Criminological theory: A life-course approach* (pp. 241–255). Sudbury, MA: Jones & Bartlett.

Dennett, D. (1995). *Darwin's dangerous idea: Evolution and the meanings of life*. New York: Simon & Schuster.

Depue, R., & Collins, P. (1999). Neurobiology of the structure of personality: Dopamine, facilitation of incentive motivation, and extraversion. *Behavioral and Brain Sciences, 22*, 491–569.

de Quervain, D., Fischbacher, U., Valerie, T., Schellhammer, M., Schnyder, U., Buch, A., et al. (2004). The neural basis of altruistic punishment. *Science, 305*, 1254–1259.

Derntl, B., Finkelmayer, A., Eickhoff, S., Kellerman, T., Falkenberg, D., Schnieder, F., et al. (2010). Multidimensional assessment of empathetic abilities: Neural correlates and gender differences. *Psychoneuroendocrinology, 35*, 67–82.

Desai, R., & Eckstein, H. (1990). Insurgency: The transformation of peasant rebellion. *World Politics, 42*, 441–465.

Deuscher, I. (1968). The social causes of social problems: From suicide to delinquency. In E. Mizruchi (Ed.), *The substance of sociology* (pp. 247–258). New York: Appleton-Century-Crofts.

de Vries, G., & Sodersten, P. (2009). Sex differences in the brain: The relation between structure and function. *Hormones and Behavior, 55*, 589–596.

de Waal, F. (1991). The chimpanzee's sense of social regularity and its relation to the human sense of justice. *American Behavioral Scientist, 34*, 335–349.

de Waal, F. (1996). *Good natured: The origins of right and wrong in humans and other animals*. Cambridge, MA: Harvard University Press.

de Waal, F. (2001). *The ape and the sushi master: Cultural reflections of a primatologist*. New York: Basic.

de Waal, F. (2008). Putting the altruism back into altruism: The evolution of empathy. *Annual Review of Psychology, 59*, 279–300.

Dickens, W., & Flynn, J. (2001). Heritability estimates versus large environmental effects: The IQ paradox resolved. *Psychological Review, 108*, 346–349.

Domes, G., Heinrichs, M., Michel, A., Berger, C., & Herpertz, S. (2007). Ocytocin improves "mind-reading" in humans. *Biological Psychiatry, 61*, 731–733.

dos Santos, M., Rankin, D., & Wedekind, C. (2011). The evolution of punishment through reputation. *Proceedings of the Royal Society: Biology, 278*, 371–377.

Du Bois, W. (1903/1969). *The souls of black folk*. New York: New American Library.

Dupre, J. (1992). Blinded by "science:" How not to think about social problems. *Behavioral and Brain Sciences, 15*, 382–383.

Durant, W. (1944). *Caesar and Christ*. New York: Simon & Schuster.

Durant, W. (1952). *The story of philosophy*. New York: Simon & Schuster.

Durant, W., & Durant, A. (1967). *Rousseau and revolution.* New York: Simon & Schuster.

Durant, W., & Durant, A. (1968). *The lessons of history.* New York: Simon & Schuster.

Durkheim, E. (1933). *The division of labor in society.* New York: Free Press.

Durkheim, E. (1951). *The division of labor in society.* Glencoe, IL: Free Press.

Durkheim, E. (1964). *The division of labor in society.* New York: Free Press.

Durkheim, E. (1982). *Rules of sociological method.* New York: Free Press.

Durkheim, E. (2005). The dualism of human nature and its social conditions. *Durkheimian Studies, 11,* 35–45.

Eagly, A., Wood, W., & Johannesen-Schmidt, M. (2004). Social role theory of sex differences and similarities. In A. Eagely, A. Beall, & R. Sternberg (Eds.), *Psychology of gender* (pp. 269–295). New York: Guilford.

Ehrenreich, B., & McIntosh, J. (1997). The new creationism: Biology under attack. *The Nation, 9,* 12–16.

Einstadter, W., & Henry, S. (2006). *Criminological theory: An analysis of its underlying assumptions.* Lanham, MD: Rowman & Littlefield.

Einstein, A. (1923). *Sidelights on relativity (geometry and experience).* New York: Dutton.

Einstein, A., & Infeld, L. (1938). *The evolution of physics.* Cambridge, UK: Cambridge University Press.

Eliaeson, S. (2002). *Max Weber's methodologies: Interpretation and critique.* Malden, MA: Blackwell.

Ellis, L., & McDonald, J. (2001). Crime, delinquency, and social status: A reconsideration. *Journal of Offender Rehabilitation, 32,* 23–52.

Ellis, L., & Walsh, A. (1997). Gene-based evolutionary theories in criminology. *Criminology, 35,* 229–276.

Ellis, L., & Walsh, A. (2000). *Criminology: A global perspective.* Boston: Allyn & Bacon.

Ellwood, D., & Crane, J. (1990). Family changes among black Americans: What do we know? *Journal of Economic Perspectives, 4,* 65–84.

Endler, J. (1986). *Natural selection in the wild.* Princeton, NJ: Princeton University Press.

Esch, T., & Stefano, G. (2005). Love promotes health. *Neuroendocrinology Letters, 3,* 264–267.

Eskridge, C. (2005). The state of the field of criminology. *Journal of Contemporary Criminal Justice, 21,* 296–308.

Evans, P., Gilbert, S., Mekel-Bobrov, N., Vallender, E., Anderson, J., Vaez-Azizi, L., et al. (2005). *Microcephalin,* a gene regulating brain size, continues to evolve adaptively in humans. *Science, 309,* 1717–1720.

Falcon, A. (2011). Aristotle on causality. In E. Zalta (Ed.), *The Stanford encyclopedia of philosophy.* Available at http://plato.stanford.edu/archives/fall2011/entries/aristotle-causality.

Fausto-Sterling, A. (2002). Gender identification and assignment in intersex children. *Dialogues in Pediatric Urology, 25,* 4–5.

Felson, R. (1991). Blame analysis: Accounting for the behavior of protected groups. *American Sociologist, 22,* 5–23.

Felson, R. (2001). Blame analysis: Accounting for the behavior of protected groups. In S. Cole (Ed.), *What's wrong with sociology?* (pp. 223–245). New Brunswick, NJ: Transaction.

Ferguson, C. (2010). Genetic contributions to antisocial personality and behavior: A meta-analytic review from an evolutionary perspective. *Journal of Social Psychology, 150,* 160–180.

Ferguson, C. (2011). Gene × environment interactions in antisocial behavior. In K. Beaver, & A. Walsh (Eds.), *The Ashgate research companion to biosocial theories of crime* (pp. 115–132). Farnham, UK: Ashgate.

Fergusson, D., Swain-Campbell, N., & Horwood, J. (2004). How does childhood economic disadvantage lead to crime? *Journal of Child Psychology and Psychiatry, 45*, 956–966.

Ferrell, J. (2004). Boredom, crime and criminology. *Theoretical Criminology, 8*, 287–302.

Ferri, E. (1917). *Criminal sociology*. Boston: Little, Brown. (Original work published 1897).

Fetchenhauer, D., & Buunk, B. (2005). How to explain gender differences in fear of crime: Towards an evolutionary approach. *Sexualities, Evolution and Gender, 7*, 95–113.

Fine, C. (2010). *Delusions of gender: How our minds, society, and neurosexism create difference*. New York: Norton.

Finkel, N., Harré, R., & Rodriguez Lopez, J. (2001). Commonsense morality across cultures: Notions of fairness, justice, honor and equity. *Discourse Studies, 3*, 5–27.

Fishbein, D. (1992). The psychobiology of female aggression. *Criminal Justice and Behavior, 19*, 99–126.

Fishbein, D. (2001). *Biobehavioral perspectives in criminology*. Belmont, CA: Wadsworth.

Fisher, H., Aron, A., & Brown, L. (2005). Romantic love: An fMRI study of a neural mechanism for mate choice. *Journal of Comparative Neurology, 493*, 58–62.

Flavin, J. (2001). Feminism for the mainstream criminologist: An invitation. *Journal of Criminal Justice, 29*, 271–285.

Fredrickson, B. (2003). The value of positive emotions. *American Scientist, 91*, 330–335.

Freud, S. (1965). *New introductory lectures on psychoanalysis*. New York: Norton.

Freud, S. (2002). *Civilization and its discontents*. London: Penguin.

Friedman, M., & Freidman, R. (1980). *Free to choose: A personal statement*. New York: Harcourt, Brace, Jovanovich.

Friedman, N., Miyake, A., Young, S., DeFries, J., Corely, R., & Hewitt, J. (2008). Individual differences in executive functions are almost entirely genetic in origin. *Journal of Experimental Psychology, 137*, 201–225.

Fromm, H. (2006). Science wars and beyond. *Philosophy and Literature, 30*, 580–589.

Galison, P. (2008). Ten problems in history and philosophy of science. *Isis, 99*, 111–124.

Gane, N. (2005). Max Weber as social theorist: "Class, status, party." *European Journal of Social Theory, 8*, 211–226.

Gangestad, S., Haselton, M., & Buss, D. (2006). Evolutionary foundations of cultural variation: Evoked culture and mate preferences. *Psychological Inquiry, 17*, 75–95.

Gannett, L. (2010). Questions asked and unasked: How by worrying less about the "really real" philosophers of science might better contribute to debates about genetics and race. *Synthese, 177*, 363–385.

Gao, Y., Raine, A., Venerables, P., Dawson, M., & Mednick, S. (2010). Association of poor childhood fear conditioning and adult crime. *American Journal of Psychiatry, 167*, 56–60.

Geary, D. (2000). Evolution and proximate expression of human paternal investment. *Psychological Bulletin, 126*, 55–77.

Geary, D. (2005). *The origin of mind: Evolution of brain, cognition, and general intelligence*. Washington, DC: American Psychological Association.

Gergen, K. (1988). Feminist critique of science and the challenge of social epistemology. In M. McCanney Gergen (Ed.), *Feminist thought and the structure of knowledge* (pp. 27–48). New York: New York University Press.

Gill, M. (2000). Hume's progressive view of human nature. *Hume Studies, 26*, 87–108.

Gintis, H. (2003). The hitchhiker's guide to altruism: Gene–culture coevolution and the internalization of norms. *Journal of Theoretical Biology, 220*, 407–418.

Glahn, D., Thompson, P., & Blangero, J. (2002). Neuroimaging endophenotypes: Strategies for finding genes influencing brain structure and function. *Human Brain Mapping, 28*, 488–501.

Glueck, S., & Glueck, E. (1934). *Five hundred delinquent women.* New York: Knopf.

Goldberg, E. (2001). *The executive brain: Frontal lobes and the civilized mind.* New York: Oxford University Press.

Goldman, A. (2006). Social epistemology *Stanford encyclopedia of philosophy.* Available at http://plato.stanford.edu/entries/epistemology-social.

Gorelik, G., Shackelford, T., & Salmon, C. (2011). Between conflict and cooperation: New horizons in the evolutionary science of the human family. In C. Salmon, & T. Shackelford (Eds.), *Oxford handbook of evolutionary family psychology* (pp. 386–398). New York: Oxford University Press.

Gottesman, I., & Hanson, D. (2005). Human development: Biological and genetic processes. *Annual Review of Psychology, 56*, 263–286.

Gottfredson, M., & Hirschi, T. (1990). *A general theory of crime.* Stanford, CA: Stanford University Press.

Gould, S. (1976). Darwin's untimely death. *Natural History, 85*, 24–30.

Gould, S., & Eldredge, N. (1977). Punctuated equilibria: The tempo and mode of evolution reconsidered. *Paleobiology, 3*, 115–151.

Gove, W., & Wilmoth, C. (2003). The neurophysiology of motivation and habitual criminal behavior. In A. Walsh, & L. Ellis (Eds.), *Biosocial criminology: Challenging environmentalism's supremacy* (pp. 227–245). Hauppauge, NY: Nova Science.

Grasmick, H. (1990). Conscience, significant others, and rational choice: Extending the deterrence model. *Law & Society Review, 24*, 837–862.

Grasmick, H., & Bursik, R. (1990). Conscience, significant others, and rational choice: Extending the deterrence model. *Law and Society Review, 24*, 837–861.

Gray, J. (1994). Three fundamental emotional systems. In P. Ekman, & R. Davidson (Eds.), *The nature of emotion: Fundamental questions* (pp. 243–247). New York: Oxford University Press.

Green, M. (1983). Marx, utility, and right. *Political Theory, 11*, 433–446.

Greenberg, D. (1981). *Crime and capitalism: Readings in Marxist criminology.* Palo Alto, CA: Mayfield.

Grosvenor, P. (2002). Evolutionary psychology and the intellectual left. *Perspectives in Biology and Medicine, 45*, 433–448.

Grusec, J., & Hastings, P. (2007). Introduction. In J. Grusec, & P. Hastings (Eds.), *Handbook of socialization: Theory and research* (pp. 1–9). New York: Guilford.

Gunnar, M., & Quevedo, K. (2007). The neurobiology of stress and development. *Annual Review of Psychology, 58*, 145–173.

Guo, G. (2006). The linking of sociology and biology. *Social Forces, 85*, 145–149.

Guo, G., Roettger, M., & Shih, J. (2007). Contributions of the DAT1 and DRD2 genes to serious and violent delinquency among adolescents and young adults. *Human Genetics, 121*, 125–136.

Guo, G., Tong, Y., & Cai, T. (2008). Gene by social context interactions for number of sexual partners among white male youths: Genetics-informed sociology. *American Journal of Sociology, 114*, S36–S66.

Hacking, I. (1999). *The social construction of what?* Cambridge, MA: Harvard University Press.

Haidt, J. (2001). The emotional dog and its rational tail: A social intuitionist approach to moral judgment. *Psychological Review, 108*, 814–834.

Hanley, R. (2012). Capitalism's two cultures. *Society, 49*, 151–154.

Hare, R. (1993). *Without conscience: The disturbing world of the psychopaths among us.* New York: Pocket Books.

Harris, A., & Shaw, J. (2001). Looking for patterns: Race, class, and crime. In J. Shelley (Ed.), *Criminology: A contemporary handbook* (pp. 129–163). Belmont: CA: Wadsworth.

Harris, K. (1991). Moving into the new millennium: Toward a feminist view of justice. In H. Pepinsky, & R. Quinney (Eds.), *Criminology as peacemaking* (pp. 83–97). Bloomington, IN: Indiana University Press.

Hawkins, D. (1995). Ethnicity, race, and crime: A review of selected studies. In D. Hawkins (Ed.), *Ethnicity, race, and crime: Perspectives across time and space* (pp. 11–45). Albany, NY: State University of New York Press.

Hawks, J., Wang, E., Cochran, G., Harpending, H., & Moyzis, R. (2007). Recent acceleration of human adaptive evolution. *Proceedings of the National Academy of Science of the USA, 104,* 20753–20758.

Hayek, F. (1976). *Law, legislation and liberty* (Vol. 2). London: Routledge & Kegan Paul.

Henrich, J., McElreath, R., Barr, A., Ensminger, J., Barrett, C., Bolyanatz, A., et al. (2006). Costly punishment across human societies. *Science, 312,* 1767–1770.

Herman, E., Putman, P., & van Honk, J. (2006). Testosterone reduces empathetic mimicking in healthy young women. *Psychoneuroendocrinology, 31,* 859–866.

Hindelang, M., Hirschi, T., & Weis, J. (1981). *Measuring delinquency.* Beverly Hills, CA: Sage.

Hines, M. (2004). *Brain gender.* Oxford: Oxford University Press.

Hines, M. (2011). Gender development and the human brain. *Annual Review of Neuroscience, 34,* 69–88.

Hirschi, T. (1969). *The causes of delinquency.* Berkeley, CA: University of California Press.

Hirschi, T., & Gottfredson, M. (2000). In defense of self-control. *Theoretical Criminology, 4,* 55–69.

Hoffmann, S. (1963). Rousseau on war and peace. *American Political Science Review, 57,* 317–333.

Howard, D. (2005). Albert Einstein as a philosopher of science. *Physics Today, Dec,* 34–40.

Huby, P. (1967). The first discovery of the free will problem. *Philosophy, 42,* 353–362.

Hume, D. (1969). *A treatise of human nature.* London: Penguin. (Originally work published 1739).

Hunnicutt, G., & Broidy, L. (2004). Liberation and economic marginalization: A reformulation and test of (formerly?) competing models. *Journal of Research in Crime and Delinquency, 41,* 130–155.

Hunter, V. (2009). Crime and criminals in Plato's laws. *Mouseion: Journal of the Classical Association of Canada, 9,* 1–19.

Hur, Y., & Bouchard, T. (1997). The genetic correlation between impulsivity and sensation-seeking traits. *Behavior Genetics, 27,* 455–463.

Inbar, Y., & Lammers, J. (2012). Political diversity in social and personality psychology. *Perspectives on Psychological Science, 7,* 496–503.

Irwin, K., & Chesney-Lind, M. (2008). Girls' violence: Beyond dangerous masculinity. *Sociology Compass, 2/3,* 837–855.

Jacoby, S. (1983). *Wild justice: The evolution of revenge.* New York: Harper & Row.

Jagger, A. (1986). Love and knowledge: Emotion in feminist epistemology. In A. Jagger, & S. Bordo (Eds.), *Gender/body/knowledge: Feminist reconstructions of knowing and being* (pp. 145–171). New Brunswick, NJ: Rutgers University Press.

Jeans, J. (1930). *The mysterious universe.* Cambridge, UK: Cambridge University Press.

Jost, J., & Amodio, D. (2012). Political ideology as motivated social cognition: Behavioral and neuroscience evidence. *Motivation and Emotion, 36,* 55–64.

Jost, J., Federico, C., & Napier, J. (2009). Political ideology: Its structure, functions, and elective affinities. *Annual Review of Psychology, 60*, 307–337.

Jost, L., & Jost, J. (2007). Why Marx left philosophy for social science. *Theory and Psychology, 17*, 297–322.

Kahan, A. (2012). *Max Weber and Warren Buffett: Looking for the lost charisma of capitalism. Society,* 49: 144–150.

Kalderon, M. (2009). Epistemic relativism. *Philosophical Review, 118*, 225–240.

Kanai, R., Feilden, T., Firth, C., & Rees, G. (2011). Political orientations are correlated with brain structure in young adults. *Current Biology, 21*, 677–680.

Kanazawa, S. (2008). Temperature and evolutionary novelty as forces behind the evolution of general intelligence. *Intelligence, 36*, 99–108.

Kant, I. (1964). *Groundwork of the metaphysics of morals.* Translated and analyzed by H. Paton. New York: Harper & Row.

Katz, J. (1988). *Seductions of crime: Moral and sensual attractions in doing evil.* New York: Basic Books.

Kaufman, S. (2000). *Investigations.* Oxford: Oxford University Press.

Kaufmann, W. (1980). The inevitability of alienation. *Revue Européenne des Sciences Sociales, 18*, 29–42.

Kennair, L. (2002). Evolutionary psychology: An emerging integrative perspective within the science and practice of psychology. *Human Nature Review, 2*, 17–61.

Kenrick, D., & Simpson, J. (1997). Why social psychology and evolutionary psychology need one another. In J. Simpson, & D. Kenrick (Eds.), *Evolutionary social psychology* (pp. 1–20). Mahwah, NJ: Erlbaum.

Kim-Cohen, J., Caspi, A., Taylor, A., Williams, B., Newcombe, R., Craig, I., et al. (2006). MAOA, maltreatment, and gene–environment interaction predicting children's mental health: New evidence and a meta-analysis. *Molecular Psychiatry, 11*, 903–913.

Kimura, D. (1992). Sex differences in the brain. *Scientific American, 267*, 119–125.

Kincaid, H. (2002). Social science. In P. Hachamer, & M. Silverstein (Eds.), *Philosophy of Science* (pp. 290–311). Oxford: Blackwell.

Kitayamama, S., & Uskul, A. (2011). Culture, mind, and the brain: Current evidence and future directions. *Annual Review of Psychology, 62*, 419–449.

Klein, R. (2012). The neurobiology of altruistic punishment: A moral assessment of its social utility. In K. Plaisance, & T. Reydon (Eds.), *Philosophy of behavioral biology* (pp. 297–313). Boston: Springer.

Knickmeyer, R., Baron-Cohen, S., Raggatt, P., Taylor, K., & Hackett, G. (2006). Fetal testosterone and empathy. *Hormones and Behavior, 49*, 282–292.

Knight, D. (1992). *Ideas in chemistry: A history of the science.* New Brunswick, NJ: Rutgers University Press.

Kochanska, G., & Aksan, N. (2004). Conscience in childhood: Past, present, and future. *Merrill-Palmer Quarterly, 50*, 299–310.

Kochanska, G., & Knaack, A. (2003). Effortful control as a personality characteristic of young children: Antecedents, correlates, and consequences. *Journal of Personality, 71*, 1087–1112.

Kohlberg, L. (1984). *Essays on moral development.* San Francisco: Harper & Row.

Kornhauser, R. (1978). *Social sources of delinquency: An appraisal of analytical methods.* Chicago: University of Chicago Press.

Krebs, D. (2008). The evolution of a sense of justice. In J. Duntley, & T. Shackelford (Eds.), *Evolutionary forensic psychology* (pp. 230–246). Oxford: Oxford University Press.

Kuhn, T. (1970). *The structure of scientific revolutions.* Chicago: University of Chicago Press.

Lacourse, E., Nagin, D., Vitaro, F., Côté, S., Arseneault, L., & Tremblay, R. E. (2006). Prediction of early-onset deviant peer group affiliation: A 12-year longitudinal study. *Archives of General Psychiatry, 63*, 562–568.

Ladikos, A. (2000). Plato's views on crime and punishment. *Phronimon, 2*, 166–174.

Lahn, B., & Ebenstein, L. (2009). Let's celebrate human genetic diversity. *Nature, 46*, 726–728.

Laks, A. (1990). Legislation and demiurgy: On the relationship between Plato's Republic and Laws. *Classical Antiquity, 9*, 209–229.

Latimer, J., Dowden, G., & Muise, D. (2005). The effectiveness of restorative justice practices: A meta-analysis. *Prison Journal, 85*, 127–144.

Leahy, T. (2012). The elephant in the room: Human nature and the sociology textbooks. *Current Sociology, 60*, 806–823.

Lee, D. (2008). Game theory and neural basis of social decision making. *Nature Neuroscience, 11*, 404–409.

Lemert, E. (1974). Beyond Mead: The societal reaction to deviance. *Social Problems, 21*, 457–468.

Lenski, G. (1978). Marxist experiments in destratification: An appraisal. *Social Forces, 57*, 364–383.

Leonard, E. (1995). Theoretical criminology and gender. In B. Price, & N. Sokoloff (Eds.), *The criminal justice system and women: Offenders, victims, and workers* (pp. 54–70). New York: McGraw-Hill.

Leslie, C. (1990). Scientific racism: Reflections on peer review, science and ideology. *Social Science and Medicine, 31*, 891–912.

Levitt, N. (1999). *Prometheus bedeviled: Science and the contradictions of contemporary culture.* New Brunswick, NJ: Rutgers University Press.

Levitt, S., & List, J. (2007). What do laboratory experiments measuring social preferences reveal about the real world? *Journal of Economic Perspectives, 21*, 153–174.

Lilly, J., Cullen, F., & Ball, R. (2007). *Criminological theory: Context and consequences.* Thousand Oaks, CA: Sage.

Lippa, R. (2003). *Gender, nature, and nurture.* Mahwah, NJ: Erlbaum.

Lipset, S. (1994). The state of American sociology. *Sociological Forum, 9*, 199–220.

Logan, C., & Gaes, G. (1993). Meta-analysis and the rehabilitation of punishment. *Justice Quarterly, 10*, 245–263.

Lovell, D. (2004). Marx's utopian legacy. *The European Legacy, 9*, 629–640.

Lubinski, D., & Humphreys, L. (1997). Incorporating intelligence into epidemiology and the social sciences. *Intelligence, 24*, 159–201.

Lutz, W. (2000). Nothing in life is certain except negative care patient outcome and revenue enhancement. *Journal of Adolescent and Adult Literacy, 44*, 230–233.

Lykken, D. (1995). *The antisocial personalities.* Hillsdale, NJ: Erlbaum.

Lytton, H., & Romney, D. (1991). Parents' differential socialization of boys and girls: A meta-analysis. *Psychological Bulletin, 109*, 267–296.

Machalek, R. (1996). The evolution of social exploitation. *Advances in Human Ecology, 5*, 1–32.

Machalek, R., & Cohen, L. (1991). The nature of crime: Is cheating necessary for cooperation? *Human Nature, 2*, 215–233.

Mackenzie, M. (1981). *Plato on punishment.* Berkley, CA: University of California Press.

Marx, K. (1967). *Capital* (Vol. 1). New York: International Publishers.

Marx, K. (1978a). Economic and philosophical manuscripts of 1844. In R. Tucker (Ed.), *The Marx–Engels reader* (pp. 66–123). New York: Norton.

Marx, K. (1978b). Theses on Feuerbach. In R. Tucker (Ed.), *The Marx–Engels reader* (pp. 143–145). New York: W.W. Norton.

Marx, K., & Engels, F. (1932). The Communist manifesto. In J. Borchardt (Ed.), *Capital and other writings by Karl Marx*. New York: Carlton House.

Marx, K., & Engels, F. (1948). *The Communist manifesto*. New York: International.

Marx, K., & Engels, F. (1965). *The German ideology*. London: Lawrence & Wishart.

Marx, K., & Engels, F. (2004). *The German ideology*. London: Lawrence & Wishart.

Massey, D. (2002). A brief history of human society: The origin and role of emotion in social life. *American Sociological Review, 67*, 1–29.

Matsueda, R., Drakulich, K., & Kubrin, C. (2006). Race and neighborhood codes of violence. In R. Peterson, L. Krivo, & J. Hagan (Eds.), *The many colors of crime: Inequalities of race, ethnicity, and crime in America* (pp. 334–356). New York: New York University Press.

Matthen, M., & Ariew, A. (2005). How to understand causal relations in natural selection: Reply to Rosenberg and Bouchard. *Biology and Philosophy, 20*, 355–364.

Matuštík, M. (1994). Kierkegaard as socio-political thinker and activist. *Man and World, 27*, 211–224.

McCrae, T., & Terracciano, A. (2005). Universal features of personality traits from the observer's perspective: Data from 50 cultures. *Journal of Personality and Social Psychology, 88*, 547–561.

McDermott, R., Tingley, D., Cowden, J., Frazzetto, G., & Johnson, D. (2009). Monoamine oxidase A gene (MAOA) predicts behavioral aggression following provocation. *Proceedings of the National Academy of Sciences of the USA, 106*(7), 2118–2123.

McIntyre, M., & Edwards, C. (2009). The early development of gender differences. *Annual Review of Anthropology, 38*, 83–97.

McKibbin, W., & Shackleford, T. (2011). Women's avoidance of rape: An evolutionary psychological perspective. In K. Beaver, & A. Walsh (Eds.), *The Ashgate research companion to biosocial theories of crime* (pp. 331–347). Farnham, UK: Ashgate.

McKinnon, J., & Humes, K. (2000). *The black population in the United States*. Washington, DC: U.S. Census Bureau.

Mealey, L. (1995). The sociobiology of sociopathy: An integrated evolutionary model. *Behavioral and Brain Sciences, 18*, 523–559.

Mears, D., Ploeger, M., & Warr, M. (1998). Explaining the gender gap in delinquency: Peer influence and moral evaluations of behavior. *Journal of Research in Crime and Delinquency, 35*, 251–266.

Mekel-Bobrov, N., Gilbert, S., Evans, P., Vallender, E., Anderson, J., Hudson, R., et al. (2005). Ongoing adaptive evolution of *ASPM, a brain size determinant in Homo sapiens. Science, 309*, 1720–1722.

Menard, S., & Mihalic, S. (2001). The tripartite conceptual framework in adolescence and adulthood: Evidence from a national sample. *Journal of Drug Issues, 31*, 905–940.

Merten, J. (2005). Culture, gender and the recognition of the basic emotions. *Psychologia, 48*, 306–316.

Merton, R. (1948). The self-fulfilling prophecy. *The Antioch Review, 8*, 193–210.

Merton, R. (1968). *Social theory and social structure*. Glencoe, IL: Free Press.

Merton, R. (1995). The Thomas theorem and the Matthew effect. *Social Forces, 74*, 379–424.

Messner, S., & Rosenfeld, R. (2001). *Crime and the American dream* (3rd ed.). Belmont, CA: Wadsworth.

Miller, D., & Vidmar, N. (1981). The social psychology of punishment reactions. In M. Lerner, & S. Lerner (Eds.), *The justice motive in social behavior* (pp. 145–172). New York: Plenum.

Miller, W. (1958). Lower-class culture as a generating milieu of gang delinquency. *Journal of Social Issues, 14*, 5–19.

Miller-Butterworth, C., Kaplan, J., Shaffer, J., Devlin, B., Manuck, S., & Ferrell, R. (2008). Sequence variation in the primate dopamine transporter gene and its relationship to social dominance. *Molecular Biology and Evolution, 25*, 18–28.

Milner, C., & Milner, R. (1972). *Black players*. Boston: Little, Brown.

Mitchell, K. (2007). The genetics of brain wiring: From molecule to mind. *PLoS Biology, 4*, 690–692.

Mithen, S., & Parsons, L. (2008). The brain as a cultural artifact. *Cambridge Archeological Journal, 18*, 415–422.

Moffitt, T. (1993). Adolescent-limited and life-course persistent antisocial behavior: A developmental taxonomy. *Psychological Review, 100*, 674–701.

Moffitt, T. (2005). The new look of behavioral genetics in developmental psychopathology: Gene–environment interplay in antisocial behavior. *Psychological Bulletin, 131*, 533–554.

Moffit, T., & the E-Risk Study Team. (2002). Teen-aged mothers in contemporary Britain. *Journal of Child Psychology and Psychiatry, 43*, 1–16.

Moffitt, T., Caspi, A., Rutter, M., & Silva, P. (2001). *Sex differences in antisocial behaviour: Conduct disorder, delinquency and violence in the Dunedin longitudinal study*. Cambridge, UK: Cambridge University Press.

Moffitt, T., & Walsh, A. (2003). The adolescence-limited/life-course persistent theory of antisocial behavior: What have we learned? In A. Walsh, & L. Ellis (Eds.), *Biosocial criminology: Challenging environmentalism's supremacy* (pp. 125–144). Hauppauge, NY: Nova Science.

Mogil, J. (1999). The genetic mediation of individual differences in sensitivity to pain and its inhibition. *Proceedings of the National Academy of Sciences of the USA, 96*, 7744–7751.

Moll, J., Krueger, F., Zahn, R., Pardini, M., de Oliveira-Souza, R., & Grafman, J. (2006). Human fronto-mesolimbic networks guide decisions about charitable donation. *Proceedings of the National Academy of Sciences of the USA, 103*, 15623–15628.

Mori, S., & Zhang, J. (2006). Principles of diffusion tensor imaging and its application to neuroscience research. *Neuron, 51*, 527–539.

Mumola, C. (2000). *Incarcerated parents and their children*. Washington, DC: Bureau of Justice Statistics.

Muñoz, L., & Anastassiou-Hadjicharalambous, X. (2011). Disinhibited behaviors in young children: Relations with impulsivity and autonomic psychophysiology. *Biological Psychology, 86*, 349–359.

Murray, J., Irving, D., Farrington, D., Colman, I., & Bloxsom, C. (2010). Very early predictors of conduct problems and crime: Results from a national cohort study. *Journal of Child Psychology and Psychiatry, 51*, 1198–1207.

Nasser, A. (1975). Marx's ethical anthropology. *Philosophy and Phenomenological Research, 35*, 484–500.

Nettler, G. (1982). *Explaining criminals*. Cincinnati, OH: Anderson.

Nettler, G. (1984). *Explaining crime* (3rd ed.). New York: McGraw Hill.

Nicholson, L. (1994). Interpreting gender. *Signs, 20*, 79–105.

Nowak, M. (2006). Five rules for the evolution of cooperation. *Science, 314*, 1560–1563.

Nowak, M., & Sigmund, K. (2005). Evolution of indirect reciprocity. *Nature, 437*, 1291–1298.

Nunnally, S., & Carter, N. (2012). Moving from victims to victors: African American attitudes on the "culture of poverty" and black blame. *Journal of African American Studies, 16*, 423–455.

Oberwittler, D. (2004). A multilevel analysis of neighborhood contextual factors on serious juvenile offending. *European Journal of Criminology, 1*, 201–235.

O'Brien, R. (2001). Crime facts: Victim and offender data. In J. Sheley (Ed.), *Criminology: A contemporary handbook* (pp. 59–83). Belmont: CA: Wadsworth.

Oderberg, D. (2007). *Real essentialism*. New York: Routledge.

Oderberg, D. (2011). Essence and properties. *Erkenn, 75*, 85–111.

Okasha, S. (2002). *Philosophy of science: A very short introduction*. Oxford: Oxford University Press.

Olson, J., Vernon, P., & Harris, J. (2001). The heritability of attitudes: A study of twins. *Journal of Personality and Social Psychology, 80*, 845–860.

O'Manique, J. (2003). *The origins of justice: The evolution of morality, human rights, and law*. Philadelphia: University of Philadelphia Press.

Osgood, D., & Chambers, J. (2003, May). Community correlates of rural youth violence. *Juvenile Justice Bulletin*. U.S. Department of Justice.

Parsons, C. (2010). Godel and philosophical idealism. *Philosophia Mathematica, 18*, 166–192.

Passas, N. (1995). Continuities in the anomie tradition. In F. Adler, & W. Laufer (Eds.), *The legacy of anomie theory* (pp. 91–112). New Brunswick, NJ: Transaction.

Paternoster, R., & Iovanni, L. (1989). The labeling perspective and delinquency: An elaboration of the theory and an assessment of the evidence. *Justice Quarterly, 6*, 359–394.

Patterson, O. (1998). *Rituals of blood: Consequences of slavery in two American centuries*. Washington, DC: Civitas Counterpoint.

Patterson, O. (2000). Taking culture seriously: A framework and an Afro-American illustration. In L. Harrison, & S. Huntingto (Eds.), *Culture matters: How values shape human progress* (pp. 202–230). New York: Basic Books.

Paul, D. (1984). Eugenics and the left. *Journal of the History of Ideas, 45*, 567–590.

Paus, T. (2010). Population neuroscience: Why and how. *Human Brain Mapping, 31*, 891–903.

Penn, A. (2001). Early brain wiring: Activity-dependent processes. *Schizophrenia Bulletin, 27*, 337–348.

Perdue, W. (1986). *Sociological theory: Explanation, paradigm, and ideology*. Palo Alto: CA: Mayfield.

Perry, B. (2002). Childhood experience and the expression of genetic potential: What childhood neglect tells us about nature and nurture. *Brain and Mind, 3*, 79–100.

Pessoa, L. (2008). On the relationship between emotion and cognition. *Nature/Neuroscience, 9*, 148–158.

Peterson, C. (1997). *Psychology: A biopsychosocial approach*. New York: Longman.

Piaget, J. (1968). *On the development of memory and identity*. Worcester, MA: Clark University Press.

Pinker, S. (2002). *The blank slate: The modern denial of human nature*. New York: Viking.

Pitchford, I. (2001). The origins of violence: Is psychopathy an adaptation? *Human Nature Review, 1*, 28–38.

Plato. (1960). *The Republic and other works*. Jowett, B. (Trans.). Garden City, NY: Dolphin.

Plomin, R. (2003). General cognitive ability. In R. Plomin, J. Defries, I. Craig, & P. McGuffin (Eds.), *Behavioral genetics in the postgenomic era* (pp. 183–201). Washington, DC: American Psychological Association.

Plomin, R., Ashbury, K., & Dunn, J. (2001). Why are children in the same family so different? Nonshared environment a decade later. *Canadian Journal of Psychiatry, 46*, 225–233.

Plomin, R., & Daniels, D. (1987). Why are children in the same family so different from one another? *Behavioral and Brain Sciences, 10*, 1–60.

Plotkin, H. (2011). Human nature, cultural diversity and evolutionary theory. *Philosophical Transaction of the Royal Society: Biological Sciences, 366*, 454–463.

Polkinghorne, J. (2002). *Quantum theory: A very short introduction*. Oxford: Oxford University Press.

Pollock, J. (1999). *Criminal women*. Cincinnati, OH: Anderson.

Polsek, D. (2009). Who has won the science wars? *Drustvena Istrazivanja (Journal of General Social Science), 18*, 1023–1047.

Pope, C., & Snyder, H. (2003). Race as a factor in juvenile arrests. In *Juvenile Justice Bulletin (NCJ 189180)*. Washington, DC: Office of Juvenile Justice and Delinquency Prevention.

Porteous, A. (1934). Platonist or Aristotelian? *Classical Review, 48*, 97–105.

Powell, K. (2006). How does the teenage brain work? *Nature, 442*, 865–867.

Price, B., & Sokoloff, N. (Eds.). (1995). *The criminal justice system and women: Offenders, victims, and workers*. New York: McGraw-Hill.

Prinz, J. (2007). *The emotional construction of morals*. Oxford: Oxford University Press.

Propper, C., & Moore, G. (2006). The influence of parenting on infant emotionality: A multilevel psychobiological perspective. *Developmental Review, 26*, 427–460.

Quartz, S., & Sejnowski, T. (1997). The neural basis of cognitive development: A constructivist manifesto. *Behavioral and Brain Sciences, 20*, 537–596.

Quinsey, V. (2002). Evolutionary theory and criminal behavior. *Legal and Criminological Psychology, 7*, 1–14.

Qvarnstrom, A., Brommer, J., & Gustafsson, L. (2006). Testing the genetics underlying the co-evolution of mate choice and ornament in the wild. *Nature, 44*, 84–86.

Rachels, J. (1986). *The elements of moral philosophy*. New York: Random House.

Radzinowicz, L., & King, J. (1979). *The growth of crime: The international experience*. Middlesex, UK: Penguin.

Raine, A. (2002). Biosocial studies of antisocial and violent behavior in children and adults: A review. *Journal of Abnormal Child Psychology, 30*, 311–326.

Rand, D., Ohtsuki, H., & Nowak, M. (2009). Direct reciprocity with costly punishment: Generous tit-for-tat prevails. *Journal of Theoretical Biology, 256*, 45–57.

Rank, M., Yoon, H., & Hirschl, T. (2003). American poverty as a structural failing: Evidence and arguments. *Journal of Sociology and Social Welfare, 30*, 3–29.

Rawls, A. (2003). Conflict as a foundation for consensus: Contradictions of industrial capitalism in book III of Durkheim's Division of Labor. *Critical Sociology, 29*, 295–335.

Rawls, J. (1971). *A theory of justice*. Cambridge, MA: Harvard University Press.

Reckdenwald, A., & Parker, K. (2008). The influence of gender inequality and marginalization on types of female offending. *Homicide Studies, 12*, 208–226.

Redding, R. (2012). Likes attract: The sociopolitical groupthink of (social) psychologists. *Perspectives on Psychological Science, 7*, 512–515.

Rennie, Y. (1978). *The search for criminal man*. Lexington, MA: Lexington Books.

Replogle, R. (1990). Justice as superstructure: How vulgar is vulgar materialism? *Polity, 22*, 675–699.

Restak, R. (2001). *The secret life of the brain*. New York: co-published by Dana Press and Joseph Henry Press.

Rhee, S., & Waldman, I. (2002). Genetic and environmental influences on antisocial behavior: A meta-analysis of twin and adoption studies. *Psychological Bulletin, 128*, 490–529.

Richerson, P., & Boyd, R. (2010). Darwin on the role of culture in human evolution. In M. Bell, D. Futuyma, W. Eanes, & J. Levinton (Eds.), *Evolution since Darwin: The first 150 years* (pp. 561–588). Sunderland, MA: Sinauer.

Richter-Levin, G. (2004). The amygdala, the hippocampus, and emotional modulation of memory. *The Neuroscientist, 10*, 31–39.

Ridley, M. (2003). *Nature via nurture: Genes, experience and what makes us human.* New York: HarperCollins.

Rieppel, O. (2010). New essentialism in biology. *Philosophy of Science, 77*, 662–673.

Romine, C., & Reynolds, C. (2005). A model of the development of frontal lobe functioning: Findings from a meta-analysis. *Applied Neuropsychology, 12*, 190–201.

Rose, H., & Rose, S. (Eds.). (2000). *Alas, poor Darwin: Arguments against evolutionary psychology.* London: Jonathan Cape.

Rose, S. (1999). Precis of *Lifelines*: Biology, freedom, determinism. *Behavioral and Brain Sciences, 22*, 871–921.

Rose, S. (2001). Moving on from old dichotomies: Beyond nature–nurture towards a lifeline perspective. *British Journal of Psychiatry, 178*, 3–7.

Rosebury, B. (2009). Private revenge and its relation to punishment. *Utilatus, 21*, 1–21.

Rosenfeld, R. (2011). The big picture: 2010 Presidential address to the American Society of Criminology. *Criminology, 49*, 1–26.

Rossi, A. (1984). Gender and parenthood. *American Sociological Review, 49*, 1–19.

Rowe, D. (1994). *The limits of family influence: Genes, experience, and behavior.* New York: Guilford.

Rowe, D. (1996). An adaptive strategy theory of crime and delinquency. In J. Hawkins (Ed.), *Delinquency and crime: Current theories* (pp. 268–314). Cambridge, UK: Cambridge University Press.

Rubenstein, D. (1992). Structural explanation in sociology: The egalitarian imperative. *American Sociologist, 23*, 5–19.

Ruden, R. (1997). *The craving brain: The biobalance approach to controlling addictions.* New York: HarperCollins.

Ruffie, J. (1986). *The population alternative: A new look at competition and the species.* New York: Random House.

Russell, B. (1988). The value of philosophy. In L. Pojman (Ed.), *Philosophy: The quest for truth* (pp. 17–21). Belmont, CA: Wadsworth.

Sagan, C. (1980). *Cosmos.* New York: Random House.

Saint-Amand, P. (1997). Contingency and enlightenment. *Substance, 26*, 96–109.

Sampson, R. (2000). Whither the sociological study of crime. *Annual Review of Sociology, 26*, 711–714.

Sampson, R., & Bean, L. (2006). Cultural mechanisms and killing fields: A revised theory of community-level racial inequality. In R. Peterson, L. Krivo, & J. Hagan (Eds.), *The many colors of crime: Inequalities of race, ethnicity, and crime in America* (pp. 8–36). New York: New York University Press.

Sampson, R., & Wilson, W. J. (2000). Toward a theory of race, crime, and urban inequality. In S. Cooper (Ed.), *Criminology* (pp. 149–160). Madison, WI: CouresWise.

Sanderson, S. (2001). *The evolution of human sociality: A Darwinian conflict perspective.* Lanham, MD: Rowman & Littlefield.

Sarukkai, S. (2005). Revisiting the "unreasonable effectiveness" of mathematics. *Current Science, 88*, 415–423.

Sawhill, I., & Morton, J. (2007). *Economic mobility: Is the American dream alive and well?* Washington, DC: The Economic Mobility Project/Pew Charity Trusts.

Sayer, A. (1997). Essentialism, social constructionism, and beyond. *Sociological Review, 45*, 453–487.

Sayers, S. (2005). Why work? Marx and human nature. *Science & Society, 69*, 606–616.

Scarpa, A., & Raine, A. (2003). The psychophysiology of antisocial behavior: Interactions with environ-mental experiences. In A. Walsh, & L. Ellis (Eds.), *Biosocial criminology: Challenging environ-mentalism's supremacy* (pp. 209–226). Hauppauge, NY: Nova Science.

Schafer, L. (2006). Quantum reality and the consciousness of the universe. *Zygon, 41*, 505–532.

Schmalleger, F. (2004). *Criminology today.* Upper Saddle River, NJ: Prentice Hall.

Schmaus, W. (2003). Is Durkheim the enemy of evolutionary psychology? *Philosophy of the Social Sciences, 33*, 25–52.

Schmitt, D., Realo, A., Voracek, M., & Allik, J. (2008). Why can't a man be more like a woman? Sex dif-ferences in big five personality traits across 55 cultures. *Journal of Personality and Social Psychology, 94*, 168–182.

Schon, R., & Silven, M. (2007). Natural parenting—Back to basics in infant care. *Evolutionary Psychology, 5*, 102–183.

Schulte-Ruther, M., Markowitsch, H., Fink, G., & Piefke, M. (2007). Mirror neuron and theory of mind mechanisms involved in face-to-face interactions: A functional magnetic resonance imaging approach to empathy. *Journal of Cognitive Neuroscience, 19*, 1354–1472.

Schuster, P. (2009). Free will, information, quantum mechanics, and biology: It pays to distinguish different forms of free choice and information. *Complexity, 15*, 8–11.

Schwalbe, M., Goodwin, S., Holden, D., Schrock, D., Thompson, S., & Wolkomer, M. (2000). Generic processes in the reproduction of inequality: An interactionist analysis. *Social Forces, 79*, 419–452.

Schwartz, M., & Friedrichs, D. (1994). Postmodern thought and criminological discontent. *Criminology, 32*, 221–246.

Sharp, B. (2006). *Changing criminal thinking: A treatment program.* Alexandria, VA: American Correctional Association.

Shi, S., Cheng, T., Jan, L., & Jan, Y. (2004). The immunoglobin family member dendrite arborization and synapse maturation 1 (Dasm1) controls excitatory synapse maturation. *Proceedings of the National Academy of Sciences of the USA, 101*, 13246–13351.

Siegel, L. (1986). *Criminology.* Belmont, CA: Wadsworth.

Silfver, M., & Klaus, H. (2007). Empathy, guilt, and gender: A comparison of two measures of guilt. *Scandinavian Journal of Psychology, 48*, 239–246.

Simon, R. (1975). *Women and crime.* Lexington, MA: Lexington Books.

Singer, P. (2000). *A Darwinian left: Politics, evolution, and cooperation.* New Haven, CT: Yale University Press.

Sisk, C., & Zehr, J. (2005). Pubertal hormones organize the adolescent brain and behavior. *Frontiers in Neuroendocrinology, 26*, 163–174.

Small, M., & Newman, K. (2001). Urban poverty after *The Truly Disadvantaged*: The rediscovery of the family, the neighborhood, and culture. *Annual Review of Sociology, 27*, 23–45.

Smith, H., & Bohm, R. (2008). Beyond anomie: Alienation and crime. *Critical Criminology: An International Journal, 16*, 1–15.

Smith, H., Pettigrew, T., Pippin, G., & Bialosiewitz, S. (2012). Relative deprivation: A theoretical and meta-analytical review. *Personality and Social Psychology Review, 16*, 203–232.

Smith, K., Oxley, D., Hibbing, M., Alford, J., & Hibbing, J. (2011). Linking genetics and political attitudes: Reconceptualizing political ideology. *Political Psychology, 32*, 369–397.

Sniderman, P., & Bullock, J. (2004). A consistency theory of public opinion and political choices: The hypothesis of menu dependence. In W. Saris, & P. Sniderman (Eds.), *Studies in public opinion:*

Attitudes, nonattitudes, measurement error, and change (pp. 337–357). Princeton, NJ: Princeton University Press.

Snowdon, C. (2011). Should we sacrifice economic growth for equality? *Economic Affairs, 31*(Suppl. 1), 4.

Soderstrom, H., Blennow, K., Sjodin, A.-K., & Forsman, A. (2003). New evidence for an association between the CSF HVA:5-HIAA ratio and psychopathic traits. *Journal of Neurology, Neurosurgery and Psychiatry, 74*, 918–921.

Sokal, A., & Bricmont, J. (1998). *Fashionable nonsense: Postmodern intellectuals' abuse of Science.* New York: Picador.

Solomon, R. (1977). The logic of emotion. *Nous, 11*, 41–49.

Sowell, E., Thompson, P., & Toga, A. (2004). Mapping changes in the human cortex throughout the span of life. *Neuroscientist, 10*, 372–392.

Sowell, T. (1987). *A conflict of visions: Ideological origins of political struggles.* New York: Morrow.

Spielberg, J., Miller, G., Engels, A., Herrington, J., Sutton, B., Banich, M., et al. (2011). Trait approach and avoidance motivation: Lateralized neural activity associated with executive function. *NeuroImage, 54*, 661–670.

Spiro, M. (1999). Anthropology and human nature. *Ethos, 27*, 7–14.

Stark, R. (1979). Whose status counts? Comment on Tittle, Villemez, and Smith. *American Sociological Review, 44*, 668–669.

Steffensmeier, D., & Haynie, D. (2000). Gender, structural disadvantage, and urban crime: Do macrosocial variables also explain female offending rates? *Criminology, 38*, 403–438.

Stohr, M., & Walsh, A. (2012). *Corrections: The essentials.* Thousand Oaks, CA: Sage.

Strauss, D. (2006). Democracy between a just public legal order and the ideal of (equitable) transformation. *Politeia, 25*, 151–167.

Sullivan, C., & Maxfield, M. (2003). Examining paradigmatic development in criminology and criminal justice: A content analysis of research methods syllabi in doctoral programs. *Journal of Criminal Justice Education, 14*, 269–285.

Sutherland, E., & Cressey, D. (1974). *Criminology* (9th ed.). Philadelphia: Lippincott.

Sutton, W., & Linn, E. (1976). *Where the money was: Memoirs of a bank robber.* New York: Viking.

Suwa, G., Asfaw, B., Kono, R., Kubo, D., Lovejoy, C., & White, T. (2009). The *Ardipithecus ramidus* skull and its implications for hominid origins. *Science, 326*, 68e1–68e8.

Syngelaki, E., Fairchild, G., Moore, S., Savage, J., & van Goozen, S. (2013). Fearlessness in juvenile offenders is associated with offending rate. *Developmental Science, 16*, 84–90.

Tancredi, L. (2005). *Hardwired behavior: What neuroscience reveals about morality.* Cambridge, UK: Cambridge University Press.

Tang, S. (2011). Foundational paradigms of social sciences. *Philosophy of the Social Science, 41*, 211–249.

Taylor, I. (1999). Crime and social criticism. *Social Justice, 26*, 150–168.

Taylor, S. (2006). Tend and befriend: Biobehavioral bases of affiliation under stress. *Current Directions in Psychological Science, 15*, 273–277.

Terranova, A., Morris, A., & Boxer, P. (2008). Fear reactivity and effortful control in overt and relational bullying: A six-month longitudinal study. *Aggressive Behavior, 34*, 104–115.

Thernstrom, S., & Thernstrom, A. (1997). *America in black and white: One nation indivisible.* New York: Simon & Schuster.

Thomas, H. (1962). *Understanding the great philosophers.* New York: Doubleday.

Tibbetts, S. (2003). Selfishness, social control, and emotions: An integrated perspective on criminality. In A. Walsh, & L. Ellis (Eds.), *Biosocial criminology: Challenging environmentalism's supremacy* (pp. 83–101). Hauppauge, NY: Nova Science.

Tibbetts, S., & Hemmens, C. (2010). *Theoretical criminology*. Thousand Oaks, CA: Sage.

Tinbergen, N. (1963). On aims and methods in ethology. *Zeitschrift für Tierpsychologie, 20*, 410–433.

Tittle, C. (1983). Social class and criminal behavior: A critique of the theoretical foundation. *Social Forces, 62*, 334–358.

Tittle, C., Villemez, W., & Smith, D. (1978). The myth of social class and criminality: Evidence of the relationship between social class and criminal behavior. *American Sociological Review, 49*, 398–411.

Toates, F. (2009). *Burrhus F. Skinner: Shaper of behaviour*. London: Palgrave Macmillan.

Trautner, H. (1992). The development of sex-typing in children. *German Journal of Psychology, 16*, 183–199.

Tremblay, R. (2008). Understanding development and prevention of physical aggression: Towards experimental epigenetic studies. *Philosophical Transactions of the Royal Society: B Biological Sciences, 363*, 2613–2622.

Trigg, R. (1999). *Ideas of human nature: An historical introduction*. Malden, MA: Blackwell.

Trudge, C. (1999). Who's afraid of genetic determinism? *Biologist, 46*, 96.

Tucker, K. (2002). *Classical social theory: A contemporary approach*. Oxford: Blackwell.

Turner, J., & Stets, J. (2005). *The sociology of emotions*. Cambridge, UK: Cambridge University Press.

Udry, J. R. (2003). *The National Longitudinal Study of Adolescent Health (Add Health)*. Chapel Hill, NC: Carolina Population Center, University of North Carolina at Chapel Hill.

Uggen, C. (2000). Class, gender, and arrest: An intergenerational analysis of workplace power and control. *Criminology, 38*, 835–862.

Ule, A., Schram, A., Rieddl, A., & Cason, T. (2009). Indirect punishment and generosity toward strangers. *Science, 326*, 1701–1704.

Unger, R. (1996). Using the master's tools: Epistemology and empiricism. In S. Wilkinson (Ed.), *Feminist social psychologies: International perspectives* (pp. 165–181). Milton Keynes, UK: Open University Press.

U.S. Census Bureau. (2012). *Statistical abstract of the United States*. Washington, DC: Author. Available at http://www.census.gov/compendia/statab.

U.S. Department of Health and Human Services. (2011). *Births: Preliminary data for 2010*. Washington, DC: U.S. Government Printing Office.

van den Berghe, P. (1990). Why most sociologists don't (and won't) think evolutionarily. *Sociological Forum, 5*, 173–185.

Velkley, R. (2002). *Being after Rousseau: Philosophy and culture in question*. Chicago: University of Chicago Press.

Vold, G., Bernard, T., & Snipes, J. (1998). *Theoretical criminology*. New York: Oxford University Press.

Vos, A. (2007). The philosophy of John Duns Scotus. *Ars Disputandi, 7*, 1566.

Wagstaff, G. (1998). Equity, justice, and altruism. *Current Psychology, 17*, 111–134.

Wallace, W. (1990). Rationality, human nature, and society in Weber's theory. *Theory and Society, 19*, 199–223.

Walsh, A. (1997). Methodological individualism and vertical integration in the social sciences. *Behavior and Philosophy, 25*, 121–136.

Walsh, A. (2002). *Biosocial criminology: Introduction and integration*. Cincinnati, OH: Anderson.

Walsh, A. (2006). Evolutionary psychology and criminal behavior. In J. Barkow (Ed.), *Missing the revolution: Darwinism for social scientists* (pp. 225–268). Oxford: Oxford University Press.

Walsh, A. (2009a). *Biology and criminology: The biosocial synthesis*. New York: Routledge.

Walsh, A. (2009b). Criminal behavior from heritability to epigenetics: How genetics clarifies the role of the environment. In A. Walsh, & K. Beaver (Eds.), *Biosocial criminology: New directions in theory and research* (pp. 29–49). New York: Routledge.

Walsh, A. (2009c). Crazy by design: A biosocial approach to the age–crime curve. In A. Walsh, & K. Beaver (Eds.), *Biosocial criminology: New directions in theory and research* (pp. 154–175). New York: Routledge.

Walsh, A. (2011a). *Feminist criminology through a biosocial lens*. Durham, NC: Carolina Academic Press.

Walsh, A. (2011b). *Social class and crime: A biosocial approach*. New York: Routledge.

Walsh, A. (2012). *Criminology: The essentials*. Thousand Oaks, CA: Sage.

Walsh, A. (2013). *The science wars: Politics, gender and race*. New Brunswick: NJ: Transaction/Rutgers University Press.

Walsh, A., & Bolen, J. (2012). *The neurobiology of criminal behavior: Gene–brain culture co-evolution*. Farnham, UK: Ashgate.

Walsh, A., & Ellis, L. (2004). Ideology: Criminology's Achilles' heel? *Quarterly Journal of Ideology, 27*, 1–25.

Walsh, A., & Ellis, L. (2007). *Criminology: An interdisciplinary approach*. Thousand Oaks, CA: Sage.

Walsh, A., & Hemmens, C. (2011). *Law, justice, and society: A sociolegal introduction* (2nd ed.). New York: Oxford University Press.

Walsh, A., Johnson, H., & Bolen, J. (2012). Epigenetics, neurobiology, and drug addiction. *Journal of Contemporary Criminal Justice, 28*, 314–328.

Walsh, A., & Stohr, M. (2010). *Correctional assessment, casework, and counseling* (5th ed.). Alexandria, VA: American Correctional Association.

Walsh, A., & Wu, H.-H. (2008). Differentiating antisocial personality disorder, psychopathy, and sociopathy: Evolutionary, genetic, neurological, and sociological considerations. *Criminal Justice Studies, 21*, 135–152.

Walsh, A., & Yun, I. (2011). Developmental neurobiology from embryonic neuron migration to adolescent synaptic pruning: Relevance for antisocial behavior. In M. DeLisi, & K. Beaver (Eds.), *Criminological theory: A life-course approach* (pp. 69–84). Boston: Jones & Bartlett.

Warneken, F., & Tomasello, M. (2009). The roots of human altruism. *British Journal of Psychology, 100*, 455–471.

Warr, M. (2002). *Companions in crime: The social aspects of criminal conduct*. New York: Cambridge University Press.

Weber, M. (1930). *The Protestant ethic and the spirit of capitalism* (Talcot Parsons, Trans.). London: Routledge.

Weber, M. (1978). *Economy and society: An outline of interpretative sociology* (Vol. 2). Berkley, CA: University of California Press.

Widom, C., & Brzustowicz, L. (2006). MAOA and the "cycle of violence": Childhood abuse and neglect: MAOA genotype and the risk for violent and antisocial behavior. *Biological Psychiatry, 60*, 684–689.

Wiebe, R. (2004). Psychopathy and sexual coercion: A Darwinian analysis. *Counseling and Clinical Psychology Journal, 1*, 23–41.

Wiebe, R. (2011). The nature and utility of low self-control. In K. Beaver, & A. Walsh (Eds.), *The Ashgate research companion to biosocial theories of crime* (pp. 369–395). Farnham, UK: Ashgate.

Williams, C., & Arrigo, B. (2006). Philosophy, crime, and theoretical criminology. In B. Arrigo, & C. Williams (Eds.), *Philosophy, crime, and criminology*. Urbana, IL: University of Illinois Press.

Williams, L., Gatt, J., Kuan, S., Dobson-Stone, C., Palmer, D., Paul, R., et al. (2009). A polymorphism of the *MAOA* gene is associated with emotional brain markers and personality traits on an antisocial index. *Neuropsychopharmacology, 34*, 1797–1809.

Williams, N. (2011). Putnam's traditional neo-essentialism. *Philosophical Quarterly, 61*, 151–170.

Wilson, D., & Wilson, E. (2007). Rethinking the theoretical foundation of sociobiology. *Quarterly Review of Biology, 84*, 327–348.

Wilson, E. O. (1990). Biology and the social sciences. *Zygon, 25*, 245–262.

Wilson, E. O. (1998). *Consilience: The unity of knowledge*. New York: Vintage.

Wilson, J. (1975). *Thinking about crime*. New York: Vintage.

Wilson, J., & Herrnstein, R. (1985). *Crime and human nature*. New York: Simon & Schuster.

Wilson, M., & Daly, M. (1997). Life expectancy, economic inequality, homicide and reproductive timing in Chicago neighborhoods. *British Medical Journal, 314*, 1271–1274.

Wood, D. (2010a). Punishment: Consequentialism. *Philosophy Compass, 5*, 455–469.

Wood, D. (2010b). Punishment: Nonconsequentialism. *Philosophy Compass, 5*, 470–482.

Wood, P., Gove, W., Wilson, J., & Cochran, J. (1997). Nonsocial reinforcement and habitual criminal conduct: An extension of learning theory. *Criminology, 35*, 335–366.

Wood, W., & Eagly, A. (2002). A cross-cultural analysis of the behavior of women and men: Implications for the origins of sex difference. *Psychological Bulletin, 128*, 699–727.

Woodger, J. (1948). *Biological principles*. London: Routledge & Kegan Paul.

Woods, T. (2004). *The politically incorrect guide to American history*. Washington, DC: Regnery.

Woolgar, S., & Pawluch, D. (1985). Ontological gerrymandering: The anatomy of social problems explanations. *Social Problems, 32*, 214–227.

Wright, J. (2009). Inconvenient truths: Science, race and crime. In A. Walsh, & K. Beaver (Eds.), *Biosocial criminology: New directions in theory and research* (pp. 137–153). New York: Routledge.

Wright, J., & Beaver, K. (2005). Do parents matter in creating self-control in their children? A genetically informed test of Gottfredson and Hirschi's theory of low self-control. *Criminology, 43*, 1169–1202.

Wright, J., & Boisvert, P. (2009). What biosocial criminology offers criminology. *Criminal Justice and Behavior, 36*, 1228–1239.

Wright, J., & Cullen, F. (2012). The future of biosocial criminology: Beyond scholars' professional ideology. *Journal of Contemporary Criminal Justice, 28*, 237–253.

Wright, J., Moore, K., & Newsome, J. (2011). Molecular genetics and crime. In K. Beaver, & A. Walsh (Eds.), *The Ashgate research companion to biosocial theories of crime* (pp. 93–114). Farnham, UK: Ashgate.

Yacubian, J. T., Sommer, K., Schroeder, J., Glascher, R., Kalisch, B., Leuenberger, D., et al. (2007). Gene–gene interaction associated with neural reward sensitivity. *Proceedings of the National Academy of Sciences of the USA, 104*, 8125–8130.

Yang, J., Baskin, L., & DiSandro, M. (2010). Gender identity in disorders of sex development: Review article. *Urology, 75*, 153–159.

Young, J. (2003). Merton with energy, Katz with structure: The sociology of vindictiveness and the criminology of transgression. *Theoretical Criminology, 7*, 389–414.

Zack, N. (2002). *Philosophy of science and race*. New York: Routledge.

Zimmerman, M. (2011). *The immorality of punishment*. Buffalo, NY: Broadview Press.

Index